A
LITERARY
HISTORY
OF
SPAIN

A LITERARY HISTORY OF SPAIN

General Editor: R. O. JONES
Cervantes Professor of Spanish, King's College, University of London

THE MIDDLE AGES
by A. D. DEYERMOND
Professor of Spanish, Westfield College, University of London

THE GOLDEN AGE: PROSE AND POETRY
by R. O. JONES

THE GOLDEN AGE: DRAMA
by EDWARD M. WILSON
Professor of Spanish, University of Cambridge
and DUNCAN MOIR
Lecturer in Spanish, University of Southampton

THE EIGHTEENTH CENTURY
by NIGEL GLENDINNING
Professor of Spanish, Trinity College, University of Dublin

THE NINETEENTH CENTURY
by DONALD L. SHAW
Senior Lecturer in Hispanic Studies, University of Edinburgh

THE TWENTIETH CENTURY
by G. G. BROWN
Lecturer in Spanish, Queen Mary College, University of London

SPANISH AMERICAN LITERATURE
SINCE INDEPENDENCE
by JEAN FRANCO
Professor of Latin American Literature, University of Essex

CATALAN LITERATURE
by ARTHUR TERRY
Professor of Spanish, The Queen's University, Belfast

A LITERARY HISTORY OF SPAIN

THE NINETEENTH CENTURY

A LITERARY
HISTORY OF SPAIN

THE NINETEENTH CENTURY

DONALD L. SHAW

Senior Lecturer in Hispanic Studies,
University of Edinburgh

LONDON · ERNEST BENN LIMITED

NEW YORK · BARNES & NOBLE INC

First published 1972 by Ernest Benn Limited

Bouverie House · Fleet Street · London EC4

and Barnes & Noble Inc. · 49 East 33rd Street · New York 10016

(a division of Harper & Row Publishers, Inc.)

Distributed in Canada by

The General Publishing Company Limited · Toronto

Printed in Great Britain

ISBN 0 510-32281-6

ISBN 0-389-04621-3 (USA)

Paperback 0 510-32282-4

Paperback 0-389-04622-1 (USA)

To
MARIELLA

FOREWORD BY THE GENERAL EDITOR

SPANISH, the language of what was in its day the greatest of European powers, became the common tongue of the most far-flung Empire the world had until then seen. Today, in number of speakers, Spanish is one of the world's major languages. The literature written in Spanish is correspondingly rich. The earliest European lyrics in a post-classical vernacular that we know of (if we except Welsh and Irish) were written in Spain; the modern novel was born there; there too was written some of the greatest European poetry and drama; and some of the most interesting works of our time are being written in Spanish.

Nevertheless, this new history may require some explanation and even justification. Our justification is that a new and up-to-date English-language history seemed called for to serve the increasing interest now being taken in Spanish. There have been other English-language histories in the past, some of them very good, but none on this scale.

Every history is a compromise between aims difficult or even impossible to reconcile. This one is no exception. While imaginative literature is our main concern, we have tried to relate that literature to the society in and for which it was written, but without sub-ordinating criticism to amateur sociology. Since not everything could be given equal attention (even if it were desirable to do so) we have concentrated on those writers and works of manifestly outstanding artistic importance to us their modern readers, with the inevitable consequence that many interesting minor writers are reduced to names and dates, and the even lesser are often not mentioned at all. Though we have tried also to provide a usable work of general reference, we offer the history primarily as a guide to the under-standing and appreciation of what we consider of greatest value in the literatures of Spain and Spanish America.

Beyond a necessary minimum, no attempt has been made to arrive at uniform criteria; the history displays therefore the variety of approach and opinion that is to be found in a good university department of literature, a variety which we hope will prove stimulating. Each section takes account of the accepted works of scholarship in its field, but we do not offer our history as a grey consensus of received opinions; each contributor has imposed his own interpretation to the extent that this could be supported with solid scholarship and argument.

Though the literature of Spanish America is not to be regarded simply as an offshoot of the literature of Spain, it seemed natural to link the two in our history since Spanish civilisation has left an indelible stamp on the Americas. Since Catalonia has been so long a part of Spain it seemed equally justified to include Catalan literature, an important influence on Spanish literature at certain times, and a highly interesting literature in its own right.

The bibliographies are not meant to be exhaustive. They are intended only as a guide to further reading. For more exhaustive inquiry recourse should be had to general bibliographies such as that by J. Simón Díaz.

R.O.J.

CONTENTS

LIST OF ABBREVIATIONS

BAE	*Biblioteca de Autores Españoles*
BH	*Bulletin Hispanique*
BHS	*Bulletin of Hispanic Studies*
BSS	*Bulletin of Spanish Studies*
CHA	*Cuadernos Hispanoamericanos*
Hisp	*Hispania*
HR	*Hispanic Review*
MLN	*Modern Language Notes*
MLQ	*Modern Language Quarterly*
MLR	*Modern Language Review*
PMLA	*Publications of the Modern Language Association of America*
RHi	*Revue Hispanique*
RHM	*Revista Hispánica Moderna*
RLC	*Revue de Littérature Comparée*
RO	*Revista de Occidente*
RR	*Romanic Review*

HISTORICAL INTRODUCTION

THREE DATES DOMINATE SPANISH NINETEENTH-CENTURY HISTORY: 1834, the return of the exiles after the death of Ferdinand VII; 1868, the 'Glorious Revolution' resulting in the fall of the Bourbon monarchy; and 1898, the Cuban Disaster. All three dates had important repercussions in Spanish literature.

Spain entered the nineteenth century still a largely static society. Three-quarters of the population lived on the land and an even larger fraction of wealth and employment remained concentrated in the primary (agricultural) sector of the economy. But agricultural pro-duction itself had failed to keep pace with a sharp rise in population at the end of the eighteenth century, and there were difficult times ahead for the countryside as war overtook much of the Peninsula. Meanwhile the embryo of manufacturing capacity was only just visible in Catalonia, and as late as 1869 it could be asserted that Spain's industry still did not provide 5 per cent of her exports. There was thus insufficient growth of industrial capacity to absorb surplus population. Still less could it bring into being a politically moderate, work-orientated middle class, large and influential enough to hold consistently the balance between reactionary conservatism and Liberal extremism—that task inevitably fell to the army.

Nevertheless, the seeds of politico-social change had already been sown by the reforms of Charles III in the late eighteenth century. Much of the progressive ideology which was to be the mainstay of Liberalism in Spain had already been formulated there before that century ended. The propaganda which accompanied the Napoleonic armies contributed more. So that the Constitution of 1812, drawn up by Spain's first Constituent Assembly in Cadiz during the French occupation, was far in advance of its time and of popular opinion. Its ideas animated Liberals for decades; but they were never to triumph. The modern history of Spain is principally the record of their failures.

The Napoleonic invasion galvanised Spain's national consciousness and led to one of her finest hours: the uprising of the *dos de mayo* of 1808 which sparked off a vast liberation movement. But the success of this movement, guaranteed by Wellington's victories, brought about no immediate change in institutions or power-groupings. If anything the anti-French struggle intensified the attachment felt by the masses to the so-called *castizo* traditions of Catholicism, nationalism, and reverence for the arbitrary power of the monarchy which formed a link with Spain's imperial past. The return of Ferdinand VII in 1814 from ignominious exile was greeted with cries of '¡Vivan las cadenas!' They heralded a period of black reaction which sent successive waves of Liberals into exile and which ended only with Ferdinand's death in 1833.

During his reign no effective opposition had been possible. Riego, who in 1820 had led the first *pronunciamiento* in favour of the Constitution of 1812, was felled by the Holy Alliance and executed. But once Ferdinand left the scene a major confrontation was inevitable. His infant daughter Isabella found her claim to the throne disputed by her reactionary uncle Don Carlos. The moderate Liberals promptly rallied to her cause, which was represented by the regency of her mother, María Cristina. The first Carlist Civil War broke out and lasted until 1839. Then a peace was patched up which, while it satisfied the extremists of neither side, at least had the effect of forcing Don Carlos out of the Peninsula for the time being. With his exit extreme traditionalism, lacking both decisive power and viable ideas, became increasingly committed to the avoidance of responsible decisions. Henceforth those on the far Right of Spanish politics remained in the wilderness, hopefully observing the contest which had emerged between the two factions of their opponents.

Power had split the Liberals. When María Cristina as regent had turned to them for support against Don Carlos, on behalf of her daughter, a section of the party seized the opportunity to ally the monarchy with the idea of gradual progress. These were the Moderates. Their aim broadly was to make Liberalism respectable by establishing about the throne a safely upper-middle-class governing élite opposed alike to the clerical absolutism of the Carlists and to revolutionary social change. They soon found themselves assailed on both fronts. The pattern of events in the second and third quarters of the nineteenth century in Spain is that of successive Carlist threats from the northern provinces, while at the same time waves of revolutionary violence led by the other wing of the Liberals, the *exaltados*, spread out from the other main cities to Madrid in 1820, 1835, 1840, and 1869-73. When successful, the *exaltados* tended to form short-lived governments chiefly characterised by well-meaning doctrinaire incompetence.

Meanwhile the most chronic problem, the economic one, remained. When the Moderates came to power Spain had neither the infrastructure (of communications in particular) nor the social structure to support industrial development. The basic tasks of responsible government until the early 1860s were to stave off the threats from the Right and the Left, to elude national bankruptcy—never far away —and to prepare the way for such modest industrial expansion as the country in the nineteenth century was to see. The land problem inevitably came first. The abolition of entail in 1836 produced the conditions for a radical redistribution of land hitherto concentrated in the hands of the nobility. In the same year the offensive against church lands and property also began. It was to last until 1859 when Pope Pius IX was finally compelled to agree to their disposal. Thus in a quarter of a century a new landowning middle class came into being and the balance of power in Spanish society shifted towards it. Between 1848 and 1858 some 500 miles of railway had been laid down. During the next decade 3,000 miles were constructed. It meant the end of internal customs barriers and cottage industries. Manufacturing development could go ahead. Beginning in the 1830s the Basque provinces and Catalonia began to experience a slow industrial revolution. Wheat-production increased by more than 30 per cent and the population continued to grow by a million every decade.

By the middle of the 1850s a fragile balance of power had begun to develop between the throne, the army, and the political figures of the centre parties. Paradoxically enough the revolutionary outbreak of 1848, which is such an important watershed in the history of other European countries, had been contained quite easily in Spain, where the new period in radical left-wing thought and the rise of working-class movements which it opened elsewhere was not apparent until 1868 and even then was not of major importance. Spanish political life enjoyed an interval of relative tolerance and conciliation. It was symbolised by the embrace of Espartero and O'Donnell, two of the chief political generals, in 1854 and the subsequent invention by the latter of the Liberal Union Party which practically took over government until 1868.

The Liberal Union Party drifted along in the wake of the new political tendency of the time. This was the progressive replacement of the power of the monarchy and the traditional Catholic ideal of the state associated with it, by the outlook of a nascent plutocracy wedded chiefly to belief in wealth and economic expansion. The myth, in the name of which the new oligarchy of merchant, landed, and industrial interests governed, was no longer that of a Christian society with a God-ordained subordination of classes under the king. It was the notion that material progress, chiefly reserved for the bourgeoisie, was the necessary starting-point for the onward march of man towards liberty and collective moral improvement. Protected on the Right by the temporary collapse of Carlism and the Concordat of 1851, while at the same time safeguarded on the Left by the outlawing of the Democratic (i.e. extreme radical anti-monarchical) Party which had been founded in 1849 from the remnants of the more uncompromising *exaltados,* the Liberal Unionists and their allies devoted themselves afresh to extending the socio-economic foundations of a modernised society and to improving its industrial, administrative, monetary, and mercantile substructure. It is noteworthy that while the Romantics, who were nearly all Liberals, had split along with the party into Moderates (Martínez de la Rosa, Rivas, Pastor Díaz, and the majority) and *exaltados* (Espronceda, Larra—with reservations—and the minority), the major writers of the mid-century (Alarcón, López de Ayala, Campoamor, and Núñez de Arce) were all Liberal Unionists. Tamayo, alas, was a Carlist.

The years of Liberal Union leadership, the 1850s and early 1860s, saw the achievement at last of some degree of political stability without undue authoritarianism, the doubling of Spain's foreign trade, vast extensions of both the road and railway systems, the completion of land redistribution, the modernisation of Spain's banking system, and a great influx of foreign capital. There was even money to finance military adventures abroad to Cochin China, Santo Domingo, Mexico, and above all to Morocco which made O'Donnell's reputation. But the new affluence was narrowly distributed and a breach opened up between the beneficiaries, grouped around the old upper-middle class, and an expanding, depressed, lower-middle class which was preparing to seize the political initiative.

There was no serious peasant unrest in Spain, in spite of inhuman conditions, during most of the nineteenth century, and no organised urban working-class movement before 1909. The major power-groups were therefore both bourgeois. As their divisions of interests grew during the 1860s, another political general, Prim, emerged as the leader of a left-wing coalition of reformist Progressives and Democrats which avoided attempts by O'Donnell and other Old Guard politicians to contain it. An economic crisis in 1867 precipitated a major revolution the following year. The immediate victim was Queen Isabella whose refusal to make political concessions to the Left brought about her fall. The Left itself made important gains: universal (male) suffrage (effective after 1875); religious freedom (not effective after 1875); liberty of the press and of association; and trial by jury (effective only after 1885). But the country remained a monarchy under Prim's imported Italian king, Amadeo of Savoy. The assassination of Prim, the collapse of the revolutionary coalition, guerrilla war in Cuba, and a big swing to the extreme Republican Left in the 1871 elections, brought Amadeo's abdication in February 1873. Meanwhile Don Carlos, seeing his opportunity, had called for a general revolt against the foreign intruder-king: the Second Carlist War had begun.

The Republic of 1873 soon found itself fighting on two fronts: against the Carlists in the north and against Federalist insurrections in some of the remaining provinces. It found saviours in a politician and —inevitably— a general: Castelar and Pavía. Reasserting governmental authority they staved off the Carlists and reduced the provinces to order by force. The way was now open for the sixteen-year-old son of Isabella, Alfonso XII, to be placed on the throne by a military *coup* (December 1874).

The restoration of the old monarchy produced a return to political stability and a resurgence of economic prosperity which lasted until the 1890s. By early 1876 the Second Carlist War had been won by the central government and the Cuban insurrection was brought under control in the following year. Meanwhile Cánovas, the dominant figure of the Restoration period, succeeded in conciliating the less extreme Catholic conservatives by agreeing to the continued control of education by the Church. At the same time he accepted a peaceful rotation of government between his party and the Liberals under Sagasta, which ensured the consolidation of Liberal reforms and the isolation of remaining Liberal extremists. A mixture of force and patronage administered by the local political bosses (*caciques*) of each party guaranteed that elections went the right way. In spite of a trade recession in the nineties, Spanish national self-confidence revived. The alarms and excursions of the earlier part of the century were forgotten; Cánovas was popularly regarded as the equal of Bismarck.

The crash came in 1898. Three years earlier rebellion had broken out afresh in Cuba. This time the United States intervened. In two naval engagements, which cost the Americans only one casualty, the antiquated Spanish fleets in the Pacific and the Caribbean were blown out of the water. Spain was forced to sign away the Philippines, Puerto Rico, and Cuba. A year earlier Cánovas had been assassinated. The death of her national hero and the loss of the last shreds of her empire left Spain at the end of the century stunned and humiliated. But already a new group of young writers and intellectuals had begun to emerge. They were eventually to be called after the disaster year: the Generation of 1898. Among their main preoccupations was the cultural and ideological regeneration of Spain.

The lesson of Spanish nineteenth-century history is that political change without corresponding social and economic advance is largely meaningless. Three major causes held up such advance. One was the selfish and reactionary attitude of Spain's ruling power-groups: the throne, the Church, the army, and the new plutocracy, expressed in the policies of their client-politicians. Another was the doctrinaire extremism and consistently revealed impracticality when in office of their opponents on the Left. The third and most important was Spain's basic poverty in material resources, which impeded such progress as was achieved. These impediments were among the chief legacies of the nineteenth century to the Spain of our own day.

Chapter 1

EARLY ROMANTICISM
MARTÍNEZ DE LA ROSA AND RIVAS

THE WORD *romántico* came into use in Spain rather late. Its first recorded appearance is in the *Crónica Científica y Literaria*, a Madrid newspaper, on 26 June 1818. Before this time the word which had been gaining acceptance was *romancesco*, but until 1814 it had had no clearly defined meaning, being used as we today would use words like 'odd', 'exaggerated', or 'far-fetched'.

In 1814 there arose between José Joaquín de Mora (1763-1864), the editor of the *Crónica*, and Johann Nikolas Böhl von Faber (1770-1864), a German scholar living in Cadiz, a controversy which opened the discussion about romanticism in Spain. Böhl, we must notice, was a monarchist of strongly reactionary ideas and a recent convert to Catholicism; Mora was a Liberal. From the first, therefore, the controversy had political overtones. In addition, since the first Spanish works that can be called Romantic even in the loosest sense were still to be published—abroad—during the 1820s by Mora himself, Blanco White, and other exiles, there were no Romantic works or doctrines at that time in Spain to discuss. Hence the debate necessarily remained abstract. It centred round the defence of Calderón (and the absolutist-theocratic ideas Böhl attributed to him) against Mora's rationalist and rather Neo-classic criticisms.

The importance of the controversy lies in the fact that it gave rise to a conception of Spanish romanticism which prevailed until our own day and has only recently been shown to be misleading in some of its major presuppositions. Böhl, under the influence of A. W. Schlegel, identified romanticism with the entire current of literature which is essentially Christian as opposed to the pagan Classic tradition of Greece and Rome. First appearing in the Middle Ages, with which it remained inextricably associated, this 'romantic' current of Western literature, though unified by its common Christian inspiration,

1

reflected (since it was written in the various vernacular tongues) the growing divergence of national characters in Europe. In contrast to Classic works which, being imitative, uniform, and rational, can be subjected to rules, these later writings cannot be so rigidly constrained and find their own forms and manner. For Böhl Neo-classicism was merely a temporary and regrettable interruption of this main current of European literature. He confidently anticipated a return to the popular, heroic, monarchical, and Christian tradition which had reached, he believed, a peak in the Golden Age and Calderón.

Böhl's two main errors of judgement: his attempt to associate romanticism too closely with Christianity and his consequent view of it as a continuous tradition from the Middle Ages to his own time, still survive to confuse critics. Only recently have writers on the movement begun to accept the distinction originally suggested by Menéndez Pelayo between the early 'historical' approach to romanticism pioneered by Böhl, and what is now variously called 'liberal', 'revolutionary', or 'contemporary' romanticism.

Böhl's broadsides were followed in October 1823 by Monteggia's article 'Romanticismo' in *El Europeo* of Barcelona and López Soler's 'Análisis de la cuestión agitada entre románticos y clasicistas' in the November issue. Monteggia's conciliatory article is chiefly memorable for marking the triumph of the word *romántico* over its various rivals: *romancesco, romanesco, romancista*, etc. López Soler reiterated with vigour Böhl's Christian interpretation of romanticism. It remained for Agustín Durán to bring to an end the first phase of critical discussion of romanticism with the publication in 1828 of his *Discurso sobre el influjo de la crítica moderna en la decadencia del teatro español*. . . . The Schlegelian conception of romanticism, transmitted and adapted by Böhl and López Soler, culminates in Durán's addition of a strong dash of Spanish cultural nationalism: the idea that the 'romantic' century *par excellence* was the Golden Century of Spain.

The 'Fernandine' critics, then, fell into various critical errors. They failed to associate romanticism with a specifically contemporary *Weltanschauung*; they failed to discuss seriously Romantic innovations in themes and literary technique; and they betrayed a marked tendency to interpret the movement in terms of the Spanish Catholic and absolutist monarchical tradition which was then, under Ferdinand VII, enjoying a revival.

The figure of exception is Alcalá Galiano. In his famous but too seldom read preface to Rivas's *El moro expósito,* written in 1833, he attempted to demolish the arguments in favour of 'historical' romanticism. Attacking the Golden Age as a period of fanatical obscurantism (joining hands here with his fellow-Liberals Mora, Blanco White, and a tradition reaching back through Quintana to the eighteenth-century literary debate) Galiano advocated recognition of what he called 'el romanticismo actual'. Mention of Dante, Shakespeare, and Calderón as 'romantic' writers was at last replaced by favourable reference to Scott, Hugo, and above all Byron. In fact acceptance of Byron, and to a lesser extent Hugo and Dumas, is the acid test of any view of romanticism advanced by their contemporaries.

The attempt by Galiano to present romanticism as a phenomenon essentially of his own time, reflecting a rigorously contemporary shift of outlook, together with his important reference to poetry on philosophical themes arising out of the poet's 'inner commotions', marks a great advance in the understanding of the movement.

After the polemic with Böhl mentioned above, Mora continued to edit progressive periodicals in Madrid until forced into exile by the French invasion of 1823. For the next twenty years he lived abroad, returning to his literary activities in Madrid only after the tide of romanticism had receded. Apart from publishing his own poems, including a collection of *Leyendas españolas* (1840) of which the earliest ones are among the first examples of the verse-*leyenda* in Spanish, he performed two valuable services to Spanish literature. In 1844 he compiled and published the critical essays of Lista, and in 1849 he translated from the French and published Fernán Caballero's *La gaviota.*

Alberto Lista (1775-1848) was, though a priest, in early life an advanced Liberal, *afrancesado,* and Freemason. Later, after a four-year exile in France, he prudently compromised with the regime of Ferdinand VII and was allowed to open a school, the Colegio de San Mateo, which included among its pupils Espronceda, Ventura de la Vega, Ochoa, Patricio de la Escosura, Roca de Togores, and several other future writers, soldiers, and statesmen. Durán too was Lista's pupil. During the Romantic period Lista was unquestionably the most learned and influential critic of the day.

Both Mora and Lista represented, in differing degrees, moderation. They are of great significance for the way they illustrate the transition from enlightened Neo-classicism to qualified romanticism. Mora, without moving away from his basic rationalist, humanitarian optimism and deism, came to admire Shakespeare, to translate Scott, and to advocate the study of English poetry, as well as that of the Classics. While rejecting 'las incongruencias de los autores románticos', he criticised rigid adherence to Neo-classic 'rules', accepted local colour and nationalism in literature, and hence modified his views considerably in favour of the Spanish Golden Age *comedia* and medieval poetry. Lista similarly sought a point of balance. Defending the 'rules' as useful guidelines, and 'imitation' against 'creation', he attacked the Romantics' reliance on genius, inspiration, and spontaneity, stressing the need for 'el gusto ejercitado y perfeccionado'. He was the first modern Spanish critic to offer a broad and systematic survey of Golden Age drama. Above all he stood for literature of Christian and moral inspiration. Embracing broadly the standpoint of 'historical' romanticism he led the attack on what he regarded as the subversive immoralism of *romanticismo actual*.

I. THE COMING OF ROMANTICISM

A glance at the state of Spanish literature under Ferdinand VII reveals a melancholy situation. Between 1814 and 1820 Quintana, Gallego, Martínez de la Rosa, and many writers and intellectuals underwent imprisonment. Moratín, Meléndez Valdés,[1] Lista, and Reinoso suffered exile. At home the censorship was crushing. Prose fiction, widely regarded as immoral and in any case an inferior branch of literature, came under especially heavy attack. In 1799 the government had attempted to suppress the publication of novels altogether and even translations of Scott remained officially forbidden until 1829. However, the *Colección de novelas*, an important series of contemporary European novels in translation, published from 1816 onwards by Cabrerizo in Valencia, did begin to prepare public taste for the work of native novelists. The advent of these was heralded by R. Húmara Salamanca's *Ramiro, Conde de Lucena* (1823), the first native historical novel, followed by López Soler's *Los bandos de Castilla* (1830), best remembered for its preface, which is an interesting Romantic manifesto.

Though the 1820 edition of his poetry was censured, Meléndez Valdés was still the main influence on the lyric. Lista, Mora, and Martínez de la Rosa all still dated a new epoch in Spanish poetry from his appearance; Quintana, who shared public esteem with him, was his pupil and biographer. The editorial group of *El Europeo* (1823-24), who are reasonably representative of younger writers, shared their admiration between Meléndez and Quintana, while enthusiastically disseminating translations of Schiller, Ossian, Gessner, Klopstock, Chateaubriand, and other European Romantic poets.

In the theatre, notwithstanding a spirited attack on Neo-classic drama by García Suelto in 'Reflexiones sobre el estado actual de nuestro teatro' (1805) and the appearance in the same year of Quintana's patriotic tragedy *Pelayo*, which portended the early dramatic works of Martínez de la Rosa and Rivas, Moratín remained the presiding genius. His influence was to outlast romanticism. For the rest the theatre had marked time. The absurd monstrosities which Moratín had satirised in *La comedia nueva* still held the stage. The smash-hit of the times was Grimaldi's *La pata de cabra*, a *comedia de magia* adopted from the French which ran for 125 performances between 1829 and 1833. (Compare García Gutiérrez's *El trovador*, the most successful Romantic play, with its twenty-five performances.) Golden Age *comedias* (mostly adapted) remained popular until the mid-1830s, after which they declined. Neo-classic survivals including Moratín's plays, bourgeois sentimental dramas, opera, and above all translations from the French also flourished.

The exiles had experienced the great changes which had been coming about in European taste and ideas at first hand and sometimes for many years: Rivas was abroad for a decade, Espronceda for seven years. Extremists (at first) in politics, the Romantics abroad were naturally open to extreme influences in thought and literary expression. Their return coincided with an easing of the censorship which suddenly allowed these influences freer play inside Spain itself. The results, far in advance of anything the 'Fernandine' critics had bargained for, led E. A. Peers to make his misleading distinction between the Romantic 'revival' and the Romantic 'revolt'. To understand what really happened it is necessary to remember a fact which Peers never squarely faced. A major change in literary forms seldom occurs unrelated to something deeper: a shift of sensibility, a change of attitude to the human condition, a new view of life.

Were this not the case, romanticism, considered as a purely literary phenomenon, could have made its appearance any time after dissatisfaction with Neo-classic models became widespread. What happened specifically in 1833 was that the ideological basis of romanticism proper, the change in the climate of ideas which came about chiefly as a result of the religious and philosophical crisis of the end of the eighteenth century, reinforced by the social, political, and economic upheavals of the French Revolution and the Napoleonic Wars, could no longer be contained at the frontier of Spain. It was now possible to question the whole pattern of religious, national, and moral absolutes on which the coherence of society and the welfare of the individual had hitherto been thought to depend. Those who seized the opportunity were a minority. Deeply nostalgic themselves for the old certainties, confused and sometimes anguished by their new insight, their work is often ambivalent. The hostility which their outlook provoked has obscured critical perspective ever since. But one fact is clear: theirs is the romanticism which has survived. There is an unbroken continuity from these Romantics' sceptical *criticismo*, however limited and sporadic, to the Generation of 1898 and into the present.

This is not to underrate the contradictions and inconsistencies inherent in the Romantic movement. There were Liberals who were not Romantics (e.g. Mora) and there were Romantics who were not Liberals (e.g. Zorilla). Lista, and later Rivas, often seem to face in both directions. In the same way, not all those who gave literary expression to anguished insight or perceived in it the hallmark of the movement, did so consistently. Rivas changed sides on this issue as he did in politics; so did Pastor Díaz. The problem is rendered more acute by the fact that all the Romantics were united by nationalism, hostility to Neo-classicism, and attraction to the Golden Age; they shared the same innovations of diction and the same *topoi*. But in the end what separates Zorrilla, for example, from Espronceda is more essential than what united them.

II. MARTÍNEZ DE LA ROSA

Two figures who emerge in the initial stages of the movement, both significantly older than the other major Romantics, are Francisco Martínez de la Rosa (1787-1862) and Ángel Saavedra (1791-1865), later to become duque de Rivas. Originally a pupil of Mora and a precocious young professor of moral philosophy at the University of Granada, Martínez de la Rosa was an influential member of the ultra-Liberal wing of the *Cortes* of 1813 and was imprisoned under Ferdinand VII for almost six years. The first group of his writings belongs to this period. It includes *Lo que puede un empleo* (1812), a daringly anti-clerical satire on his traditionalist political opponents, followed in the same year by *La viuda de Padilla*, a slow and repetitive, five-act, heroic tragedy in verse, modelled on Alfieri. Its theme was the topical one of liberty or death. *La niña en casa y la madre en la máscara* (1821) illustrates the continuing predominance of the Moratinian manner in comedy. *Morayma* (1818), another heroic tragedy, is too like the first. The last work in the group is still completely Neo-classic: an elegant translation of Horace's *Epistola ad Pisones* (1819).

Martínez de la Rosa's political views had meanwhile become more moderate. When after his release he became Prime Minister for a few months in 1822, he was opposed by the left wing and finally forced into exile in France (1823-31). During this exile most of Martínez de la Rosa's best-known works were written. They include, apart from the *Poética* (1822): *Aben Humeya*, another Moorish play on the theme of liberty; *Edipo*, a rewrite of the Classical tragedy; and above all *La conjuración de Venecia*; three plays which cannot be dated exactly, though they were probably written in this order between 1827 and 1830. The *Poetica*'s appendices reveal a patriotic desire to make the best defence possible of Spanish literature from the Neo-classicist position which still tries to subject taste to rules. This in itself illustrates Martínez de la Rosa's undogmatic position. Not surprisingly, in the prologue to his poems he writes of the *clásicos* and *románticos*: 'tengo como cosa asentada, que unos y otros llevan razón'—provided that both avoided extremes! Similarly his rule in the composition of *Aben Humeya* was to 'olvidar todos los sistemas y seguir como única regla . . . el código del buen gusto'.

Martínez de la Rosa's early heroic tragedies contain sundry Romantic trappings: local colour including music and choruses, which he was the first to introduce and advocate in Spain; crowd scenes; Spanish medieval and Moorish settings; spectacular effects such as the fire in *Aben Humeya*; libertarian ideals; and even a certain degree of on-stage violence and horror. But missing are a genuine sense of irresistibly adverse fate, its attendant pathos, and any formulation of the Romantic love-ideal. *La conjuración de Venecia* comes significantly closer to the true Romantic pattern in that we dimly perceive in Rugiero features of the Romantic hero. His mysterious origin, his melancholy, his tendency to relate life itself to love, and his subjection to hostile fatality show Martínez de la Rosa groping towards a new type-figure. But *La conjuración de Venecia*, though marking the first real attempt to express the new sensibility in dramatic terms, falls short of success. Rugiero, though young, handsome, and successful, is portrayed as deeply unhappy merely because he is illegitimate. Even this is simply a device to bring about the recognition scene at the end. Rugiero in fact lacks both the insight and the symbolic role of the genuine Romantic hero. The conspiracy rather than the theme of love and fate is the centre of the play. Martínez de la Rosa, while recognising vaguely 'what was in the air', failed to formulate it adequately.

The rest of Martínez de la Rosa's work includes an over-documented historical novel, *Isabel de Solís* (published in parts 1837-46), and three minor plays: *Los celos infundados* (1833), *La boda y el duelo* (1839), and *El español en Venecia* (1840).

III. RIVAS

The literary career of Ángel de Saavedra, duque de Rivas, has points of comparison with that of Martínez de la Rosa. Like him, Rivas began by writing pastoral *romances cortos* in the tradition of Meléndez, interspersed with declamatory patriotic odes ('A la victoria de Bailén', 1808; 'A la victoria de Arapiles', 1812), before evolving in the direction of romanticism. Like Martínez de la Rosa also, Rivas was among the writers in Cadiz in 1812 and remained for some years afterwards a Liberal *exaltado*. From 1823 to 1834 he lived successively in Britain, Malta, and France, married, started a family, and for a time earned his living by teaching painting. During his stay in Malta he enjoyed the friendship of Sir John Hookham Frere, whose encouragement of his already strong interest in Spanish medieval and Golden Age literature was gratefully acknowledged in the dedication of *El moro expósito*. His swing towards romanticism in middle life took him with *Don Álvaro* into the centre of the movement and momentarily to the leadership of it. This renders all the more striking the insignificance of his later plays and his relapse into the superficiality of the *leyendas* in the 1850s.

Rivas's shorter lyric poems, though fresher in inspiration than those of Martínez de la Rosa, are none the less, with a few exceptions, disappointingly conventional in both theme and manner. In his main set of love-poems, to the mysterious Olimpia, the note of real passion is rarely heard above the plaintive tone inherited from a century which identified poetry with soft sentimental emotion. Here only two themes stir Rivas to memorable poetry. One is that of exile and the spectacle of his country prostrate under the heel of Ferdinand VII. In 'El desterrado' and his most famous lyric 'El faro de Malta', Rivas at length achieves noble expression of genuine feeling. But although the theme, tone, and manner of 'El desterrado' all point in the Romantic direction, Rivas was still only on the edge of Romantic sensibility, as we see from the comparison in the other poem of the Maltese lighthouse to the light of reason amid the swirling passions, a comparison nearer to the outlook of the Enlightenment than to that of the younger generation.

The other important theme of Rivas's shorter poems is that of the inexorable passage of time. 'El tiempo', 'Brevedad de la vida', 'El otoño', and 'El sol poniente' are Rivas's nearest approaches to that poetry of 'sesgo metafísico' which Alcalá Galiano, Martínez de la Rosa, and others considered especially characteristic of romanticism. But like Meléndez, from whom he borrowed the theme, Rivas recoiled from its deeper implications. From contemplating the ephemerality of existence and the inevitability of death, which brought him close to that awareness of the human predicament which is so prominent in Espronceda, he took refuge in resignation to the will of God.

Rivas's longer narrative poems: El paso honroso (1812), Florinda (1826), and El moro expósito (1834), together with the Romances históricos (first collected edition 1841), belong to that type of poetry essentially nationalist in inspiration, set for preference in the Middle Ages or the Siglo de Oro, glorifying traditional Spanish values (and all that they imply), which conforms to the ideas of Böhl von Faber and Durán. In the preface to the Romances históricos Rivas in fact embraced their outlook.

Neither El paso honroso nor Florinda exhibits the conflict of love and fate which is one of the most basic Romantic themes; in both poems physical strife is more important than emotional conflict. With El moro expósito, written in romantic real metre between 1829 and 1833 and published in 1834, the emphasis shifts markedly. While the poem still falls broadly within the bounds of 'historical' romanticism, love now occupies the central position. Hostile fate (unlike the merited fate which overtakes Rodrigo in Florinda) is prominent both when Mudarra, like Don Álvaro later, inadvertently kills the father of his beloved, and when in Canto III the young Gonzalo Gustios unwittingly sets it in motion against his family at the banquet. Noteworthy in the latter case is the triumph of the hostile principle over the divine protection symbolised in the relic of the True Cross given to Gonzalo. These two features indicate the direction in which Rivas was now moving.

Much in the later part of *El moro expósito* portends *Don Álvaro*. But in comparison with it the basic conception of the poem appears confused and unsatisfying. Arbitrary hostile fate plays a large part in the misfortunes of Gonzalo Gustios and his son Mudarra. It is that same fate which strikes relentlessly at Don Álvaro. Yet at the end ' f *El moro expósito* Providence triumphs over it and is repeatedly declared to be instrumental in favouring Mudarra's vengeance. Ruy Velázquez, the agent of fatality, is a figure of satanic evil, but there is no element of cosmic rebellion in his character; on the contrary, he attempts desperately in *Romance* X to conciliate Heaven. Finally, when the love-principle triumphs at last, it is suddenly subordinated to religious belief, as Kerima, at the very altar where she is to be married, decides dramatically to take the veil. In each of these features we perceive an element of vacillation, which ultimately is what robs *El moro expósito* of really deep human significance.

What is lacking in Rivas's poetry in fact, and indeed in his work as a whole, is that consciousness of life's enigma, that often despairing preoccupation with human destiny in a universe no longer ruled by a benevolent Providence, which is part of the legacy of the Romantics to our own age.

IV. 'DON ÁLVARO'

The exception in Rivas's work is *Don Álvaro* (1835). It follows a respectable number of earlier, though markedly inferior, dramatic productions which the author later found unworthy of inclusion in the first edition of his *Obras completas* (1854). These plays comprise *Ataúlfo* (1814), which was prohibited by the censorship and has not survived complete; *Aliatar* (1816); *Doña Blanca* (1817), the only manuscript of which was destroyed in 1823; *El Duque de Aquitania* (1817); *Malek-Adhel* (1818); *Lanuza* (1822); *Arias Gonzalo* (1826 or 1827); and *Tanto vales cuanto tienes* (written in Malta in 1828, but

*

not published until 1840). All of these merit much the same judgment as the plays of Martínez de la Rosa except for *La conjuración de Venecia*: they incorporate certain semi-Romantic features (such as Moorish and medieval settings, passion and violence, and libertarian declamation), but they are not genuinely Romantic in spirit. This is far from the case with *Don Álvaro*. It stands alone, enigmatically, in the middle of Rivas's work, different in manner and outlook from anything he wrote before or after. Its theme, the triumph of fate over love, is the basic theme of all the major Spanish Romantic dramas.

This interpretation is confirmed by Don Álvaro's reflections about life in the famous soliloquy (Act III, Scene iii);

> ¡Qué carga tan insufrible
> es el ambiente vital
> para el mezquino mortal
> que nace en signo terrible!

reflections which include the dawning realisation that love itself is merely a trick of hostile fate:

> Así, en la cárcel sombría
> mete una luz el sayón,
> con la tirana intención
> de que un punto el preso vea
> el horror que lo rodea
> en su espantosa mansión.

The coincidences in the play, which Azorín found so unconvincing, are deliberately designed to illustrate further the operation of the malignant force which drives Don Álvaro inexorably to suicide, a suicide which, far from being inexplicable, as N. González Ruiz asserts,[2] is the natural climax of the action: the rejection by the Romantic hero of a life from which the last existential prop has been removed with the death of Leonor. 'El cadáver romántico', in Casalduero's words, 'es un testimonio de la falta de sentido de la vida'.[3]

For the rest, *Don Álvaro* represents in its mixture of verse and prose; in the use of local colour (the *aguaducho*, the *posada*, and the *sopa* scenes which open Acts I, II, and V); and in the striking use of contrast (the tragic climax of Act I followed by the noisy gaiety of the *posada*, followed in turn by the emotional exaltation of Leonor's renunciation of the world), the most striking example of Romantic

2 *

stage-technique. Especially noteworthy is the brilliant use of the three local-colour scenes as exposition and re-exposition designed to give the audience the information required to understand the following incidents.

Two further features merit brief attention. These are the prison and the monastery/convent as Romantic symbols. Nearly every Spanish Romantic hero from Rugiero of *La conjuración de Venecia* to Adán of *El diablo mundo* has a spell in prison. The reference in Don Álvaro's soliloquy to

este mundo
¡qué calabozo profundo . . .!

sufficiently explains the attraction of the prison for Romantic writers. It symbolises existence. We find it re-echoed as late as Baroja's *Vidas sombrías* in *El amo de la jaula*. Similarly in *El travador* and elsewhere entry into a convent or monastery symbolises retreat from the new awareness of the modern human predicament, which we have seen finding dramatic expression in terms of hostile fate, back into the old serenity and confidence of the religious belief. But always as here in *Don Álvaro* the world of insight, the anti-vital principle, breaks in afresh. Retirement to the cloister is for the Romantics a reaction of despair, not a solution. It merely indicates a certain nostalgia in their minds for the time when it was.

After *Don Álvaro*, which was not initially a box-office success, Rivas returned to his earlier creative pattern and in 1840 published the first edition of his *Romances históricos*. To its important preface defending the ancient verse-form against the contempt of Hermosilla, reference has already been made. The eighteen *romances* themselves seem to have been written chiefly between 1833 and 1839, though the dates of most are uncertain. They constitute Rivas's best-known contribution to the current of Romantic poetry dedicated to traditional and patriotic themes and look forward to the *Leyendas* of Zorrilla which were soon to follow. The typical *romance* of Rivas describes in strikingly vivid terms either a characteristic anecdote from Spanish history: the murder by King Pedro I of his brother Don Enrique; the death of Villamediana; the *castizo* gesture of the Conde de Benavente ('Un castellano leal'); or a memorable national triumph ('La victoria de Pavía', 'Bailén'). In either case Rivas's now fully developed gifts of painter-like presentation and dramatic expression are prominently displayed, though in general the shorter *romances* concerned with a single incident compressed into a small number of visually effective scenes in rapid succession are superior.

How far Rivas moved away in later life from the extreme romanticism of *Don Álvaro* is revealed by his later *comedia de magia*: *El desengaño en un sueño* (1842), his Academy Speech (1860), and his preface to *La familia de Alvareda* (1861) by Fernán Caballero. In the central character of *El desengaño en un sueño*, Lisardo, a monster borrowed from the Golden Age *comedia*, we perceive features which suggest that Rivas also had in mind to attack the satanism and cosmic defiance prominent in several Romantic figures. The Academy Speech and preface to *La familia de Alvareda* confirm the extent of Rivas's change of heart. In the former he attacks the 'doctrinas disolventes, impías y corruptoras' which literature, and the novel especially, were spreading. In the latter he praises Fernán Caballero for combating them. He was unfortunately not alone in taking this reactionary stand, as we shall see in a future chapter.

NOTES

1. For discussion of Quintana, Moratín, and Meléndez Valdés, see Nigel Glendinning, *A Literary History of Spain: The Eighteenth Century*, pp.83–4, 111 ff., 75 ff.
2. N. González Ruiz, *El duque de Rivas* (Madrid, 1944), p. 13.
3. J. Casalduero, *Forma y visión de El diablo mundo* (Madrid, 1951), p. 29.

Chapter 2

ESPRONCEDA AND LARRA

I. ESPRONCEDA

THE TWO WRITERS associated with the more despairing and rebellious (in the view of the times, more subversive) kind of romanticism are Espronceda and Larra.

José de Espronceda (1808-42) was originally a pupil of Lista's, but soon became impatient with his teacher's prudent Liberalism and qualified acceptance of Romantic literary doctrines. After a flamboyant attempt in adolescence to found a revolutionary secret society to avenge the death of Riego, he was banished to a monastery, where with Lista's encouragement he began writing *Pelayo*, an epic on the theme of the Moorish conquest of Spain, fortunately left unfinished. In 1827 he found it wise to emigrate. After his return from exile in 1833 he continued to be politically active on the extreme conspiratorial Left of the Liberal Party and in 1840 became a founder-member of the Republican Party. He died suddenly, probably from a throat infection, in May 1842 not long after entering parliament.

There is little in *Pelayo* (written, like Rivas's similar *Florinda*, in stiff *octaves reales*) to suggest Espronceda's future evolution. It is not in fact until Espronceda tried his hand at fiction in a rambling and undistinguished historical novel, *Sancho Saldaña* 1834), that we perceive signs of his future outlook. The core of Sancho's character is the Romantic formula 'vacío del alma' combined with a deep desire to recover his lost belief in some enduring principle, leading to despair when love fails to provide it. Like Rugiero's in *La conjuración de Venecia*, Sancho's misery is quite arbitrary and unrelated to his actual situation. His repeated exclamations of horror at the prospect of further existence can be interpreted only in terms of Espronceda's own growing spiritual and intellectual malaise.

The growth of this pessimistic insight can be followed in his

14

poetry. Three groups of lyrics stand out. The first is that of the
patriotic and libertarian political poems beginning with 'A la patria'
(1829) which like Rivas's more popular 'El desterrado' attacks the
prevailing despotism in Spain and bewails the exiles' lot. This was
followed by the much more aggressive sonnet on the death of Torrijos,
and the lament for Joaquín de Pablo in whose futile *pronunciamiento*
Espronceda had taken part in 1830. Finally, in 1835 Espronceda
wrote a call to arms against the Carlists, which is simply a rabble-
rousing demand for bloodshed and violence:

> ¡Al arma, al arma! ¡Mueran los carlistas!
> Y al mar se lancen con bramido horrendo
> de la infiel sangre caudalosos ríos
> y atónito contemple el Océano
> sus olas combatidas
> con la traidora sangre enrojecidas.

The intemperate and exalted tone of this poem and the 'Dos de
Mayo' (1840), at a time when the older Martínez de la Rosa and
Rivas were in rapid retreat from their earlier principles, sufficiently
marks the gap between the two Romantic generations.

A second group of lyrics includes 'El canto del cosaco', 'Canción
del pirata', 'El mendigo', 'El reo de muerte', and 'El verdugo'. These
poems in different ways illustrate the Romantics' hostility to social
bonds and conventions, and their aspiration to absolute individual
liberty. 'El mendigo' in particular with its rancorous tone of protest
marks the beginning of 'social' poetry in Spanish. But the poems
of real importance are 'El reo de muerte' and 'El verdugo'. In the
former we note the absence of any reference to the condemned
prisoner's crime or sense of remorse. It is fate, not his own actions,
which the prisoner curses, while the end of the poem, with its
emphasis on illusion shattered by bitter reality (Espronceda's favourite
theme), further emphasises the underlying meaning. We are all in the
prison-house of life, condemned by fate to inexorable death: *el reo
de la muerte* is Everyman. 'El verdugo' is more explicitly symbolic.
At the climax of the poem the headsman is identified with an eternal
force of evil willed into existence by a cruel God against whom man
strives in vain.

Closely associated are the poems of the third group which includes
'A Jarifa en una orgía', 'A una estrella', and most of all the 'Himno
al Sol'. This last occupies a unique place among Espronceda's shorter

poems as the only one of them which is exclusively philosophic. In the body of the poem a carefully organised series of contrasts with time's mutability establishes the Sun as a symbol of all that is dependably eternal and enduring. But at the climax this pattern of absolute dependability is brutally shattered:

> ¿Y habrás de ser *eterno*, inextinguible,
> sin que *nunca jamás* tu inmensa hoguera
> pierda su resplandor, *siempre* incansable
> . . . y solo, *eterno*, *perenal*, sublime
> monarca poderoso, dominando?
> No; . . .

Nothing can be conceived of as eternal: not merely love, glory, and happiness, but even truth and certainty. Ideals and beliefs, the sun-symbol reminds us, have no absolute time-defying existence.

It is superficial in this connection to relate Espronceda's sceptical pessimism simply to his unhappy love-affair with Teresa Mancha. Teresa as a woman of flesh and blood was far less important than what she represented: the attempt to promote human love to fill the gap left by the collapse of faith in religion or reason. Casalduero is right in his assertion:

> No debemos partir de Teresa para llegar al sentimiento de la vida de Espronceda, sino que partiendo del sentimiento que de la vida tiene el poeta debemos llegar a ver la forma que debía adquirir su amor.[1]

El estudiante de Salamanca, which appeared, in two parts, in 1836 and 1837, is one of the first and best examples of the *leyenda*, a favourite narrative genre of the Spanish Romantics, who cultivated it both in verse and prose. It tells the story of a corrupt and arrogant young nobleman, Don Félix de Montemar, who, after killing the brother of his abandoned mistress, is drawn by a spectre to a macabre punishment, meeting his own funeral on the way. Hardly longer than some of the *Romances históricos* which Rivas was already writing, it has all their vivacity and suspensefulness, if not their brilliant use of visual effects. It differs from the *Romances*, however, in being completely a work of imagination, in its audacious diversity of metres, and most of all in the characters of Don Félix and Elvira. She illustrates the Romantic conception of love as, at one and the same time, both an illusion and the only vital ideal. Once the illusion is outlived, her hold on life is broken. Like the lovers of Hartzenbusch's *Los amantes de Teruel*, where the symbolism is identical, she simply dies of grief. Don Félix is at first glance anything but a figure of Romantic insight. The element of abstract thought which (in Don Álvaro's soliloquy, for example) occasionally allows the Romantic hero to express the author's deeper vision of life, is conspicuously absent from his make-up. But Espronceda cannot resist turning him, without warning, into a figure of cosmic rebellion:

> . . . alma rebelde que el temor no espanta,
> hollada, sí, pero jamás vencida;
> el hombre, en fin, que en su ansiedad quebranta
> su límite a la cárcel de la vida,
> y a Dios llama ante él a darle cuenta,
> y descubrir su inmensidad intenta.

The victim of the prison-house no longer groans, but rattling the bars of his cell calls his unjust gaoler to account. In contrast, the *gemido* of the phantom in the middle of the poem, largely uncon-nected with the story, represents an outcry of the poet himself once more against the bitter reality behind the world of appearances, against the irreparable loss of protective illusion:

> ¡Ay! el que descubre por fin la mentira;
> ¡Ay! el que la triste realidad palpó; . . .

II. 'EL DIABLO MUNDO'

These lines might serve as an epigraph for Espronceda's last and most ambitious poem, *El diablo mundo*, which began to be published in 1840 and was unfinished at the time of his death. It is an allegory of existence. In it Adán, who stands for man, is allowed to choose between death and understanding of ultimate truth or eternal life. Inevitably he chooses the latter, and the poem records his discovery of the bitter consequences. Most of the principal elements of Espron-ceda's final outlook are contained in the prologue to the poem. The chorus of voices expresses his doubts and disillusionment; the Spirit of Man his rebellion against a malign God who is in turn perhaps only a hypothesis. In the body of the poem Adán comes, like man, naked and guileless into the world, only to find himself according to Romantic precept at once immured (literally and figuratively) in the prison-house. Here his bitter introduction to reality begins. As yet, however, he is possessed of the fount of illusion—Youth; and at the touch of love his shackles are broken. So far the poem is worked out in detail. But from here on difficulties of interpretation supervene because of the poem's unfinished state. It is clear that disillusionment follows. Two further phases are incompletely mapped out: Adán's dissatisfaction with the love-ideal and finally his dawning tragic insight. Beside the corpse of Lucía, an innocent child, arbitrarily struck down by Death, Adán suddenly becomes aware of the problems posed by her inexplicably undeserved fate. In the voice and language of the luciferine Spirit of Man in the prologue he questions defiantly:

> El Dios ese . . .
>   que inunda a veces de alegría,
> Y otras veces, cruel, con mano impía
> Llena de angustia y de dolor el suelo

and is suddenly aware of 'La perpetua ansiedad que en él se esconde': the Romantic (and modern) quest for a satisfying answer to life's enigma. Here the poem breaks off. But although its climax was never written, we can hardly doubt its nature. It is foreshadowed in the grim warning of the Spirit of Life in Canto I that if Adán ever came to regret his decision, he was to remember that the responsibility for it was his alone.

Espronceda's plays and the articles he contributed to various periodicals are disappointing. He had little ability to present conflict and mistook horrific effects for dramatic ones. Like many creative writers he was a poor critic and only one brief article, the amusing 'El Pastor Clasiquino' satirising the bucolic Neo-classical tradition of poetry, is nowadays remembered.

III. LARRA

The chief meeting-place of the Romantics in Madrid in the middle 1830s was the café of the Teatro del Príncipe (now the Español). Here publishers like Carnerero and Delgado and the manager of the Príncipe itself met Espronceda, Mesonero, Bretón, García Gutiérrez, and their fellow-Romantics in what came to be known as El Parnasillo. In 1838 this group formed the short-lived Liceo Artístico y Literario which for a time rivalled the Ateneo (founded 1820) as a centre for literary life, with debates, lectures, poetry readings, and other similar functions. Apart from Espronceda, the major figure of the *Parnasillo* was Mariano José de Larra (1809-37). In 1828, rebelling against his family background, he abandoned his studies and founded his first periodical, *El Duende Satírico del Día*. Only five numbers appeared, but the best of these already reveal extraordinary powers of observation and particularly mordant humour in a boy of nineteen. The following year, against parental opposition, he married Pepita Wetoret. The marriage, whose reflections can be seen in 'El casarse pronto y mal', was a disastrous failure and though the couple had three children, they separated in 1834, the year, ironically, of Larra's drama *Macías* with its exalted vision of the love-ideal. During the interval he had founded another short-lived satirical review, *El Pobrecito Hablador* (1832-33), and translated a number of plays from the French, chiefly by Scribe, as well as staging his own full-length *No más mostrador* (1831), based on a one-act piece by a French author. *El Conde Fernán González*, Larra's only other original play, though extant, was never performed.

Macías stands as an early monument in Spain to Romantic passion. In it Larra may be said to have invented the great Romantic formula for drama: love thwarted by fate leading to death. Again and again in the play Macías asserts that life without love is meaningless torment, and in the lyrical climax of Act III proclaims explicitly the Romantic love-ideal:

> Los amantes son solos los esposos
> su lazo es el amor ¿Cuál hay más santo?
> . . . ¿Qué otro asilo
> Pretendes más seguro que mis brazos?
> Los tuyos bastaránme, y si en la tierra
> asilo no encontramos, juntos ambos
> moriremos de amor. ¡Quién más dichoso
> que aquél que amando vive y muere amado!

Macías reveals a curiously hybrid technique, since it both attempts clumsily to observe the unities and to follow the fashion of imitating the Golden Age *comedia*.[2] The imitation is of course doctored. There is significantly no *gracioso* and no sub-plot. The ending especially, with its loud Romantic overtones, contrasts completely with the sensibility of the Golden Age. The play as a whole is defective both as a work of art and of stagecraft. The verse-medium is stiff and the imitation of the Golden Age manner self-conscious. Macías, for all his exaltation, is something of a light-weight. Above all, not enough of the passion is expressed in action. But its influence on later plays, *El trovador* of Gutiérrez and *Los amantes de Teruel* of Hartzenbusch in particular, compels us to regard it as a seminal work.

Apart from *Macías* and a historical novel, *El doncel de don Enrique el doliente* (1834), Larra's major writings are the theatre criticism, literary and political satire, and *costumbrista* articles he published in his own two periodicals and a half a dozen others. They show him to have been at once the most intellectually analytic and the most unhappy of the Spanish Romantics. He struggled to believe in the triumph of truth over error, the inevitable progress of humanity, and in his own phrase, 'la regeneración de España'. But the consistent betrayal of Liberal ideas by successive Liberal ministries in the 1830s, which disillusioned Rivas and exasperated Espronceda, produced in Larra a cold and bitter despair. This combined with his own more abstract scepticism, his failure to get into parliament, and his break with his mistress, Dolores Armijo, to produce his suicide.

Larra's early articles in *El Duende* are very unequal, but they already illustrate some of his basic characteristics: his interest in ideas rather than things; the faith in the truth which underlies his biting exposure of shams and hypocrisy; and the deep, indignant, patriotism which kept him always among the opposition. 'El café' above all, his first really memorable article, places him, while still in his teens, far ahead of the still feeble efforts of his fellow-*costumbristas*.

The characteristic of *costumbrismo* was its interest, not in observed reality as a whole, but in those aspects of reality which were both typical of a given region or area in Spain and at the same time pleasingly picturesque and amusing. The field of the *costumbrista* writers, that is to say, was deliberately limited. Their concern was not to describe popular life and behaviour as it really was. Their aim was to select only what gave a striking impression of 'local colour', especially if it represented a pleasant survival from the past. They helped to bring into being what we now call *la España de pandereta*: the peninsular equivalent of 'Merrie England', and just as artificial. The *costumbrista* movement has a long history in Spanish letters before the early nineteenth century. It was reinforced by the emergence of a general European interest in short visual descriptions of local types and customs, and especially by the 'historical' Romantics' attachment to what was intrinsically *castizo* and Spanish. A good example from Larra is 'La diligencia' of 1835. But while this is typical *costumbrismo*, it is not typical Larra—except in the brilliance of its technique. It is a piece of satirical description for its own sake. It lacks the outright social criticism and genuine reformist intention which are inseparable from Larra's best work. For it is not only that Larra portrays individuals while the *costumbristas* usually portray types; it is not only that he excels in neat construction, humorous dialogue, and irony, while their articles are so often replete with rambling description; what makes Larra a great writer, rather than merely a great *costumbrista*, is the deep personal involvement which brings the man constantly into his writings, and the courageous discussion of the problem of Spain which these writings contain.

The typical *costumbrista* article by Larra deals either with some specific aspect of *madrileño* life—cafés, housing, parks, a masked ball —or more usually of Spanish social life in general—education, cultural life, the class system, the public services. After an opening generalisation, Larra passes swiftly to concrete illustrations. His own participation and first-person description frequently add impact and conviction to his criticism. Observed detail, artfully humorous dialogue, and ironic asides combine with comic exaggeration to present recognisable people and situations in a satirical light. The result is usually amusing and sometimes hilarious, but in many of Larra's representative articles an undertone of despair is present at the close. Despite his opposition to negativism, defeatism, and self-deception by Spaniards, the picture which emerges from his *costumbrista* articles is that of a corrupt, empty society rotted by inefficiency, idleness, and apathy.

Larra's political articles have, with a few exceptions, proved less durable than his *costumbrista* social criticism, though he himself undoubtedly regarded them as more important. Indeed this is perhaps the reason. For in his political writings Larra often took his *papel de redentor* so seriously as to compromise his satirical manner. They present the rare spectacle of a young man who began as a moderate and became continuously more radical with age. But since Larra tends to attack attitudes of mind rather than socio-economic evils, and sees the remedy in education and enlightenment rather than in specific measures of reform, we see no very definite doctrinal content in his work.

As a literary critic Larra began conventionally in *El Duende* from a Neo-classic standpoint. But in his review of Martínez de la Rosa's *Poesías* in 1833 he took his stand firmly beside Alcalá Galiano in asserting a necessary connection between literature (which for him always meant literature of ideas) and the spirit of his own times. Early in 1836 he developed the idea into his major statement of opinion, 'Literatura. Rápida ojeada sobre la historia e índole de la nuestra', which ranks as a major Romantic manifesto. Attacking, with Mora and Galiano, the religious intolerance and ideological stagnation of the Golden Age, and hailing in the Reformation the origins of 'las innovaciones y el espíritu filosófico', Larra called for a literature which reflected recent intellectual progress 'rompiendo en todas partes antiguas cadenas, desgastando tradiciones caducas y derribando ídolos . . . una literatura nueva, expresión de la sociedad nueva que componemos'. Its guiding principles were to be liberty and truth.

Larra was able to identify this new literature largely with romanticism and his articles on major Romantic plays, Spanish and French, are of central importance. By far the most revealing of them, however, are the two in which he attacks Dumas's *Antony*. For here Larra suddenly found himself face to face with a truth which was neither 'útil', 'bueno', nor the 'expresión del progreso humano'. It was on the contrary Byron's 'fatal truth', Leopardi's 'infausta verità', Espronceda's 'verdad amarga': the Romantics' realisation that the truth about human existence might be in total disharmony with an optimistic interpretation of life. Larra states this, indeed, as a fact, which he not only does not attempt to deny, but even holds to be the inevitable discovery of the rest of mankind in the future. His recognition of it and at the same time his desire to shield his fellow-men from it, we shall see also in the work of Valera and Unamuno.

NOTES

1. Casalduero, *Forma y visión de El diablo mundo* (Madrid, 1951), p. 129.
2. See Edward M. Wilson and Duncan Moir, *A Literary History of Spain: The Golden Age—Drama, 1492–1700.*

Chapter 3

ROMANTICISM'S FULL TIDE

AMONG THE VARIOUS LITERARY PERIODICALS published and staffed by
the Romantics were *El Artista,* founded by Eugenio de Ochoa and
Federico de Madrazo in January 1835 with the collaboration of
Espronceda, Pastor Díaz, Escosura, Ventura de la Vega, Tassara, and
eventually Zorrilla, among others, and its successor *No Me Olvides,*
edited by Jacinto de Salas y Quiroga. This began in May 1837 and
soon had among its contributors many of the earlier group as well as
Mora and Miguel de los Santos Álvarez. In the columns of these two
publications and those of the more important middle-of-the-road
Semanario pintoresco, founded in 1836 by Mesonero Romanos, it is
possible to survey the work of most of the second-rank Spanish
Romantic writers.

I. GARCÍA GUTIÉRREZ

Indubitably the foremost among these, for their contributions to the
theatre—the battleground of the Romantic movement—are Antonio
García Gutiérrez (1813-84) and Juan Eugenio Hartzenbusch (1806-
80). García Gutiérrez arrived in Madrid from Cadiz, where he had
been a poor medical student, in 1833. After living precariously as a
journalist and—inevitably—translating several French plays he
joined the *Parnasillo* and gained the friendship of its leading members.
Through the intervention of Espronceda, García Gutiérrez succeeded
in staging in March 1836 the longest-running Spanish Romantic
drama, *El trovador.* It exhibits most of the outer trappings of romanticism and from this point of view makes an illuminating study. But
while it perhaps ranks higher than *Don Álvaro* as theatre, it lacks a
fully developed Romantic *theme.* Plot alone predominates and this is
probably the clue to the play's popularity. The great criticisms of it

23

apply first to Act I, Scene i, where García Gutiérrez was evidently at a loss for an idea and resorts to a cold and undramatic narrative exposition in total contrast to the brilliant *aguaducho* scene in Rivas's drama, and second to the incredible nature of Azucena's mistake in burning her own child. But the effective distribution of events in Act I after the opening scene; the delayed climax in the middle of the play when the abduction of Leonor is postponed until the end of Act III; the striking curtain-scenes; and the superb finale of Act V with its cunning use of pause-scenes in the minor key combine to make *El trovador* a model of dramatic craftsmanship. But dramatic competence alone is not enough. While in *La conjuración de Venecia* we perceive a struggle between love and duty, and in *Macías, Don Álvaro,* and *Los amantes de Teruel* a struggle between love and fate, the real conflict in *El trovador* is between Nuño and Manrique *as people.* There is no attempt to invest it with any sort of universality. In Acts II and III love and religion are brought into opposition, when, as at the end of *Don Álvaro,* retreat into the cloister is seen to offer no final solution. But although the conflict between human love and faith is traditionally a central Romantic theme, it is not developed here. The explanation lies partly in the fact that Manrique's character lacks the necessary dimension of thought and introspection: significantly he has no soliloquies. This leaves Leonor with the key-lines, specifically subordinating her religious vows to the fulfilment of the Romantic love ideal:

> ¡Ay! todavía
> delante de mí le tengo,
> y Dios, y el altar y el mundo
> olvido cuando le veo.

and later at the foot of the crucifix itself

> Cuando en el ara fatal
> eterna fe te juraba
> mi mente ¡ay Dios! se extasiaba
> de la imagen de un mortal
> Imagen que vive en mí,
> hermosa, pura y constante . . .
> No, tu poder no es bastante
> a separarla de aquí.

Like Don Álvaro, at the first test, she abandons the attempt to find solace in religion and follows Manrique in the full knowledge of the spiritual consequences. When the sacrifice for love even of her hope of salvation proves vain she too dies by her own hand.

García Gutiérrez's later plays of significance include *El rey monje* (1837), *El encubierto de Valencia* (1840), *Simón Bocanegra* (1843), *Venganza catalana* (1864; with the young Galdós in the audience), and *Juan Lorenzo* (1865), in all of which the historical element predominates. But although he wrote nearly sixty other plays, he never matched the success of *El trovador*.

II. HARTZENBUSCH

Hartzenbusch was the son of a poor German immigrant. Though his father managed to give him a good education, he was forced to follow the family trade of cabinet-making until he obtained a post as a parliamentary shorthand-writer. Meanwhile he had gained a foothold in the Madrid theatre in the usual way by translating from the French and adapting from the Spanish Golden Age *comedia*, as well as staging minor pieces of his own without success. In January 1837, using the contacts he had made, he succeeded in having put on at the Teatro del Príncipe his new play: *Los amantes de Teruel*.

In this play the Romantics' 'existential' concept of love, love as the only life principle, achieves its most direct expression. An interesting feature of the circumstances connected with the play is that as originally composed it was so similar to Larra's *Macías* that Hartzenbusch had to rewrite it extensively. Something of the same is true also of García Gutiérrez's *El trovador*. There is, of course, no suggestion of plagiarism. But the identity of conception cannot be lightly passed over. It implies an identity of outlook and sensibility. When three dramatists write major plays on the same theme, it must be concluded that the theme itself has a very special significance for the movement to which they belong. In each of the three plays, as is equally the case in *Don Álvaro*, the frustration of love is inevitably followed by the death of the lovers. But there is a distinct evolution. Martínez de la Rosa, a transitional writer, had avoided linking love and death directly together in *La conjuración* . . .; Rugiero is executed by the Council of Ten for political reasons. The two parts of the theme are merely juxtaposed. Larra takes the major step: Macías is killed, Elvira kills herself. In *Don Álvaro* the formula is reversed; while in

El trovador both hero and heroine in practice bring about their own deaths. In every case the issue is death. Loss of love allows no other solution, since to conceive of any other would be to accept a higher law than that of human love. We have seen that even when divine love is the alternative, this is unacceptable. What we have not so far seen is a direct connection between frustrated love and death. Here it is. Neither Mansilla nor Isabel dies from any external cause. There is no recourse either to murder or suicide. When the lovers find themselves deprived of their last hope of love-fulfilment they die as simply and inevitably as a watch stops when its mainspring breaks.

Hartzenbusch's essential problem in the play is that of creating and maintaining in the audience the suspension of disbelief necessary to prevent the pathos of the ending collapsing into bathos. Aided by the fact that the story is a familiar legend and the ending therefore known in advance, Hartzenbusch combines constant reiteration of the love-life theme with an intensely lyrical and poetic atmosphere. Here also the hero's ill-fate is appropriately balanced by the heroine's, when she too is independently involved in an adverse current of circumstances. With the aid of this new and effective device Hartzenbusch was able to refurbish effectively Larra's original theme.

Hartzenbusch followed *Los amantes* with a series of plays on historical subjects, culminating in *La jura en Santa Gadea* (1845) based on an incident in the life of El Cid, which marks the peak of his later production. His other plays, which include comedies of magic and thesis-drama, plays for children, and a large number of translations and adaptations, have been justly forgotten even by scholars. So too are most of his critical and editorial labours, though these anticipate, in some cases, the methods of modern systematic criticism.

III. OTHER DRAMATISTS AND POETS

Other significant Romantic dramatists include Joaquín Francisco Pacheco (1808-45), remembered above all for his exaltedly Romantic play *Alfredo* (1835) which drew important comments from Espronceda, Ochoa, and Donoso Cortés. Like most of the other Romantic dramatists he cultivated historical drama on national themes such as *Los Infantes de Lara* and *Bernardo del Carpio*. In a similar category to *Alfredo* is *Carlos II* (1837) of Antonio Gil y Zárate (1793-1861).

A third figure of interest is Patricio de la Escosura (1807-78) with *Bárbara de Blomberg* (1837). He is also the author of a well-known, highly-coloured, and melodramatic *romance histórico* on the theme of love and death, 'El bulto vestido de negra capuz' and several novels including *Los desterrados a Siberia* which, in line with the Romantic impatience with separate literary genres, was written in a mixture of verse and prose.

The disenchanted and sceptical wing of romanticism was ably represented by Nicomedes Pastor Díaz (1811-63). This is especially true of his often-quoted poems 'La mariposa negra' and 'A la luna'. However, in his unjustly neglected novel *De Villahermosa a la China* (published in sundry parts 1845-58), the last major piece of Romantic subjective fiction, Pastor Díaz, like Rivas and others, defected from this wing of the movement.

A fair-sized anthology of compositions in Pastor Díaz's earlier sombre vein could be made up from other minor Romantics, including Salvador Bermúdez de Castro (1814-33) and Mariano Roca de Togores, marqués de Molins (1812-89). *María* (1840), a lengthy poem by Espronceda's intimate friend Miguel de los Santos Álvarez (1818-92), is in a like category. The existence of this broadly united group in line with the outlook of Espronceda, in contrast to the orthodoxy and traditionalism of the later Rivas and especially of Zorrilla, who broke away from it, provides further evidence of the ideological split which divided the Spanish Romantics.

While Pastor Díaz along with Enrique Gil, to whom further reference will be made presently, were said by Menéndez Pelayo to represent the northern regional group of Spanish Romantic lyricists, Pablo Piferrer (1818-48) and Padre Juan Arolas (1805-49) represent Barcelona and Valencia respectively. Piferrer's early death from tuberculosis robbed Spain of a promising poet and critic. Only a handful of his poems, a mere sixteen, survive and of these more than half are trivial. But of the remainder two at least are highly original —'Retorno de la feria' and 'Canción de la Primavera'—and reveal the influence of folk-ballads, which Piferrer collected. The latter of the two poems was included by Menéndez Pelayo among the *Cien mejores poesías líricas de la lengua castellana*. Piferrer's major prose-work, *Recuerdos y bellezas de España* (1839), probably suggested to Bécquer in 1854 the idea for his unfortunate *Historia de los templos de España*. J. F. Gómez de las Cortinas has summarised Piferrer's position in the history of Spanish literature, describing him felicitously, if a little over-enthusiastically, as 'el schlegeliano español más puro y el prebecqueriano de más hondura'.[1]

IV. AROLAS

Padre Juan Arolas, a priest of the Spanish teaching order of the *Escuelas Pías,* is one of the more curious and pathetic figures of the Romantic movement. After completing his studies he taught from 1835 to 1842 in the Colegio Andresino of Valencia but divided most of his time between journalism and poetry. Like Zorrilla he wrote with astonishing facility and his production was considerable. His first collection of verse, published in 1840, was followed by a three-volume edition in 1843 with posthumous editions in 1850, 1860, and 1879. The title of the 1860 edition, *Poesías religiosas, caballerescas, amatorias y orientales,* reflects the categories to which the majority of his poems belong. The last, *orientales,* suggests his indebtedness to Victor Hugo and the most summary comparison reveals its extent. Lamartine similarly is the source of all too many of Arolas's religious poems, in which the imitation is often slavish. Portending the later evolution of Romantic verse, Arolas wrote chiefly narrative poems, including *Leyendas* and *romances históricos* under the influence of Zorrilla and Rivas. But in spite of this excessive derivativeness Arolas has a special place in Spanish romanticism for two reasons. The first is the strongly erotic tendency of his verse, in contrast to the conspicuous Romantic tendency to idealise and spiritualise love as the existential principle. (Cf. Espronceda's characteristic reference to the 'mujer que nada dice a los sentidos' and the non-consummation of love-affairs in the Romantic theatre and narrative.) The opening of 'La favorita del sultán':

> Marcha despiadada y cruda
> Pues me quemas con tus besos
> Al lucir casi desnuda
> Tantas gracias y embelesos.
>
> . . . Tú te ríes y te alegras
> Cuando en mí los bríos faltan
> Mientras tus pupilas negras
> Ebrias de placer te Saltan.

is typical. This carnal approach to the feminine, with woman presented purely in terms of her sensual physical attractions:

> ¡Qué hermosas son tus pomas!
> Parecen dos palomas
> De venturosa cría
> Nacidas en un día . . .

is not only almost unique in the Spanish poetry of its time but looks forward to one of the major themes of *modernismo*: Darío's 'Carne, celeste carne de mujer'. The other important characteristic of Arolas is his use of intense images of colour, in contrast to (for example) Espronceda's marked preference for black and white. Arolas's use of rich, warm, and brilliant hues, reds, golds, and purples, similarly portends the *modernista* manner.

A strain of deep frustration and melancholy, perhaps due to the tension between his erotic temperament and clerical obligations, appears in some of his best-remembered poems, especially the moving 'Sé más feliz que yo' and 'Plegaria'. This, combined with the constant drain on his energies imposed by his rapid literary production and with the abuse of stimulants, unbalanced his mind and he died insane after several years of mental disturbance.

V. TASSARA

The poetry of Gabriel García Tassara (1817-75) represents the transition from romanticism to that poetry of politico-social preoccupation which Darío so aptly called 'baritonante'. Most of the verse which survives in his collected *Poesías* (1872) belongs to the short period 1839-42 and probably does not illustrate very fully his early evolution. He was proud of his Classical formation in Seville. But he was powerless to resist the attraction of the new school. The influence of Espronceda on Tassara's romanticism is unmistakable, most of all in those poems which reflect his religious crisis during these years ('La Noche', 'Dios', 'Meditación religiosa') and in his approach to nature, which is the opposite of E. Gil's:

> Dame nevados montes
> Ceñudos horizontes
> Y bosques ¡ay! de la creación hermanos:

Y playas y arenales
y fieros vendavales
y siempre embravecidos océanos,

. . .

But with his return to orthodoxy Tassara turned his talent for grandiloquence (already evident in his taste for the epic rhythms of the *octava real*) to poetic commentaries on the European political and social scene. An intimate friend and correspondent of Donoso Cortés and now no less deeply traditionalist, he became increasingly aware of himself as the poet of 'un mundo que se desmorona'. Henceforth he thundered out in verse his own and his friend's version of a Europe madly bent on its own destruction, and his prophecy of its ruin:

Los tronos derretidos como cera,
Tronos y altares, leyes y blasones;
Los pueblos consumiéndose en la hoguera,
La Europa ardiendo como cien Iliones.

('A Napoleón', 1841)

The upheavals of 1848 confirmed his pessimism and called forth his most apocalyptic verse, the Epistles to Donoso and 'El nuevo Atila', balanced by the religious confidence of 'Himno al Mesías'. Thereafter he was practically silent. Significantly, however, his poems were collected and published during the aftermath of the Revolution of 1868, only three years before the appearance of *Gritos del combate*. Critics have thus been able to see in Tassara the poet who, in a sense, handed on to Núñez de Arce his own heritage from Quintana.

VI. LA AVELLANEDA

Gertrudis Gómez de Avellaneda (1814-73) emerges as the major poetess of the period. The antithesis in many ways of her older contemporary Fernán Caballero, she gravitated via Quintana, Heredia, Madame de Staël, Scott, and Chateaubriand to the more extreme Romantic attitudes of Rousseau, Byron, and above all George Sand. Born in Cuba, she left the island in 1836 to settle in Madrid where she did not hesitate to carry Romantic principles, especially that of freedom, into her private life.

Her first collection of verses, *Poesías* (1841), included a number of poems, especially the fine sonnet 'Al partir' and an invocation 'A la poesía', which reveal that even before her arrival in Spain she was a highly accomplished and dedicated poetess. In 1845 she carried off both first and second prizes at a poetry competition organised by the Madrid *Liceo Artístico y Literario* and henceforth was an established literary figure. The death of her first husband inspired two 'Elegías' which are among her finest works. Thereafter she increasingly turned to religious subjects, publishing, after a long delay due to the loss of the manuscript, a *Devocionario poético* in 1867. Meanwhile a second augmented edition of her *Poesías* had appeared in 1851.

Inevitably love is the major theme of Avellaneda's verse, though only a few of her poems, notably the two entitled 'A él', refer directly to her own experiences. In her reference to sadness rather than joy as the bond with the beloved, one perceives a belated flicker of the naïver sort of Romantic *mal de siglo,* but Avellaneda's insight is into the states of mind and inner emotional conflicts associated with love, rather than its role in relation to life generally. Her verse has been compared with that of non-Hispanic poetesses, especially Luise-Victorine Ackermann and Elizabeth Barrett Browning, in its alternations of unrestrained, almost ferocious emotion and tender submission, and in its clear-sighted resignation to selfishly exercised masculine attraction. In 'Dedicación de la lira a Dios', Soledad del alma', and 'La Cruz' Avellaneda turned to God from the emptiness she described in a poem written shortly before her first marriage:

> Yo como vos para admirar nacida,
> Yo como vos para el amor creada,
> Por admirar y amar diera mi vida,
> Para admirar y amar no encuentro nada.

The highly effective change of metre from hendecasyllables to *eneasílabas* in the middle of 'La Cruz' reveals Avellaneda's technical ability, which found expression in metrical innovations such as those of 'La noche de insomnio y el alba' and 'Soledad del alma'. They include the thirteen-syllable line (4 + 9), a novel *alejandrino* (8 + 6 or 5 + 9), and fifteen- and sixteen-syllable lines, which like the innovations of Zorrilla look forward to *modernismo*.

While Avellaneda's claim to fame rests on her poetry, her contributions to drama and fiction are of genuine significance. Three of her novels are remembered. *Sab* (1841), the most original, is regarded as a landmark in Latin American literature, being one of the first novels to exploit the New World's natural and social background for fictional purposes. *Dos mujeres* (1842) is more extreme and contains a strong attack on the institution of marriage. *Guatemocín* (1846) is an over-documented historical novel, but one whose setting in Mexico at the time of the Conquest is original enough to make it memorable. Avellaneda's other novels lack the force of these earlier ones with their courageous attacks on social conventions.

Her plays are among the most distinguished of the unhappy interregnum which intervened in the Spanish theatre between 1845 and the rise of the *alta comedia* in the middle 1850s. They include *Leoncia* (1840), which has the originality for its time of belonging neither to the Moratinian comedy nor to high Romantic drama, and a number of historical plays (*Alfonso Munio*, 1844; *El Príncipe de Viana*, 1844; and *Egilona*, 1846) which combine Romantic passion, exaggeratedly striking *escenas madres*, and the slightly anachronistic influence of Quintana. Later she scored striking successes with two biblical dramas, *Saúl* (written 1846, published 1849) and *Baltasar* (1858), her masterpiece. The two plays could be interpreted as expressing respectively the manic and depressive aspects of romanticism. *Saúl* strikes well-worn attitudes of cosmic rebellion, while *Baltasar* complains in familiar tones of

> este infecundo fastidio
> contra el cual en balde lidio
> porque se encarna en mi ser.

As in all the outstanding dramas in the Romantic tradition after 1845, what we notice is the survival of stock attitudes and situations, often as in these two plays of Avellaneda or in the case of Tamayo's *La locura de amor,* very memorably reworked but lacking that symbolic expression of life's enigma and sense of the 'fatal truth' which are among the hallmarks of the great Romantic masterpieces.

The other Romantic poetess of relative significance is Carolina Coronado (1823-1911). Precocious like Avellaneda, she published her first and only collection of *Poesías* in 1843 (republished in 1852, 1872, and 1953). Subsequently she wrote both plays (*Alfonso IV de*

León, Petrarca) and novels (*Paquita,* 1850; *La Sigea,* 1954), but these met with little success. She is remembered for a few poems, in particular 'El amor de los amores', a well-known anthology piece expressing in terms of almost mystical idealisation every young woman's dream of the perfect lover. Many of her other poems are on themes connected with nature, especially on individual flowers (her famous 'La rosa blanca' and 'Al lirio', 'A la amapola') or birds or on conventionally sentimental themes which fitted her habitual gentle melancholy tone.

VII. ZORRILLA

Larra's funeral, which was attended by practically every literary figure of note except Espronceda, who was ill, became something of a public meeting on behalf of romanticism with speeches and poetry-reading before a large crowd. At the end of the ceremony, with an elegy read at the graveside, there came into sudden prominence the last figure of importance to emerge in the 1830s. This was José Zorrilla (1817-93). The son of an unbending Carlist functionary whom the advent of Liberalism sent into exile, Zorrilla had abandoned his studies of law at Valladolid University and was living in bohemian squalor in Madrid. From the cemetery he was taken in triumph to the *Parnasillo* and introduced to all its leading members. Shortly afterwards, he found himself on the staff of *El Español,* Larra's old paper, along with Espronceda, his idol and soon his close friend. The same year, 1837, saw the appearance of his first book of verse. It was followed in such astonishingly rapid succession that by August 1839 Zorrilla already had six collections of poems and two unpublished plays to his credit. In that month he married Doña Florentina O'Reilly, an attractive but impoverished widow some sixteen years his senior, and published his seventh collection of poems. This, together with the immensely popular *Cantos del trovador* which had also already begun to appear, show him at the height of his creative powers. A chance collaboration with García Gutiérrez had led him to the theatre with *Juan Dándolo,* written in three or four days, in July 1839. It was followed at the same amazing speed by others, and in March 1840, only a fortnight after staging his third play, he achieved a resounding success with *El zapatero y el rey,* Part I. The next two years saw the production of a dozen more plays, including the famous one-act *El puñal del godo* written in twenty-four hours, and the rest of the *Cantos del trovador*, the third volume of which appeared in June 1841. Finally, in March 1844, Zorrilla staged the last really memorable Romantic drama, and the greatest money-spinner of them all, *Don Juan Tenorio*.

Throughout his later life Zorrilla went on turning out new collections of verse, *leyendas*, and in his sixties two long historical poems, *La leyenda del Cid* (1882) and *Granada mia* (1885); but apart from his entertaining memoirs, *Recuerdos del tiempo viejo* (1883), little of what he produced after *Don Juan* is republished nowadays. Essentially a narrative poet and dramatist, his fame rests on his verse *leyendas* and *tradiciones,* the *Cantos del trovador,* and a small number of plays headed by the ever-popular *Don Juan* itself.

His shorter lyrics lack depth of feeling and original insight. A small number of the earlier ones bear the mark of Romantic pessimism. But there is nothing in his work as a whole or in what we know of his life to suggest that he ever experienced anything approaching an intellectual or spiritual crisis. He saw poetry not as the fruit of meditation, expressing truth memorably, but as the spontaneous outpouring of inspiration, appealing primarily to the emotions and senses of the reader. Not least he saw it in terms of popular success, as a source of fame and reputation for the poet himself. He lacked a critical and enquiring mind and was content to take his ideas ready-made from the same traditional nationalist sources in which he found his themes. His outlook never varied substantially from its expression in prose in the dedication of his second volume of poems and its expression in verse in the introduction to his *Cantos del trovador,* both equally famous. In the first he writes:

Al publicar el segundo [tomo] he tenido presentes dos cosas, la patria en que nací y la religión en que vivo. Español, he buscado en nuestro suelo mis inspiraciones. Cristiano, he creído que mi religión encierra más poesía que el paganismo.

In the second:

Mi voz, mi razón, mi fantasía
La gloria cantan de la patria mía.

Venid, yo no hollaré con mis cantares
Del pueblo en que he nacido la creencia;
Respetaré su ley y sus altares.
En su desgracia a par que en su opulencia
Celebraré su fuerza o sus azares,
Y fiel ministro de la gaya ciencia,
Levantaré mi voz consoladora
Sobre las ruinas en que España llora.

This implicit recognition by Zorrilla in both these passages that a
poetry of unorthodox tendencies existed is no less important than
his explicit rejection of it. The latter marks him out, after Rivas
(whose *romances históricos* exerted a basic influence on his formation as a poet), as the outstanding poet of 'historical' romanticism in
opposition to Espronceda who represented the other tendency. For
the rest of the century literary-minded young people divided into
partisans of one or the other. It may be argued in Zorrilla's favour
that poems are made with words and not with ideas. But it follows
that the words must be carefully chosen and subtly arranged so as to
produce a maximum of aesthetic effect. The speed at which Zorrilla
habitually wrote often precluded any such possibility, and led to his
characteristic faults: the predominance of imagination over feeling,
description over action, and grandiloquence over natural poetic
expression. But this was not always the case. His well-known verse

Yo soy la voz que agita, perdida en las tinieblas,
La gasa trasparente del aire sin color,
que sobre el tul ondula de las flotantes nieblas,
que del dormido lago se mece en el vapor

is as diaphanous as Bécquer's characteristic manner. His use of
expressions of colour, his mastery of rhythms and verse-forms, as
well as his absolute dedication to poetry, look forward to Darío.
Critics who investigate the origins of the *modernista* renovation of
poetic diction would do well to re-examine Zorrilla.

Zorrilla's most original contribution to Romantic poetry was the
tradición, in which with striking effect he applied Rivas's dramatic
and colourful manner to miraculous tales which had been part of
popular belief for generations. In the best of the *tradiciones* ('Para
verdades el tiempo y para justicia Dios', 'A buen juez, mejor testigo',
'El capitán Montoya', 'Margarita la tornera') suspense alternates with

pathos, dramatic dialogue with lyrical description, and miraculous intervention provides a compelling climax. But his stories are unidimensional with no significance beyond their intrinsic basis in popular belief. Here, as elsewhere, Zorrilla's facility is his great limitation.

During the 1840s Zorrilla's success as a dramatist rivalled his fame as a poet. After *El zapatero y el rey* (1840-41) and *El puñal del godo* (1842), at the end of the decade, in *Traidor inconfeso y mártir* (1849) Zorrilla scored a last really resounding success. But his dramatic work had already reached its climax in 1844 with *Don Juan Tenorio*. The significance and much of the popular success of this play is owing to the way Zorrilla reconciles it in the Romantic love-ideal with his own and the audience's traditional allegiances. In earlier plays we have seen the love-ideal in conflict with religion as the ultimate existential support. Here it is deposed from that position and restored to one of its conventional roles: that of providing a channel through which divine grace and forgiveness can reach the hardened sinner. Whereas Leonor's love for Manrique in *El trovador* displaces religion in her own mind, triumphing over it at the first test, Inés's love for Don Juan creates no such conflict for her. It merely makes up for Don Juan's lack of religion. Heavily sentimentalised and stripped of any existential implication, it finds its place in the religious framework of the play as an acceptable sacrifice by Inés to God on behalf of Don Juan. Instead of posing a problem it solves one. It is simply a credit balance accumulated by Inés, which she is allowed to transfer to Don Juan's spiritual account.

With the Romantic love-ideal thus brought comfortably into line with traditional belief, the brief period of prominence of the Romantic theatre proper comes to a close and our consideration of romanticism itself may be brought to an appropriate end.

NOTE

1. 'La formación literaria de Bécquer', *Revista Bibliográfica y Documental*, IV (1950), 77.

Chapter 4

POST-ROMANTIC PROSE. *COSTUMBRISMO*, FERNÁN CABALLERO, AND ALARCÓN

THE COLLAPSE OF THE ROMANTIC MOVEMENT, hastened by its own internal divisions and by the violent opposition of traditional-minded critics, came prematurely in the early 1840s. It is marked by the death of Espronceda in 1842 at the age of thirty-four. This, following Larra's suicide five years before, removed two of the leaders of the movement at the height of their powers. While, as Peers has pointed out,[1] 1840 was the *annus mirabilis* of the lyric, with major collections by Espronceda, Pastor Díaz, S. Bermúdez de Castro, García Gutiérrez, Arolas, and M. de los Santos Álvarez, to say nothing of an early volume of poems by Campoamor; and while 1841 saw *El diablo mundo*, Zorrilla's *Cantos del trovador*, Rivas's *Romances históricos* as well as collections by Ochoa and others, most of the work which thus appeared belongs to earlier years. It was a retrospective exhibition: and already the debates in the *Ateneo* and the *Liceo* during the first half of 1839, which centred—surprisingly enough—on the question of the Unities, and included very colourless contributions by Alcalá Galiano, Hartzenbusch, Escosura, and Espronceda, had indicated that the Romantic movement was beginning to run out of steam.

The surviving Romantics continued to exploit the safe possibilities of 'historical' romanticism, above all on the stage and in narrative poetry. But until 1868 'contemporary' romanticism largely succumbed to a period of ideological reaction, which arraigned its new-found insight as false, or if true, as something subversive and *disolvente*, to be withheld from public knowledge. It was this reaction, rather than 'eclecticism', which was the predominant feature of the middle decades of the nineteenth century.

I. THE CONTINUING DEBATE

The link between the Romantic movement and the literature of *nuevas ideas* which now began to emerge is therefore provided by the second stage of the debate about romanticism. This continued to rage furiously as long as the movement lasted, with a peak year in 1837. We left it in an earlier chapter at the critical moment when Alcalá Galiano launched the concept of a *romanticismo actual* in contrast to the 'Fernandine' critics' interpretation. An important extension of the idea was noticed in Larra's 1836 manifesto, only to be precipitately abandoned in his review of *Antony* the same year. But in the meantime the most illuminating and penetrating analysis of those aspects of romanticism which link it via the *fin de siglo* to our own time had been made by Pastor Díaz in his introduction to a collection of Zorrilla's poems in 1837. Placing the emphasis squarely on doubt and despair as the dominant theme of Romantic poetry and explaining this in turn by reference to the collapse of collectively-accepted beliefs, intellectual, religious, or moral, he exposes the central feature of the movement and explains the violent hostility which it provoked. Little known and less quoted, his statement deserves to be reproduced at length:

> En el estado actual de nuestra indefinible civilización, la poesía como todas las ciencias y artes, como todas las instituciones, como la pintura, la arquitectura y la música, como la filosofía y la religión, han perdido su tendencia unitaria y simpática, y sus relaciones con la humanidad en general, porque no existiendo sentimientos ni creencias sociales [i.e. socially cohesive, collectively-accepted beliefs] carece de base en que se apoye . . . Hay [in contrast to periods in which people are happily united by 'la comunión de sus ideas'] épocas tristes para la humanidad en que estos lazos se rompen, en que las ideas se dividen y las simpatías se absorben; en que el mundo de la inteligencia es el caos, el del sentimiento el vacío; en que el hombre no ejercita su pensamiento sino en el análisis y en la duda, y no conserva su corazón sino para sentir la soledad que le rodea y el abismo de hielo en que yace. Entonces el genio puede volar aun, pero vuela como el Satanás de Milton, solitario por el caos: el sol le causa pena, la belleza del mundo envidia. Su poesía es solitaria como él, y como él triste y desesperado. Canta o más bien llora sus infortunios, su cielo perdido, el fuego concentrado en su corazón, las luchas de su

inteligencia y las contrariedades de su enigmático destino . . .
los himnos que debían consagrarse a una religión de amor serán
solamente gritos de desesperación y de impío despecho, o
extravíos de un abstracto y estéril misticismo. Tal es a mis ojos
el carácter de la época presente, tal es también su poesía dominante,
la poesía elegíaca actual, poesía de vértigo, de vacilación y de
duda, poesía de delirio, o de duelo, poesía sin unidad, sin sistema,
sin fin moral, ni objeto humanitario, y poesía sin embargo que se
hace escuchar y que encuentra simpatías, porque los acentos de
una alma desgraciada hallan dondequiera su cuerda unísona, y van
a herir profunda y dolorosamente a todas las almas sensibles en el
seno de su soledad y desconsuelo.

But already, before Pastor Díaz had written these words or Larra
recoiled before their expression in dramatic terms, Lista had uttered
frequent warnings that romanticism was diverging from the attachment to Christian moral values which, along with the 'Fernandine'
critics, he laboured to see as its essence. His words were echoed with
increasing severity as Spanish authors followed French example.
Between 1837 and 1842 Salas y Quiroga, Mesonero Romanos, E. Gil,
Ventura de la Vega, and Mora all accused romanticism of fostering
immorality and impiety.

Some of the Romantics were quick to reject the charges. Ochoa,
as early as 1835, had noted that people existed 'para quienes la
palabra *romántico* equivale a hereje, a peor que hereje, a hombre
capaz de cometer cualquier crimen' and ridiculed the idea. The
editors of *No Me Olvides* in their first number two years later denied
indignantly that the essence of the movement was 'esa inmoral
parodia del crimen y de la iniquidad, esa apología de los vicios', as
was so often suggested, and asserted instead that 'en nuestra creencia
es el romanticismo un manantial de consuelo y pureza'.

Other Romantic writers were less disingenuous and like Ochoa
and Pastor Díaz pleaded the spirit of the age. Among these the most
candid was Salvador Bermúdez de Castro who, in the introduction to
his *Ensayos Poéticos* (1840), wrote:

Tal vez en estos ensayos hay algunos que son triste muestra de un
escepticismo desconsolador y frío. Lo sé, pero no es mía la culpa:
culpa es de la atmósfera emponzoñada que hemos respirado todos
los hombres de la generación presente: culpa es de las amargas
fuentes en que hemos bebido los delirios que nos han enseñado

como innegables verdades. La duda es el tormento de la humanidad, y ¿ quién puede decir que su fe no ha vacilado? Solo en las cabezas de los idiotas y en las almas de los ángeles no hallan cabida las pesadas cadenas de la duda.

II. THE ANTI-ROMANTIC REACTION: BALMES, DONOSO CORTÉS

In the light of the repeated accusations of atheism and immorality and the open admission by the more honest of the Romantics that moral and religious absolutes had been seriously undermined, it is not difficult to see why a reaction now took place. Once the implications of statements such as those of Pastor Díaz and Bermúdez de Castro sank in, orthodox intellectual opinion clamoured for reassurance that the ideas and beliefs on which the stability and cohesion of society were thought to depend were still surely founded. Two figures above all emerged to meet this demand: Balmes and Donoso Cortés, of whom Menéndez Pelayo could write 'Ellos compendian el movimiento católico en España desde 1834 a 1852'. Jaime Balmes (1810-48), a priest and teacher in the seminary of Vich, is remembered for his strenuous attempts to revive philosophical studies in Spain on an orthodox scholastic basis, tempered by more recent developments of thought and above all by the use of commonsense. His *El protestantismo comparado con el catolicismo en sus relaciones con la civilización europea* (1844) and *Cartas a un escéptico en materia de religión* (1846) were vigorous reassertions of traditional belief, while *El criterio* (1845), his most popular work, was a naïve appeal over the heads of contemporary philosophers to the general reading public. In it he avoids any attempt to deal seriously with the problems raised by contemporary critical philosophy, now treating them with derision, now endeavouring to relegate them to the category of mysteries which it was not given to man to understand, the study of which was not only fruitless but dangerous to individual and society. The whole of this approach lay in its appeal to robust practical 'sentido común' and was clearly aimed at the middle-class mind. His importance to our survey lies in the fact that he blamed the Romantics for bringing about the situation which called forth his efforts. Stigmatising Romantic writings as a public calamity, he advocated in their place a literature based exclusively on a return to the soundest principles of religion and morality.

Juan Donoso Cortés, afterwards marqués de Valdegamas (1809-53), politician, diplomat, and orator, was during the same period the great spokesman of traditional conservatism. Originally of Liberal leanings, he wrote, like Espronceda, a favourable review of his friend Pacheco's *Alfredo* (*La Abeja; 25* May 1835), though this play was one of the most subversive Romantic dramas. Subsequently he abandoned Liberalism and after a clamorous conversion, the first of several among prominent nineteenth-century writers, sprang to the defence of traditional values. His *Ensayo sobre el catolicismo, el liberalismo y el socialismo* (1851) eventually complemented that of Balmes on Catholicism and Protestantism. Meanwhile, he had inevitably ceased to support 'contemporary' romanticism and found his natural place among the advocates of the 'historical' branch of the movement. Declaring in the *Ensayo* . . . that 'analysis' was blasphemous, and condemning like the others the 'negativity' of the epoch, Donoso praised on practical and utilitarian grounds 'la belleza de las soluciones católicas.

The hint was not long in being taken up. In a letter to a friend, Fernán Caballero, soon to be praised by Rivas for the soundness of her Catholic and moral literary standpoint, defined her intention as a novelist as being to 'hacer una inovación, dando un giro nuevo a la apasionada novela, trayéndola a la sencilla senda del deber'. 'Bajo este punto de vista,' she states, 'admiro y simpatizo con el Marqués de Valdegamas'. The avowed aim of her work was to 'inocular buenas ideas en la juventud contemporánea'.

The novel had hitherto not been successfully revived in Spain. We have already referred to the attempt by the government in 1799 to suppress publication of novels of any kind. Moralists deplored their pernicious influence, men of letters derided them as essentially frivolous, unworthy of the name of literature. From the beginning of the century until 1823, the date of Rafael Húmara's *Ramiro, Conde de Lucena,* from which the vogue of the Romantic historical novel can be said to date, not a single significant original novel in Spanish appeared. But foreign novels, in the original and in translation, were still avidly read. The novels known to a cultivated Spaniard in the early 1820s belonged broadly to two groups: moral novels chiefly by lady writers such as Mesdames Cottin, Genlis, and Montolieu and their English equivalents, along with Florian, Richardson, and Fielding, and 'libertine' novels by Voltaire, Crébillon, Rousseau, and Laclos, which were imported clandestinely, being on the prohibited list along with even Bernardin de Saint-Pierre and Chateaubriand.

III. THE HISTORICAL NOVEL

With the appearance of a score of translations of Scott between 1829 and 1832 the ground was prepared for the vogue of the Romantic historical novel, which lasted without interruption until the middle of the century. We have already noticed contributions to it by López Soler (1830), Espronceda (1833), Larra (1834), and Martínez de la Rosa (1837-46). Ochoa with *El auto de fe* (1837), Escosura with *Ni rey ni Roque* (1835), Miguel de los Santos Álvarez with *La protección de un sastre* (1840), and numerous others followed their example. Among the others we may mention especially Joaquín Telesforo de Trueba y Cossío (1799-1835), whose novels in English (*Gómez Arias,* 1828; *The Castilian,* 1829; *The Incognito,* 1831), published in exile in London, not only antedate and surpass those of López Soler but, while foreign influences were about to swamp original writers in Spain, were carrying the war successfully into the enemy camp. At the other end of the decade *Lorenzo* (1836) and *El templario y la villana* (1840) by the Catalan Juan Cortada y Sala earn R. F. Brown's special commendation.[2]

The culminating work of the Romantic historical novel is, however, beyond all question *El señor de Bembibre* (1844) by Enrique Gil y Carrasco (1815-46). Arriving in Madrid as a law student in 1836, Gil was befriended, like García Gutiérrez, by Espronceda, who introduced him to the *Liceo* and later found him a post in the National Library. Later Gil was to witness his friend's will and read an elegy at his graveside. Appointed by González Bravo to a diplomatic post in Berlin, he died there of tuberculosis.

Gil's poetry reflects the influence of Espronceda, but is in a more minor key, and he is remembered chiefly for his contemplative and nature poems, such as 'La violeta' (1839), which, in a movement largely insensitive to nature except in her most violent moods, has a unique place. His earlier prose-writings include interesting criticism of contemporary poetry and some expository *cuadros de costumbres* dealing with his native León. What especially characterises his fiction, however, is the conflict of religion and adverse fate, already noticed as a prominent feature of certain Romantic dramas. Here Gil, without abandoning the despairing melancholy and spiritual malaise visible in his poetry, like Zorrilla in *Don Juan Tenorio* (published in the same year as *El señor*), comes down solidly on the side of religion.

Few works illustrate more clearly than *El señor de Bembibre* the conflict of Romantic outlook and traditional allegiances. This is not a novel in which faith and conformity with the will of God are seen as the answer to life's problems. It is one which on the ideological plane exhibits the characteristic Romantic tendency to reveal in stories of repeated arbitrary misfortunes a lack of confidence in any divinely ordained scheme of things. But at focal points in the narrative Gil's Christian convictions reassert themselves. Álvaro carries off Elvira from a convent, but on the intervention of her confessor he allows her to return to it; Elvira, struck down at the very moment when marriage to Álvaro at last becomes possible, dies edifyingly. Álvaro becomes a monk. No thought of the flagrant contradiction between these events and the general theme of the work seems to have struck the author. There is no attempt at the end to harmonise them with it. The discord so apparent to the modern reader remains unresolved: the two aspects of the book are simply juxtaposed and we are left to make what we can of them.

The novel is distinguished also by its Leonese setting. Though it is not the first novel to introduce regionalism into Romantic fiction, it is the best-known case and in view of its popularity certainly contributed to the later vogue. More memorable still are the fine and sensitive descriptions of landscape and natural scenery which are a major feature of the novel's originality. Though its tempo slackens towards the end and its characters, especially the villainous Conde de Lemus, are heavily overdrawn, it remains the most readable of the major Romantic historical novels.

El señor de Bembibre was one of the last historical novels of the time to make serious use of documentation, after the fashion set by Scott. In the later 1840s there is a marked shift of emphasis towards adventure stories of pure imagination set in a conventional past with no regard for historical accuracy or the reinterpretation of past events. Prominent among the writers who contributed most to this phase of disintegration of the serious historical novel were Manuel Fernández y González (1821-88), Francisco Navarro Villoslada (1818-95), and Wenceslao Ayguals de Izco (1801-73).

Meanwhile, an important new foreign influence had appeared. That of Eugène Sue, six of whose novels were translated in 1844.

3 * *

His success soon dwarfed even that of Scott and produced a similar flood of imitations. These included Ayguals's *María o la hija de un jornalero* (1845-46), dedicated to Sue, and incorporating his characteristically sentimental social protest and vaguely socialistic championship of the poorer classes. By situating the action in his own century Ayguals joins hands with Escosura (*El patriarca del valle*, 1846-47) and José M. Riera y Comas (*Misterios de las sectas secretas o el francmasón proscrito*, 1847-52), both of whom, while also imitating Sue, were concerned with recent events and with the expression of social and political ideas. While in *María* we have the germ of a naturalist novel, in *El patriarca* and *Misterios* we begin to approach the world of the *Episodios nacionales* of Galdós. The popularity of *novelones*, often published in weekly instalments in newspapers and magazines (hence the name *novelas por entregas* or *folletines*), coincided with the extension of literacy from 10 per cent in 1841 to 25 per cent in 1860 and thence progressively to 47 per cent in 1901.

IV. THE 'CUADRO DE COSTUMBRES': MESONERO ROMANOS AND ESTÉBANEZ CALDERÓN

What the Romantic historical novel and the *folletín* have in common is their indifference to observed contemporary reality. Neither Gil y Carrasco nor Fernández y González thought in terms of a novel set against the background of the Spanish society they lived in; while both Mesonero Romanos and Fernán Caballero state explicitly that such a novel simply would not find an audience. Professor R. F. Brown's researches have disproved this statement.[3] But the fact remains that before the mid-century the *novela de costumbres* remained marginal. The main role in preparing the public for novels with a recognisable contemporary setting still belongs to the *cuadro de costumbres*. Although the origins of the genre are frequently said to go back at least as far as Cervantes's *Rinconete y Cortadillo* and the picaresque novel generally, the *cuadro de costumbres* as we know it came into being at the end of the 1820s in the *Cartas Españolas* magazine, essentially under the influence of the French writer Jouy. Practically every major Romantic writer (including such figures as Rivas and Espronceda) wrote at least an occasional *cuadro* and the genre covered a wide variety of subjects, ranging from regional dress and customs to the more picturesque features of politics, city life, and administration, and employed many different styles from the merely factual and expository to the savagely satirical. In the absence of a genuinely Spanish novel reflecting the life of the times, the *cuadro de costumbres* must be regarded as the nearest approach to reality which the prose of the period offers.

Its relationship with traditionalism and 'historical' romanticism is close, in two respects especially. Like Larra, the *costumbristas* generally were uncomfortably aware that Spanish society was in a phase of rapid transition, amounting almost to a crisis of nationality. But unlike Larra, part of whose frustration arose from the contrast between his ideal of progress and the failure of the government and bourgeois society of his time to bring it into being, they were in literature at least broadly conservative in outlook. Among their chief anxieties was to 'fijar lo perecedero'[4]: to preserve descriptions of the typically Spanish way of life before it disappeared. *Casticismo* is a fundamental feature of *costumbrismo*. So also is moralism. It is no accident that Mesonero Romanos was one of the leaders of the reaction against the supposed immorality of romanticism. In describing the typical Spanish pattern of life it was inevitable that the *costumbristas* should defend its traditional values. In line with these two a third and minor element contributing to the vogue of the *cuadro de costumbres* was the desire to counteract the effect of the caricaturesque descriptions of *la España de pandereta*, which French Romantic writers in particular naïvely circulated.

Apart from Larra, whose *Duende Satírico* of 1828 contains early examples of the *cuadro*, to be developed triumphantly in his later work, the two major exponents of the genre are 'El curioso parlante': Ramón de Mesonero Romanos (1803-82) and 'El solitario': Serafín Estébanez Calderón (1799-1867). Mesonero was the more prolific and precocious, beginning his contribution to *costumbrismo* with *Mis ratos perdidos* (1822), a youthful work, whose twelve short chapters are nonetheless already *cuadros de costumbres* in miniature, portending his later work. Having described the physical setting in his *Manual de Madrid* (1831), a guidebook of the city, he began to publish articles the next year which were to become *Panorama matritense* (1835), his first and better collection of mature *cuadros* which describe the city's life and folk-ways. Henceforth he found on the streets of the capital a rewarding, though in the end limited and limiting, source of material. In the middle 1830s he made two major contributions to Spanish literary life by resuscitating the defunct

Ateneo (1835) and by founding *El Semanario Pintoresco Español* (1836-57) which at once became the leading literary periodical and printed the main body of *costumbrista* articles, as well as work by most of the contemporary writers. Mesonero's second collection of *cuadros, Escenas matritenses,* appeared from 1836 to 1842 and already shows signs of exhaustion of the material. His *Tipos y caracteres* (1862) deals more with persons. Mesonero's other important book is his *Memorias de un setentón,* which ranks alongside Zorrilla's *Recuerdos* as a fascinating source of literary anecdote.

Mesonero defined his *cuadros* as

> ligeros bosquejos o cuadros de caballete en que, ayudado de una acción dramática y sencilla, caracteres verosímiles y variados, y diálogo animado y castizo, procurase reunir en lo posible el interés y las condiciones principales de la novela y del drama

and his method as

> escribir para todos en estilo llano, sin afectación ni desaliño; pintar las más veces, razonar pocas, hacer llorar nunca, reir casi siempre ... y aspirar en fin ... a la reputación de verídico observador.

He took as his motto 'la moral y la verdad en el fondo, la amenidad en la forma, y la pureza y el decoro en el estilo'. These three quotations, however, reveal his aims rather than his achievements. Although the best of his *cuadros* (e.g. 'De tejas arriba' 'El recién venido') contain narrative elements, dramatic quality is largely absent. Mesonero's work is thus prevailingly descriptive as the titles of well-known *cuadros* ('La calle de Toledo', 'El prado', 'Paseo por las calles') indicate. It constitutes a vast inventory of picturesque usages, ceremonies, types, customs, pastimes, and typical scenes of life in Madrid, humorously and at times satirically described, but always seen from the outside. Morality and *casticismo* provided Mesonero's only analytic categories and together with his nostalgia for the past led to an excessively selective vision of reality. But it was he who, more than any other contemporary writer, opened the pages of literature to ordinary daily life, discovering in the process themes and types which were to continue evolving for the rest of the century. His influence is visible in the work not only of later *costumbristas,* including Fernán Caballero, Alarcón, Pereda, but even in that of Galdós and the realists.

While Mesonero's vision is limited to Madrid so that he fails miserably in his depiction of non-*madrileños*, Estébanez's *Escenas andaluzas* (1846) are notable wholly for his enthusiastic portrayal of southern types and scenes. Though less productive than Mesonero, he was more creative and his work as a whole contains less that is commonplace. In characteristic *costumbrista* fashion he declared his 'ciega pasión por todo cuanto huele a España', and set himself the task of preserving from oblivion some vestiges of 'castiza' Andalusia. Among his most memorable *cuadros* are the satirical portraits of southern bravos in 'Pulpete y Balbija' and 'Manolito Gásquez'; the descriptions of picturesque ceremonies and events: 'La feria de Mayrena', 'La rifa andaluza', and 'Un baile en Triana'; and especially the inspired fooling of 'El Roque y el Bronquis', which rivals Larra, though without the seriousness of intention.

The *costumbrista* movement outside the novel reached its peak in 1843 with the publication of *Los españoles pintados por sí mismos*. This was a two-volume anthology of *cuadros* by more than thirty writers, spanning two generations and including Rivas, Mesonero, Estébanez, Bretón, Hartzenbusch, García Gutiérrez, E. Gil, Ochoa, and Zorrilla. In the mediocrity of the younger contributors can be seen reflected both the decline of the genre itself and the drift of Spanish literature as a whole into the unhappy interregnum which separates the decline of romanticism from the rise of the new creative pattern, which was not to appear fully until after the Revolution of 1868.

V. FERNÁN CABALLERO

The major figure in prose fiction during this was Cecilia Böhl de Faber (Fernán Caballero, 1796-1877), daughter of Johann Nikolas Böhl von Faber. Her literary work is intimately bound up with her three marriages. The first, at the age of nineteen, to a young infantry captain, Antonio Planels, was a disastrous failure. We see its reflection in *Clemencia*. Fortunately it was brief. The following year Planels died in Puerto Rico and Fernán returned to Spain. In 1822 she married the marqués de Arco-Hermoso and for the next thirteen years lived happily with him in Seville and on his country estate of Dos Hermanos, where she was able to observe at first hand, listen to, and describe the country people whom she regarded as the repositories of all that was unspoiled in the Spanish national personality. Here she accumulated during the 1820s a vast store of popular tales and anecdotes, traditions, descriptions of events and scenery, people and daily life, proverbs, *coplas*, *consejas*, songs, and verses, usually written down there and then as they came to her notice and deposited with her father. These, which she later called her 'mosaic' and 'jewel box', were to provide the raw materials for the novels she was already preparing to write.

Even before this time, perhaps as early as 1815, she had begun to put together brief narratives, among them the first drafts of *Sola* and *Magdalena*, to be followed by the description of Puerto Rico included in *La farisea* (1863). Now, perhaps in 1826, she wrote in German the first draft of *La familia de Alvareda*, a translation of which into Spanish was shown to Washington Irving in 1829. Soon after this came *Elia* (in French) and a number of stories included in later novels.

By this time Fernán probably enjoyed some local reputation in her husband's circle as a writer. But she seems to have needed more incentive than this to publish: her story 'La madre', which came out in *El Artista* in 1835, was submitted by her mother without her consent. Arco-Hermoso died in 1835 leaving Fernán far from rich. She retired to Jerez and began to write seriously, producing in succession *La gaviota* (still in French), *Una en otra*, and *Lágrimas*. Meanwhile she married again in 1837. Her new husband, Antonio de Ayala, was seventeen years her junior and in poor health. His administration of her financial affairs was disastrous. But it is probably to him that we owe Fernán's belated decision to publish her work.

She turned to her father's old adversary José Joaquín de Mora as translator and agent. In May 1849 *La gaviota* appeared as a *folletín* in *El Heraldo,* followed in rapid succession by *La familia de Alvareda* and *Una en otra,* and finally *Elia* in *El Español. Lágrimas,* finished in 1849, came out in *El Heraldo* in the spring of 1850. During the same period a score of minor pieces appeared in different periodicals also. Fernán had arrived.

Her theory of the novel is not altogether easy to elucidate. She advocated five principles: *naturalidad*, truth, patriotism, morality, and poetry. Her grandeur as a novelist is associated with the first two; her unfortunate legacy to the Spanish novel with the last two. By *naturalidad,* Fernán meant rejection of the novelesque:

No pretendo escribir novelas, sino cuadros de costumbres, retratos, acompañados de reflexiones y descripciones—privo a mis

novelas de toda esa brillante parte del colorido de lo romanesco y
extraordinario . . . Todo lo novelesco tiende a exaltar a la criatura;
yo busco ablandarla, excluyendo o poniendo en mala luz todas
estas pasiones, ya enérgicas, ya exaltadas, que son venons que
vierte el corazón en la buena y llana vida . . . Pongo, pues, lo
romanesco en lo no romanesco.

Thus, for example, in *Clemencia* (1852), the unhappily married young
heroine, instead of resorting to adultery, suicide, or even excessive
self-pity, accepts her lot with Christian resignation. One hesitates to
think of how edifyingly monotonous the result would have been had
the husband not died. Similarly, in *Elia* the heroine, caught between
conflicting passions and duties, quietly retires to a convent.

By truth, Fernán meant foundation on fact and observed detail.
Repeatedly she insists on the lack of invention and creative imagination in her writing. Hence the claim sometimes made that she is a
realist writer. It is false. Realism depends not only on the faithful
reflection of observed reality: it depends also on *which aspects* of
reality are reproduced. What Fernán possessed was a realist *technique*
—the same technique which Galdós describes himself using in the
prologue to *Misericordia*. But what she used that technique to record
was merely picturesque. It was only *part* of reality which interested
her: that part which could be aligned with her moral presuppositions.

Here we come to her second group of principles: morality and
poetry. Most great art is ultimately moral; few works of art are
obtrusively so. It is no part of the task of the writer to seize the
reader by the cuff and shout urgently into his ear that virtue is the
only way. Unfortunately Fernán Caballero disagreed. While declaring
herself to be 'instintiva e indesprendiblemente apegada a la verdad'
she proclaimed at the same time that the novel must be an instrument
for moral improvement: 'la ética es parte tan esencial de la novela, que
si ésta le faltara, podría colocársele en la categoría de un culto, fino,
tutti li mundi'. Hence it is not truth as it is that she reflects, but
truth as she wished it to be. This is what she meant by 'poetizar la
verdad', to submit it to a process of selection, and (inevitably) of
deformation, to fit her ideas. How far she was unconscious of this is
shown both by her apparent failure to perceive that truth and
morality are frequently irreconcilable in or out of fiction and, con-
cretely, by her naïve belief in *Un servilón y un liberalito* (1855) she
had done perfect justice to both parties, when the *liberalito* in

question is nothing but an inconsiderate, rude, and foolish boy whose actions and manner contrast violently with the honesty, charity, and forbearance of his traditionalist hosts.

To these four principles we must add a fifth, that of patriotic *españolismo,* and especially *andalucismo.* Thus, as she defined her work (see above, p. 48) in terms of *cuadros* combined with descriptions and reflections, so elsewhere she described it as 'un ensayo sobre la vida íntima del pueblo español, su lenguage, sus creencias, cuentos y tradiciones' from which the European public could obtain for once an accurate idea of Spanish and especially Andalusian life. The numerous translations of her works reveal that the European public was willing to seize the opportunity.

Fernán's major work, consisting of the seven novels so far mentioned, was complete by 1857. In addition to her novels she published collections of short stories including *Relaciones* (1857), *Cuadros de costumbres* (1857), and *Cuentos y poesías andaluces* (1859).

Characteristic of her novels are their simple and often undramatic plots. The rapid novelesque action of the *folletín,* against which she was reacting, is replaced by interpolated stories and anecdotes, usually of popular Andalusian origin, by descriptive digressions, and by excessive commentary by the authoress, usually of a moralising trend. Subordinate characters and events connected with them are frequently introduced for their own usually picturesque sake rather than for their contribution to the onward movement of the narrative (e.g. Galo Pando, Tía Latrana, Don Modesto of *La gaviota*), while the major figures tend to be idealised or sacrificed according to their religious and political affiliations, or the country they belong to.

Finally, although Fernán usually avoids trite 'happy endings', a certain providentialism tends to prevail over the free play of chance in the working-out of her novels.

These are now unfashionable.

A disciple of Fernán Caballero was Antonio de Trueba (1819-89), not to be confused with Trueba y Cossío. By virtue of his admiration for the founder-figure of the modern Spanish novel and his influence on the youthful Pereda, Trueba may be said to link together the two ends of the *novela de buenas ideas.* Originally a shop-assistant in Madrid, he made his name with a collection of verse and went on to write a couple of historical novels. But his real vocation was that of a short-story writer. Beginning with *Cuentos populares* (1853) and *Cuentos de color rosa* (1859), he went on to publish eight further collections with general success. The last was the posthumous *Cuentos populares de Vizcaya* (1905). Like Fernán's, his short stories are generally of popular and traditional origin, rural in setting and deliberately moralising in intention.

VI. ALARCÓN

Pedro Antonio de Alarcón (1833-91) remains, in spite of his immense contemporary popularity and the polemics caused by his work, probably the least studied of the major nineteenth-century novelists. There can be no doubt that the neglect is due to his being foremost among the writers who inherited Fernán Caballero's view of the novel as a vehicle for 'buenas ideas'.

Born in Guadix (Granada), he soon revealed talent. Before he was seventeen he had written and staged three light comedies and a historical drama, all of them improvised with the astonishing speed and facility which was to mar much of his later work. The character of Pepito in *El niño de la bola* is believed to be a portrait of Alarcón himself during these youthful years. In 1853, after failing to break into the Madrid literary world, he returned to Granada, where in the following year he led a short-lived Liberal uprising. Later, however, he followed the example of Rivas and so many other *exaltados* and became strongly conservative. In 1857 he staged his only mature play, *El hijo pródigo,* on the theme of youthful folly and error. Though the characters are overdrawn and the action marred by melodrama and sentimentality, the play is by no means inferior to the general run of drama at that period. The African War provided Alarcón with the opportunity for a patriotic gesture and he joined the expeditionary force as a volunteer. His excited eyewitness account, *Diario de un testigo de la Guerra de África,* was a best-seller. His Spanish travel books deserve notice also. It is too often asserted that only with the Generation of 1898 did Spanish writers set out to explore their own countryside. *La Alpujarra* (1873) and *Viajes por España* (1883) disprove this.

Up to 1861 Alarcón's contributions to fiction proper had comprised his first novel, *El final de Norma,* written at the precociously early age of seventeen and published in 1855; and some thirty short stories published between 1853 and 1859, at first in his own *Eco del Occidente* and later in other periodicals. Together with these may be mentioned a collection of rather belated *cuadros de costumbres,* written during the same years and later collected in part as *Cosas que fueron* (1871). Although Alarcón allowed himself to believe that he was bringing something fresh to it, his *cuadros* are chiefly notable as representing the decay of the genre, whose historical role of preparing for the novel of increasingly realist observation was now completed. A curious feature of the short stories is the absence of any clearly distinguishable evolution in Alarcón's creative ability. He seems to have had no apprenticeship and to have needed none. 'El amigo de la muerte' (1852) and 'La buena ventura' (1853), written at the beginning of his career, are the equal of any stories he wrote later, with the exception of 'La comendadora' (1868). The painful process of rewriting which 'El clavo' underwent between 1853 and the appearance of the final version of *Obras completas,* analysed by Montesinos,[5] reveals similarly the difficulties encountered by the older Alarcón in improving his youthful work. In all these stories the major influences were probably Dumas, Balzac, and also Fernán Caballero, some of whose short stories on the Spanish struggle against Napoleon are not unlike Alarcón's *Historietas;* both presage Galdós's *Episodios nacionales.* Before leaving the short story, to whose evolution in Spain Alarcón undoubtedly contributed significantly, it should also be mentioned to his credit that he was probably the first Spanish writer of any importance to recognise the genius of Edgar Allan Poe. He praised his work in an article in 1858, the only one of its kind written by Alarcón to have any importance in literary history.

Alarcón held fast to two principles only. The first was that art and everyday reality were antithetical:

> el cuadro, la estatua, el drama, la novela, siempre versaron acerca de lo *excepcional, heroico* y *peregrino* . . . o la *literatura* y el arte no son nada o son algo distinto de la prosaica *realidad conocida por todos.* Porque hay otra realidad, la de las regiones *superiores* del alma . . .;

the second was that art must exert a socially useful, that is moral, influence:

> Las obras de arte . . . deben ser una lección dada por el autor al público.

This is not to say, of course, that Alarcón mistook mere moralising for great artistry. What he did assert, however, was that beauty was inseparable from goodness, which he confused with morality and above all with sexual morality. His views illustrate one of the most widespread misconceptions of Spanish literary criticism in the nineteenth century: the belief that the essence of literature was somehow indissolubly linked to the 'poeticisation' of reality, that is, the belief that the principle of artistic selection of the elements presented by observation must always operate in an idealising direction.

In 1874 Alarcón returned triumphantly to fiction with his masterpiece, *El sombrero de tres picos*. It illustrates many of the salient characteristics of Alarcón's work. Two features in particular stand out. First the speed at which the story was written. It was completed in less than a fortnight. This was Alarcón's normal rate of writing. *El capitán Veneno* was composed in little more than a week and *La pródiga*, which is over 70,000 words long, took him less than a month. The unevenness of much of Alarcón's production is thus easily explained. But for once *El sombrero de tres picos* is free from the defects of rapid improvisation.

The second feature is Alarcón's brilliant handling of suspense. This explains the relative popularity, even now, of his first full-length novel, *El final de Norma*, written about 1850 before Alarcón escaped from Guadix, but not published until five years later, after it had been partly rewritten. The narrative is a tissue of absurdities with no intrinsic literary qualities. But it is partly redeemed by its inventiveness, readability, and especially by Alarcón's dramatic distribution of the episodes. These culminate with the arrival of the hero in the nick of time to unmask his rival as he is in the act of marrying the heroine. That Alarcón possessed in his teens the ability to organise his plot so effectively is a tribute to the precocity of his talent.

This mastery of suspense and distinctive dramatic ability is seen at its peak in *El sombrero de tres picos*. First in the slow descriptive opening leading into the Corregidor's declaration and first humiliation. Then in the quickening rhythm of the narrative to its first climax with Lucas's alluring reflection 'También la Corregidora es guapa'. In the middle of the story two of the three strands of narrative are cunningly knitted together with a second climax in Chapter 27, the last sentence of which underlines Alarcón's deft transfer of interest from the Corregidor's chances with Frasquita to those of her husband with the Corregidora. The conclusion is thus able to centre on the Corregidora herself, with the other major characters grouped round her in an atmosphere of mutual suspicion. By keeping the Corregidor off stage during the explanations Alarcón retains the element of suspense to the last and brings his narrative symmetrically to a close with the discomfiture of the initial actor.

The magnificent ease with which Alarcón handles the arrangement of the narrative, together with his characteristic interest in dramatic situation rather than character, remains prominent in his longer novels: *El escándalo* (1875), *El niño de la bola* (1880), and *La pródiga* (1882). The first of these, whose composition was actually interrupted by the Revolution of 1868, illustrates perhaps more than any other single work the enormous effect of that event on the Spanish novel described by López-Morillas.[6] Alarcón himself, like Clarín, saw 1868 as a watershed in the struggle between Catholic traditionalists and the frequently anti-Catholic Liberal progressives. The Revolution clearly crystallised his religious and political outlook. He was now a supporter of the conservative régime of Cánovas and, though without Carlist sympathies, ultra-Catholic. His three major novels, while retaining many of the characteristics of his *cuentos,* are characterised by a new doctrinaire religious aggressiveness which involved Alarcón in violent polemics. Each is concerned with an act of heroic sacrifice; in the case of *El escándalo* and *El niño de la bola* for motives connected with religious belief, in the case of *La pródiga* for passion. *El escándalo,* which Alarcón regarded as his most important work, is the most extreme of the three. In it the hero, Fabián Conde, whose circumstances and personality are not unrelated to Alarcón's, is guided through a severe test of character by a Jesuit. Emerging triumphantly with renewed religious faith, he voluntarily renounces honour, reputation, fortune, and social position for reasons of conscience, but is allowed to save his prospects of marriage from the wreck. The story is told largely in dialogue between Fabián and Padre Manrique, in which Alarcón makes full use of the opportunity for religious commentary by the latter. *El niño de la bola,* possibly, in the opinion of Montesinos,[7] the best Spanish Romantic novel, exploits the familiar motif of the lover returning to find the woman he loves already married. The hero, Manuel Venegas, is persuaded by his local priest to accept the situation, until an act of folly by the heroine, ignobly exploited by the leader of the local Liberals, produces in high melodramatic fashion both her death and Manuel's. The novel contains moments of vivid description and great tension, but the lengthy, overwritten ending and the figure of the Liberal leader Vitriolo, which, like that of Diego in *El escándalo,* is a repulsive caricature designed to contrast with the idealised priest, detract from the novel's quality. Both *El escándalo* and *El niño de la bola,* then, belong to the polemic novels associated with the 1868 Revolution. They represent a frontal attack on what Fabián Conde calls 'la enfermedad de mi siglo', irreligion, in which Alarcón chose to see the main source of human and social failings. Sacrifice, as in Fernán Caballero's *Elia,* is the answer. But while Fernán strove deliberately to avoid overdramatising this sacrifice, with some risk to the interest of her narrative, Alarcón, giving free run to his dramatic instincts, raises it to a sensational level with an even greater risk to the credibility of the events he describes.

Between *El niño de la bola* and Alarcón's last novel, *La pródiga,* comes *El capitán Veneno* (1881), a charming and humorous taming-of-the-shrew story in reverse, the last occasion on which Alarcón reveals that *gracejo* which is so vital an element in *El sombrero de tres picos* and which is so conspicuously absent in his full-length novels.

La pródiga (1882), though a love-story, is Alarcón's most un-Romantic and indeed anti-Romantic work. Again it is a story of sacrifice. The heroine gives up not only the remains of her fortune but also her painfully reacquired good name and serenity of mind. But this time it is for the wrong reason: an illicit liaison with a man too young for her to marry. Earlier, in the epilogue to *El niño de la bola,* Alarcón had openly attacked Romantic art as un-Christian. Here the Romantic love-ideal is wilfully distorted, set in impossible conditions, and portrayed as squalidly immoral. The suicide of the heroine is now no longer a protest against the incomprehensibility of life, but the deplorable outcome of moral aberration. With this final tribute to edification Alarcón left the literary stage.

NOTES

1. *A History of the Romantic Movement in Spain* (Cambridge, 1940), II, 206.
2. *La novela española 1700-1850* (Madrid, 1953).
3. Ibid., esp. p. 32.
4. J. F. Montesinos, *Fernán Caballero* (Mexico, 1961), p. 83.
5. J. F. Montesinos, *Pedro Antonio de Alarcón* (Saragossa, 1955), pp. 81-112.
6. *RO,* 67 (1968).
7. op. cit., p. 180.

Chapter 5

POST-ROMANTIC POETRY.
CAMPOAMOR, NÚÑEZ DE ARCE, AND PALACIO

BY THE MIDDLE 1840s (a convenient point of reference is the publication by Zorrilla of *Recuerdos y fantasías* in 1844 and *La azucena silvestre* in 1845, followed in the same year by his retirement to France) Spanish lyric poetry, so recently revived by the Romantics, was already beginning to show signs of premature exhaustion. A renewal of its themes and manner was about to be begun, single-handedly, by Campoamor. But valiant and immensely influential as Campoamor's attempt to change the course of Spain's poetic development was, it proved in the end unprofitable and was increasingly abandoned by younger poets after the 1860s. Meanwhile, a new influence, this time external, from Germany, had emerged which was to culminate in the work of Bécquer.

I. MAIN CURRENTS OF POETRY

We may thus postulate three overlapping and at times mingled currents of Spanish poetry in the mid-century. First, the prolongation and ulterior development of Romantic themes and sensibility parallel to that which took place in the theatre and in the historical novel. Second, the current of renovation associated with the momentous success of Campoamor's *Doloras* and *Pequeños poemas*. Thirdly, the gradual fusion of the ballad-tradition and German influences (especially of Heine) to produce the *ambiente pre-becqueriano* which has only come to be recognised and studied as such since Dámaso Alonso launched the idea in the mid-1930s.

Of these three the first is the most complex. It includes at one extreme the survival of pre-Romantic and transitional sensibility in the poets of the Sevillian school, still dominated by Lista even after his death in 1848. The struggle between traditionalism and *criticismo* remains a central feature. The former is represented by the phalanx of poets who continue to develop, along with Zorrilla, 'historical' Romantic themes, and by a scarcely smaller host of poets whose work is strongly orientated towards similarly *casticista* religious, moral, and political subjects. The latter survives in the poets of despair, doubt, and pessimism, and is associated at times, just as it had been in the case of Espronceda, with Liberal progressive ideas. Finally, it includes an increasing body of 'social' poetry, for the most part middle-class in allegiance and self-important in tone. Humour and satire remain, as in the Romantic period proper, curiously segregated and apart (if we except the gently malicious irony of Campoamor).

The prolongation of 'historical' romanticism is most clearly visible in the continued production, until well into the 1880s, of *romanceros*, collections of *tradiciones*, volumes of verse *leyendas*, and the like. The inspiration of Zorrilla, who himself went on exploiting these forms for the rest of his long life (cf. *Ecos de la montaña*, 1868; *Le leyenda del Cil*, 1862; *El cantar del romero*, 1886), was constant. His example stimulated no less a poet than Rivas to follow it with *La azucena milagrosa* and other *leyendas*. But the Duke was only the most illustrious of those who followed where Zorrilla led. Other cultivators of the legend-form included Antonio Hurtado y Valhondo (1825-78), with a cycle of poems on the exploits of Cortés (1849), and later his *Madrid dramático* (1870), with scenes from the life of the city in the sixteenth and seventeenth centuries. Manuel Cano y Cueto (1849-1916), an even closer follower of Zorrilla, published eight sets of *Tradiciones sevillanas* between 1875 and 1895. Alfonso García Tejero, Gregorio Perogordo, José Castillo y Soriano, and a host of other lesser poets published or contributed to collections of *romances* in the 1860s and 1870s. Like the historical novel, which flourished at the same time, the genre eventually came to include more contemporary historical and social happenings (e.g. José Gutiérrez del Alba's *Romancero español contemporáneo*, 1863). Its educative role in popularising knowledge of Spanish history, often through carefully planned coverage of specific events and periods, cannot be overlooked. A noteworthy feature of the *leyenda* in its final phase of evolution is the change of tone and manner which occurs with the publication in 1869 of Campoamor's 'El drama universal' and more especially with Núñez de Arce's 'Raimundo Lulio' (1875) and the amazingly successful 'El vértigo' (1879) which

¿ Por qué cruza la tierra el inocente,
de espinas o de sombras coronado?
¿Por qué feliz y próspero, el malvado
alza orgulloso la atrevida frente?
¿Por qué Dios, que es el bien, mira y consiente
el eterno dominio del pecado?
¿Por qué desde Caín, la humana raza,
sometida al dolor, con sangre traza
la historia de sus luchas giganteas?
Y si es ficción la gloria prometida,
si aquí empieza y acaba nuestra vida
¿Por qué, implacable Dios, por qué nos creas?

Similar timidity can be found in the work of Rivas's son, Enrique
Saavedra, later the fourth duque (1828-1914). Characteristic is his
'Dos ángeles' in the collection *Sentir y soñar* (1876), which drew
from Valera a perceptive review distinguishing between true (philosophic) pessimism and its merely literary (aesthetic) counterpart—
Saavedra's kind. Manuel de la Revilla (*Dudas y tristezas*, 1875), J. M.
Bartrina (*Algo*, 1874), F. Balart (*Dolores*, 1894), and José Alcalá
Galiano also complained with greater or lesser consistency of what
the latter called 'este don espantoso de la vida', but their work reveals
all too frequently the vacillation which lay beneath their attitudinising. 'Fray Candil's' (the critic Emilio Bobadilla, 1862-1921) criticism
of Balart quoted by Cossío:[2] 'tan pronto se declara creyente a
machamartillo, como se entrega a una duda retórica, digna de un
seminarista', is not without more general applicability. The per-
sistence of this defect is illustrated as late as 1895 by Reina's 'La
canción de las estrellas' in which the heroine Blanca

> Traza con mano trémula en su frente
> la señal de la cruz, cierra los ojos,
> y arrójase a las aguas que, piadosas,
> le abren su tumba de cristal.

A supreme act of ideological confusion! Fortunately for the seriousness of Spanish poetry, authentic insight into the human predicament had by then found expression in the work of Rosalía de Castro.

Orthodoxy, on the other hand, emerged reinvigorated during the
post-Romantic period with, as we have seen, important contributions
in poetry from Tassara and later on Avellaneda. Among younger

poets representative of what soon became a definite reaction against the Romantics' frequently overt scepticism was Antonio Arnao (1828-89). In his first book of verse, *Himnos y quejas* (1851), one can perceive that blend of sentimentality and religio-moral pre-occupation (owing something in his case to Lamartine's early manner) which is revealed also by Fernán Caballero and Tamayo when they are not being aggressive. Arnao here emerges as the poet of serene goodness and piety expressed in predominantly brief poems with appropriately simple diction. His later collections, which include *Melancolías, rimas y cantigas* (1857), *Ecos del Táder* (1857), *La voz del creyente* (1872), *Un ramo de pensamientos* (1878), *Gotas del rocío* (1880), and the posthumous *Soñar despierto* (1891) show a continuous development but broadly illustrate Arnao's desire to soothe 'las hondas heridas de nuestra convulsa sociedad' with his gentle melancholy musicality. Like Selgas, his close friend, Arnao was among those instrumental in producing the fertilisation of the Spanish lyric by the German *Lieder*.

Arnao's reference to 'nuestra convulsa sociedad' reminds us that social preoccupations grew in importance in lyric poetry during the post-Romantic period. While elements in the work of the Romantic generation itself can properly be called 'social', they had largely taken the form of broad libertarian affirmation and rebelliousness against certain features of social class and convention, though Tassara's poems are an exception. What now came to the fore were more specific problems. Cossío cites S. Bermúdez de Castro's earlier-mentioned prologue to his *Ensayos poéticos* with its question '¿qué ha de escribir [el poeta] sino sus impresiones que son las impresiones de la sociedad?' as marking the change.[3]

II. RUIZ AGUILERA, QUEROL, AND BALART

Nine years later, in 1849, Ventura Ruiz Aguilera published the first of two sets of *Ecos nacionales*; the second followed in 1854. In the prologue he takes up the point made by Rivas with regard to his *Romances históricos*, that the great popular *castizo* lyric form, the *romance*, had lost its appeal. But instead of attempting, like Rivas, to rescue it, Aguilera set himself to produce on the model of the *balada* a new form of essentially popular poetry. Dramatic in manner, with emphasis on dialogue and the spoken word, the *Ecos* were designed either to focus the average reader's interest on some moral issue connected with social or political behaviour or to stimulate his national or local pride, his sense of recent Spanish tradition, his patriotism, or the like. Nor are society's rejects (the orphan, the prostitute) overlooked. For, as with most of the poetry of the time, sentimentality was also a prominent feature. Aguilera's combination of morality with patriotic and social preoccupation met with the same immediate success as did Trueba's combination of morality with scenes of everyday provincial life. Rosalía de Castro paid her tribute to them and Giner de los Ríos, a friend and admirer of Aguilera, insisted on their use in the *Institución Libre de Enseñanza*.

Apart from a collection of satirical verse (*Las sátiras*, 1849) and two collections of *cantares* which, along with those of Ferrán and Campoamor, illustrate the emergence of this popular poetic form to literary respectability, Aguilera's other major contribution to Spanish poetry is *Las elegías* (1862). Here also we perceive a refreshing novelty of subject and manner. Just as in the theatre bourgeois values reasserted themselves, with marriage replacing romantic love as a theme, so in the lyric the home, the family, the poet's wife and children became an increasing source of inspiration, bringing with them the charm of simplicity and sincerity. In the thirty-eight poems of this collection, the best of which are deeply appealing, Aguilera expresses his grief at the death of his daughter, his happy memories of her girlhood, and his prayers for her.

With his last collection, *La leyenda de Nochebuena* (1871), whose title sufficiently indicates its theme, Aguilera joins the current of specifically Christian poetry already mentioned.

Alongside Aguilera's poetry on domestic themes must be placed that of the Valencian Vicente Wenceslao Querol (1837-89), which may well have influenced it. His output was small and restricted to one volume: the *Rimas* (1877), republished posthumously in 1891 in an augmented form. Other poetry of Querol has since come to light. The major poems of the *Rimas*, most of which were written in the period 1859-76, fall broadly into four groups: odes on the model of Quintana, using religious or semi-religious themes ('Jesucristo', 'Al eclipse de 1860') or concerned with contemporary events ('Canto épico a la Guerra de África', 'A la patria'); love-poetry, of which the most memorable are the three 'Cartas a María', whose note of plaintive tenderness and serene intimacy is in refreshing contrast to Romantic overtones of passion; epistles to fellow-artists; and above all Querol's charmingly sincere and appealing poetry of family life.

These last two categories are of special importance. In the epistles Querol formulates his poetic *credo*. We perceive the powerful influence of his Classical formation in the heavy emphasis laid on the dignity of poetry and the sacred mission of the poet to transmit from age to age the spirit of the past and to keep alive ideals and hopes for the future:

> guiar a la humanidad por su camino
> es la misión sagrada del poeta.

Hence Querol's contemptuous rejection of most of what he saw as the prevailing poetry in his day: the insincere and trivial productions 'eco fugaz de la mentira', which constituted the great mass of published verse; the 'forma nebulosa y triste de los poetas germáni-cos', whose *sensiblerie* he repudiated; the 'realist' genre brought into vogue by Campoamor 'que el vulgar asunto/flaca y cobarde aspira-ción denota'; and the pessimistic, discouraging accusations of national decay in which Núñez de Arce specialised. But in spite of the high ideal enunciated in the Epistle to Núñez de Arce:

> Es el poeta
> fiel sacerdote que custodia oculto
> del viejo dogma el profanado culto
> o es del lejano porvenir profeta

Querol's own most original and sincere poetry is to be found in the small group of his *Poesías familiares* dating chiefly from the 1870s. The memory of his dead sister is kept alive in verses whose simplicity of imagery unashamedly conveys direct emotion:

> Como en el bosque solitario el ave,
> cual flor nacida en el cerrado huerto,
> como en el mar la ola,
> cuya breve existencia nadie sabe,
> tu, en el hogar donde naciste has muerto
> desconocida y sola.

> Pero al orgullo vano de la ciencia,
> y a las fútiles pompas de la gloria
> o al opulento brillo,
> prefiero yo tu cándida inocencia,
> y esa vida sin mancha y sin historia
> de un corazón sencillo.

The family scene is charmingly evoked:

> Mi madre tiende las rugosas manos
> al nieto que huye por la blanda alfombra.
> Hablan de pie mi padre y mis hermanos,
> mientras yo, recatándome en la sombra,
> pienso en hondos arcanos.

Presiding over all, simple faith links children with parents and all in turn to a unifying family tradition inherited from the past to be handed down uncorrupted to the future. Against the background of the rhetorical manner passed on by Tassara to Núñez de Arce, and even against that of Querol's own odes, these poems stand out with all the appeal of authentic feeling. Unamuno greatly admired them.

Among poets who subsequently continued to explore the possibilities of love in the context of the family is Ricardo Sepúlveda (1846-1909). His almost unnoticed *¡Dolores!* (1881), inspired by the death of his wife, was the direct predecessor of the collection of the same name published in 1894 by Federico Balart (1831-1905). Few men in their early sixties can have published a first book of poetry destined for such exceptional success. A distinguished Liberal journalist, Balart had been unknown as a poet until the death of his wife in 1879 provoked in him the emotional and spiritual crisis of which *¡Dolores!* was the record. The two themes of the book, inseparably connected, are those of the poet's outpouring of grief and plaintive nostalgia for his lost domestic happiness, together with his recovery of faith under the stimulus of his bereavement. Much of the book's success, apart from the obvious appeal and sincerity of the first theme, was due to the harsh criticism from both clerical and anti-clerical quarters which the poems describing the poet's clamorous, but rather unorthodox, conversion evoked. Balart's later collections of verse, *Horizontes* (1897), *Sombras y destellos* (1905), and *Fruslerías* (1906), the last two posthumous, were undistinguished.

During a period in which Spanish poetry was so often characterised by insincerity, sanctimoniousness, and over-anxiety to conform to the public image of the poet; a period in which the accepted value-pattern, whether 'progressive' or 'traditionalist', was all too often hostile to the exploration of the poet's inner sensibility, this current of domestic and often sincerely elegiac poetry comes in retrospect to seem one of the most original and attractive. Nor was it without impact later. Marti's *Ismaelillo* (1882), Villaspesa's *Viaje sentimental* (1909), Nervo's *La amada inmóvil* (1929), and—dare one add?—even A. Machado's unforgettable poems inspired by his own young wife's death, owe something to the discovery of Ruiz Aguilera, Querol, and Balart.

III. CAMPOAMOR

Before the origins in the middle 1850s of the movement which led to the emergence of Bécquer, only one serious attempt to initiate a renovation of Spanish poetry can be recorded. This was undertaken by Ramón de Campoamor (1817-1901). Born in the same year as Zorrilla and Tassara, only four years later than García Gutiérrez, Campoamor's first verses, *Ternezas y flores,* were published in the *annus mirabilis* 1840, at the expense of the *Liceo Artístico y Literario.* Previously he had toyed successively with the idea of entering the Society of Jesus and with that of becoming a doctor. Subsequently, like Alarcón and Ayala, he entered politics, and rose through various governorships to minor governmental office. He was elected to the Academy in 1861. His marriage to a lady of some wealth, was, though childless, most successful and Campoamor seems to have enjoyed an enviably happy and uneventful life, without material worries. At bottom, in spite of the recurrent notes of bitterness and cynicism which appear in his work, he remained unshakeably serene and optimistic, much as did his fellow-Asturian Palacio Valdés and his close friend Valera. His literary career was no less happy. After publishing a second unimportant collection, *Ayes del alma,* together with a book of newly fashionable poetic fables in 1842, he brought out in 1845 his famous *Doloras,* which seemed to herald a revolution in the field of lyric poetry. After unfortunate attempts at epic compositions (*Colón,* 1853; *El drama universal,* 1869) Campoamor scored a further triumph in 1872 with the first set of his *Pequeños poemas,* to be followed equally successfully by others in the 1880s and early 1890s. Finally, in 1886, he brought out an augmented edition of the *Doloras* and published for the first time his lapidary *Humoradas.* His poetic career closed with a further attempt at an extensive philosophico-narrative poem, *El licenciado Torralba* (1888), no more fortunate than his earlier ones. The success of *Doloras* was immense. It rivalled that of Espronceda's *El diabló mundo,* one of the bestselling poetic works of the century. The *Pequeños poemas* and *Humoradas* were equally popular. All three collections are still frequently republished and along with Bécquer's *Rimas* are probably the only poetic collections of the period which still command a wide audience. But the gulf which separates Campoamor from Bécquer is unbridgeable. No residual popularity of the former among the unsophisticated can make up for the stark fact that the only attempt to bring about a poetic renovation in nineteenth-century Spain which was not derived from outside sources failed miserably.

It would be a mistake, however, to attribute this failure to shortcomings in Campoamor's poetic theory. Here, as Gaos has amply demonstrated,[4] Campoamor was in possession of an extremely coherent and consistent body of ideas, interesting alike in relation to his own poetry and that of his period. His implication that the brevity and thought-content of the *Doloras* were forced on him by the fact that Zorrilla 'ocupaba a la sazón hasta el último recodo del atributo de la extensión' has led to the idea that Campoamor's poetry was essentially anti-Romantic, but this is only true if Zorrilla is regarded as the major Romantic poet. When we consider Espronceda the picture alters at once. Not only are *El drama universal* and *El licenciado Torralba* and shorter poems such as 'Buenas cosas mal dispuestas' obviously influenced by *El diablo mundo,* but the whole conception and technique of *humorismo* (so central to Campoamor's work) are initially imported into Spanish verse by Espronceda. To attempt to divorce Campoamor's poetry of ideas from its origins in Espronceda's is to lack critical perspective.

All Campoamor's most memorable pronouncements on his art: 'La poesía es la representación rítmica de un pensamiento por medio de una imagen y expresado en un lenguaje que no se pueda decir en prosa ni con más naturalidad ni con menos palabras'; 'la poesía verdaderamente lírica debe reflejar los sentimientos personales del autor en relación con los problemas proprios de su época'; 'El arte consiste en dar forma al pensamiento, en convertir lo intelectual en sensible'; 'Yo soy apasionado, no de lo que se llama el arte docente, sino del arte por la idea o, lo que es lo mismo, del arte trascendental'; 'La poesía no consiste sólo en los buenos versos, sino en los buenos asuntos'; reveal the same ultimate filiation with the poetry of *sesgo metafísico* in a contemporary context, referred to by Alcalá Galiano in 1833 in his definition of *romanticismo actual*. Analysing them we may define Campoamor's ideal of poetry in the following terms.

First, emphasis on significant content (cf. his references above to *pensamientos, problemas, lo intelectual, la idea*) as indispensable. Second, the transmutation of this thought-content into imagery. Third, the expression of it in rhythmical language. Fourth, the avoidance of specialised 'poetic' diction ('solo el ritmo debe separar el lenguaje del verso del propio de la prosa'). The sum of all this is 'poesía clara, precisa, y correcta'. The *Pequeños poemas* and longer compositions add two further elements: a strictly narrative approach ('No debe ser materia de versos lo que no sea contable') and dramatic manner ('Hacer de toda poesía un drama'). Though these elements, apart from the stress laid on transmitting content via imagery, may not add up to what we normally think of as *lyric* poetry, they certainly constitute a reasoned doctrinal statement. Sadly, Campoamor's actual poetry, which long preceded his *Poética* (1883), was not on the level of this theory. The discrepancy, though concealed by the acclaim his work enjoyed at the time, is the great tragedy of a writer who might have revolutionised Spanish poetry in a period when it was desperately in need of new horizons.

Campoamor's two principal themes are, as we might expect, the philosophico-religious problem inherited from Espronceda and Pastor Díaz's 'poesía de vértigo, de vacilación y de duda', together with love in its various manifestations. Both are Romantic themes also. What separates Campoamor from the Romantics is not, therefore, his subject matter, but the tone and manner with which he treats it. Familiar images ('este cilicio atroz del pensamiento') and overt expressions of despairing scepticism ('Horrible es la ciencia, sí/que hasta de la fe el consuelo/mata') abound, but Campoamor was not tough-minded enough to exploit the possibilities of this position consistently. Side by side with his contemplations of 'las noche sin estrellas de la nada' we find poems of trivial agnoticism ('Las dos linternas'), of mere cynicism ('Justos por pecadores', 'El origen del mal'), and finally of conventional belief ('El buen ejemplo', 'La fe de las mujeres'). Despite Campoamor's protest that what matters is not the idea itself, but its expression in poetic terms, the impression which is left is of superficiality and insincerity. His poetry on the theme of love and the human (especially feminine) foibles associated with it reveals a similar oscillation between impersonal observation and cloying sentimentality. What constitutes his originality and appeal in both cases is first of all the pose of humorous detachment, tending at times towards trenchant satire, subtly combined with disillusioned melancholy, in total contrast to the overtones of passion and despair beloved of the Romantics. Secondly, in reaction against Romantic verbosity, the pointed and condensed, sententious, and epigrammatic form of the *Doloras* and *Humoradas*. Though their jingling rhythms and frequently jejune imagery fall short of the ideals Campoamor expressed so eloquently in prose, they stick in the mind. Campoamor described his *Pequeños poemas* as 'cuentos en verso' in contrast to 'la novelería en prosa'. Characteristic of them is the alternation of narrative with interspersed reflections. Here it should be noted that the moralism often attributed to Campoamor by critics who have failed to analyse his outlook carefully is far from conspicuous. Campoamor's cynical scepticism extended as much to morality as to anything else; though his subversiveness is veiled by an elegant urbanity, it is nonetheless present. No one less like Trueba and Arnao than Campoamor can be imagined.

Campoamor also wrote two pseudo-philosophical treatises, *El personalismo* (1835) and *Lo absoluto* (1865), which remain among the quainter manifestations of Spanish nineteenth-century thought. But their importance in the context of the pathetic search for an *armonismo* conciliating traditional belief and progressive scientific positivism, which characterised Spanish nineteenth-century thought, should not be overlooked. Once the impact of the work of Bécquer and Rosalía de Castro had been felt widely enough, and more especially as *modernismo* began to make its appearance, Campoamor's poetry fell into disfavour with the cultured minority. Azorín's savage attack on Campoamor in *La voluntad* (1902) typifies the outlook of a generation, though later in *Leyendo a los poetas* and *Clásicos y modernos* Azorín modified his strictures. Darío spoke for the *modernistas* when he referred in 1907 to 'las fórmulas prosaico-filosóficas de maestros aunque ilustres, limitados' and more recently Salinas criticised Campoamor's poetry as palming off on the audience 'aforismos morales por poesía'. But though in the end it was infertile, Campoamor's influence was for a time immense. It was felt by Bécquer in the 1860s, by the Mexican *modernista* Nájera, and more obviously by the Colombian José Asunción Silva a little later, and most of all by Darío himself in the *Doloras* he wrote in the 1880s.

In Spain Campoamor's principal follower was Joaquín María Bartrina (1850-80), remembered for his collection *Algo* (1874), and its influence, parallel with that of Campoamor, in the early works of Silva.

'Hoy no se escribe para cantar conquistas de naciones, sino para lamentar derrotas del alma'. So Campoamor wrote à propos of the poetry of his time. His phrase serves admirably to introduce the work of the 'cantor de la duda', Gaspar Núñez de Arce (1832-1903). Born in obscure circumstances and educated in Toledo, Núñez de Arce moved to Madrid in 1857 and worked as a journalist. During the African War he served with Alarcón as war correspondent, and like him came to the notice of O'Donnell. Both subsequently joined the General's *Unión Liberal* Party (to which López de Ayala also belonged) and went into politics. From 1860 on, Núñez de Arce held a succession of provincial governorships and well-paid government posts, culminating in 1883 with a short spell as Foreign Minister. He was elected to the Academy in 1874.

Although he began to write poetry in his early twenties, his first-published productions were plays written in collaboration with Antonio Hurtado (1825-78), one of the host of mid-century historical dramatists. His only significant original production for the theatre was *El haz de leña* (1872) referred to below (p. 78). His revelation as a poet came after the Revolution of 1868, with the publication in 1875 of *Gritos del combate,* which collected poems written since the middle 1850s and included 'Raimundo Lulio', his first narrative poem, in three cantos of tercets. 'Un idilio' and 'Una elegía' appeared in 1878; 'La última lamentación de Lord Byron', 'El Salón oscuro', and 'El vértigo' in 1879; 'La visión de Fray Martín' in 1880; and 'La pesca' in 1884. His place in history is that of the poet of the exaltedly polemical ten or fifteen years which followed 1868. It was, as we see from the evolution of the novel in the same period, a time characterised essentially by violent conflict of ideas and Núñez de Arce's production, which contains practically no authentic love-poems, is pre-eminently poetry of ideas. His remarks concerning poetry insist no less than Campoamor's on this point. Like the latter, Núñez de Arce reacted strongly against the continuing influence of Zorrilla's so often empty musicality, dismissing his poems as

arcaicas reproducciones, frías como el retrato de un muerto, de nuestros tiempos gloriosos y caballerescos, con sus galanes pendencieros, sus damas devotas y libidinosas y su ferviente misticismo, entreverado de citas y cuchilladas.

If Zorrilla was pre-eminently the poet of the nation's past, Núñez de Arce appeared to be the poet of its present. He advocated poetry whose themes were strictly contemporary. '¡Cante lo que debe cartar la joven poesía para volver a las almas la perdida fe!' he advised his young disciple Ferrari,

> es, a saber, las alegrías, y las tristezas, las esperanzas y los desengaños, las aspiraciones y las realidades de la época en que vivimos. No olvide Vd. que sólo los ancianos y las naciones decaídas se alimentan de recuerdos.

Chief among these 'graves y trascendentales cuestiones que se ventilan en el seno de las sociedades modernas' inevitably was the problem of doubt. In common with Bermúdez de Castro thirty-five years earlier Núñez de Arce blamed his preoccupation with it on the times:

> Sobrecogido por los arduos problemas políticos, sociales y religiosos que ha planteado nuestro siglo sin haber podido resolverlos hasta ahora, y cegado por el polvo de las ruinas que, incesantemente, van cubriendo el suelo de Europa, ¿es, por ventura, extraño,

he asked, 'que la duda, la duda inquieta y dolorosa, se haya infiltrado en mi corazón y en mi inteligencia?'.

His famous poem 'La duda' (1868) proclaims categorically that

> en este siglo de sarcasmo y duda
> sólo una Musa vive. Musa ciega,
> implacable, brutal . . .
> La Musa del análisis

and about half the poems of *Gritos del combate* are wholly or partly dedicated to the theme of the poet's own spiritual vacillation, or that of his epoch. Memorable among these are 'Problema', 'Velut umbra', 'Luz y Vida', and most of all 'Tristezas' in which Núñez de Arce lays bare his own personal loss of faith with a sincerity of tone which is absent from the other more declamatory poems. His narrative poem 'La visión de Fray Martín' presents Luther as similarly tormented, just as in 'La última lamentación de Lord Byron' he had expressed, rather than conventional Byronic attitudes, his own reactions to the state of his country and his own attachment to libertarian ideals.

Núñez de Arce's second major source of inspiration derives from his conviction, stated in the preface to *Gritos del combate*, that poetry must reflect specifically the politico-social issues of its time. Like

Quintana he saw in poetry an instrument for educating his readers and fostering civilised ideas. The main problem for him here was the failure of Spain in the 1870s to combine liberty and progress with order. He believed himself to be a progressive:

> Hijo soy de mi siglo
> y no puedo olvidar que por el triunfo
> de la conciencia humana
> desde mis años juveniles lucho

he wrote proudly in 'Raimundo Lulio'. But, when the masses demanded a share of the benefits, his progressivism waned suddenly. In 'A España', 'Cartagena', and 'A Emilio Castelar' he prophesied tyranny and called timorously on the political leadership to come to the country's rescue. The state of Spain, devoid of ideals and threatened with anarchy, calls forth from him repeated complaints which to the present-day reader seem, like his ironic attack on Darwinism and his anathema of Voltaire, mere poetic anachronisms. In his own time, however, they deeply stirred the national conscience and provoked violent controversy. Querol, for example, in a typical poetic epistle took strong issue with his fellow-poet. He wrote complaining that:

> en bronce esculpas
> con un buril de fuego nuestros males
> y hagas eterno, en versos inmortales
> el infame baldón de nuestras culpas

and asserted the poet's obligation to safeguard hope and idealism. Finally, of interest to the historian of literature is Núñez de Arce's repeated lament for the state of poetry no less than for the state of his country:

> Hoy la estéril república no tiene
> ni un cantor, ni un artista, ni un soldado.
> Ni nos defiende ya, ni el golpe embota,
> partido en mil pedazos nuestro escudo.
> El vulgo, el necio vulgo nos azota.
> Yace el arte decrépito, está mudo
> el genio, el arpa destemplada y rota.

His *Discurso sobre la poesía* (1887) is a spirited defence of poetry against the external threat to it from the materialistic and positivistic spirit of the age and the internal threat of 'poesía prosaica, en la cual me figuro ver a una princesa estrambótica, que recibe corte en zapatillas, con el cabello crespo y el manto desceñido': a clear criticism of his rival Campoamor.

J. R. Arregui has defined the secret of Núñez de Arce's success happily in the phrase 'la maestría en la forma y la oportunidad en el fondo'. Of the latter what has been said of his themes is sufficient illustration. His mastery of poetic technique is more difficult to assess. Historically he stands equidistant from the suave musicality of Zorrilla and the lapidary concision of Campoamor. At the time when Spanish poetry was struggling away from a tradition of grandilo-quence towards subjective intimacy and what Valera called 'conversación interior' Núñez de Arce unexpectedly revived the emphatic declamatory manner with its characteristic exploration of the sonority of Spanish vowels and fricatives, its accumulations of obvious epithets, its heavy rhythmic stresses, obtrusive alliteration, and the like. His verses were meant to be read aloud and owed in fact much of their success to their public recitation by the actor Rafael Calvo. His ideal of sculpturesque grandeur is illustrated by his fondness for the *octava real* in which he wrote 'La última lamentación de Lord Byron', and his attempt to modify it in 'El reo de la muerte' by lengthening the lines to fourteen syllables. He reintroduced the Dantesque tercet and popularised the Aa b, cc B type of *sextina* in 'Tristezas' and his longer narrative poems 'El idilio' and 'La Pesca'. The *décimas* of 'El vértigo', according to Menéndez Pelayo, produced a host of servile imitations.

Núñez de Arce's chief failing as a poet, apart from the mediocrity of his ideas, lies in the conventionality of his comparisons and the virtual absence from his work of original imagery, without which rhetoric declines into mere bombast. But however conscious we are of these failings today Núñez de Arce's influence up to the early years of this century is not to be underestimated. It is patent in Manuel Reina and in Ricardo León. A number of early Latin American *modernistas*, above all the Mexican Díaz Mirón, felt it also. Darío said of Arce in *España contemporánea*: 'reavivaste el amor de lo bello'; and his own poems of doubt contain clear echoes of 'Tristezas'. Indeed it is Núñez de Arce, more than any other single figure, who hands on the theme of anguished scepticism from the Romantics to Unamuno and the Generation of 1898. We can even find, notwithstanding Valera's sneer that Núñez de Arce's 'poesías políticas, sin excepción, son artículos de fondo de periódicos, declamatorios y huecos, con metro y rima', more than one point of contact between his picture of Spain 'entre lágrimas y cieno' and the 'malherida España, pobre, escuálida y beoda' of A. Machado.

V. PALACIO

When Clarín in 1889 spoke of Spain's possessing only two poets and a half,[5] the half-poet to whom he referred was Manuel del Palacio (1831-1906). Born in Lérida, he moved in 1846 to Madrid, where he was befriended by Ruiz Aguilera, and later to Granada where he joined the literary group *La cuerda granadina*, which also included Alarcón and Fernández y González. Much of his early poetry was violent political satire of the type we associate above all with Martínez Villergas; like the latter's it has not survived the political circumstances by which it was inspired. After 1868, however, Palacio joined the diplomatic service and was posted to Italy. Here his poetry gained in range and variety, though not, unfortunately, in depth or originality. Between 1870 and 1894 he published half a dozen collections of verse. The two major influences on his work appear to have been Quevedo and Campoamor. Perhaps his most characteristic poems are his humorous sonnets, which owe something to the former's, though lacking their mordancy and irony. Their skilfully prepared anticlimactic or epigrammatic endings (cf. 'Idilio', 'La recompensa', 'Trabajo perdido') were regarded as a considerable novelty in their day. Palacio's serious sonnets possess a certain elevation of tone, borrowed from their seventeenth-century model, but this generally accompanies a disappointingly conventional theme ('En el calabozo', 'Beatriz'). His love-poems, like those of Campoamor, tend to develop a mental concept ('Problema', 'Las dos islas') rather than to express an emotion. His *leyendas* ('El Cristo de Vergara') illustrate the survival practically unchanged of Zorrillaesque narrative verse well into the 1880s. Nothing of the spirit of Bécquer or Rosalía de Castro seems to have touched Palacio. Time has not confirmed his claim to have been a nightingale in a nest of sparrows.

NOTES

1. In his review of Núñez de Arce's *Gritos del combate*. See his *Obras completas* (Madrid, 1949), II, 448.
2. *Cincuenta años de poesía española (1850-1900)* (Madrid, 1960), p. 1230.
3. Ibid., p. 194.
4. V. Gaos, *La poética de Campoamor* (Madrid, 1955).
5. Cossío, op. cit., p. 775.

Chapter 6

DRAMA FROM ROMANTICISM TO THE END OF THE CENTURY

I. GOROSTIZA AND BRETÓN

THROUGHOUT THE ROMANTIC PERIOD the popularity of Moratinian comedies never completely waned either with dramatists or with audiences. We have seen that Martínez de la Rosa produced them at intervals throughout his career, beginning with *Lo que puede un empleo* (1812), continuing with *La niña en casa y la madre en la máscara* (1821), *Los celos infundados* written in exile, and ending only with his comedy *La boda y el duelo* (1839), written in exile, of course, and staged later. Rivas, too, contributed *Tanto vales cuanto tienes* (1828) and *El parador de Bailén* (1844). Espronceda (*Ni el tío ni el sobrino*, 1834), Hartzenbusch (*La visionaria*, 1840), and sundry other Romantic writers including Escosura and Gil y Zárate sporadically composed comedies in the Moratinian manner. But worthy of separate mention are three dramatists who were especially responsible for preserving the continuity of the genre throughout the Romantic period and even adding to its lustre. These are Manuel Eduardo de Gorostiza (1789-1851), Manuel Bretón de los Herreros (1796-1873), and Ventura de la Vega (1807-65). Two of Gorostiza's three original full-length comedies considerably antedate the Romantic theatre and situate him as Moratín's most immediate heir. They are *Indulgencia para todos* (1818) and *Don Dieguito* (1820), both based on the use of an elaborate stratagem to convey a moral lesson to the central character. Both these plays were still being successfully presented as late as 1842.

Gorostiza's masterpiece and only other full-length play, *Contigo pan y cebolla*, was not produced until 1833, on the eve of the Romantic theatrical revolution. As Gorostiza had earlier satirised male foppery and affectation in *Don Dieguito*, so now he ridicules the

73

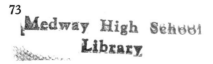

foibles of a young girl whose head has been turned by reading too many pre-Romantic novels. The play is of considerable importance and interest not only for its characteristically Neo-classic defence of rational moderation and conformity in behaviour, but also for its satire of nascent Romantic attitudinising. In this it looks forward to Bretón's *Me voy de Madrid*.

In contrast to Gorostiza's tiny output, Bretón himself wrote more than sixty full-length works, beginning at the age of twenty when he was inspired by a chance reading of Moratín's works. Only nine years younger than Martínez de la Rosa, his work shows the same mixture of styles and types of play, ranging from translations of French tragedies and Golden Age *refundiciones*, through Moratinian comedy, to high Romantic drama, anti-Romantic satire, and tragedy. His writings on the theatre reveal a similar attachment to a prudent *justo medio* between Horatian precept and modern practice.

Bretón's first success came with *A Madrid me vuelvo* in 1828, following *A la vejez viruelas* (composed in 1817 but not performed until 1824) and *Los dos sobrinos* (1825). *Marcela o ¿a cuál de los tres?* in 1831 was hailed as a new departure in his work, owing to its less rigidly Neo-classical structure, novel variety of verse metres, and occasionally highly comic plot. It was Bretón's greatest box-office success. The story of a young widow courted by several suitors, it illustrates his ability to find freshness and diversity of incidents within the framework of a conventional situation. His satire, unlike Larra's, is rarely mordant and deals for preference rather with middle-class foibles and pretentiousness than serious issues. It is just this lightness of touch and gentleness of irony which characterise Bretón's typical works.

1835, the year of Rivas's *Don Álvaro*, was a key year for Bretón. The previous October he had staged, in startling contrast to his earlier comedies, a Romantic melodrama in four acts entitled *Elena* which in the opinion of Alonso Cortés had a marked influence on *El trovador*, *Los amantes de Teruel*, and possibly even the final version of *Don Álvaro*. Now, in the same twelve months, he was to bring out an anti-Romantic satire, *Me voy de Madrid*, with Larra as its special butt; a new comedy, *Todo es farsa en este mundo*; a Classical tragedy, *Mérope* (which failed); and a translation of Casimir Delavigne's *Les enfants d'Édouard*. Such was his extraordinary facility and versatility. Though he subsequently wrote a couple of historical dramas following the Romantic fashion, *Don Fernando el emplazado* (1837) and

Vellido Dolfos (1839), these were not his real bent and he wisely returned to comedy and popularity with *Muérete y verás* (1837) and *El pelo de la dehesa* (1840). Thereafter, during his tenure of office as chief librarian of the National Library, his output declined, but his last play, *Los sentidos corporales*, was not produced until 1867. Pereda in *Pedro Sánchez* pays homage to his prestige in the early 1850s and as late as 1860 Valera would still refer to him as 'El príncipe de nuestros poetas cómicos'.[1] The work of Gorostiza and Bretón, covering as it does the entire Romantic period, illustrates in its inclusiveness the danger of generalising about the Spanish theatre in the 1830s and 1840s. Romantic lyrical dramas and anti-Romantic satires, Moratinian comedies, Classical tragedies, and historical melodramas succeeded one another in the Madrid theatres, the public remaining indifferent to all (with contradictory exceptions such as Martínez de la Rosa's *Edipo* and García Gutiérrez's *El trovador*) with a fine impartiality.

II. VENTURA DE LA VEGA

When Martínez de la Rosa's *La boda y el duelo* was staged in 1839 by the dramatic section of the Madrid *Liceo*—which significantly had just revived Moratín's *La comedia nueva*—among the cast of distinguished amateurs was Ventura de la Vega, who played Carlos. Six years later, when the Romantic movement had virtually collapsed, Ventura scored the last resounding success of the regular comedy with *El hombre de mundo* (1845). Before, he had been notorious as a tireless translator of French plays for the Spanish stage. Vega wrote some thirteen original plays between the early 1840s and 1862. Of these *Don Fernando de Antequera* (1844, performed 1847) and *La muerte de César* (1862, performed 1863) deserve mention. In the former, like Bretón shortly afterwards, he submitted to the vogue for historical drama, frequently mentioned in this chapter, but the play is largely a chronicle, with little evidence of the Romantic spirit either in style or in manner. The latter, on the other hand, stands beside Tamayo's *Virginia* (1853) as one of a handful of brave attempts at tragedy to be made in the nineteenth-century Spanish theatre. It is memorable on that score alone, and also, perhaps, for its curious pseudo-realism. Thus Ventura was able to write naïvely to the actor Romea:

4 * *

He procurado hacer una tragedia tal en su forma pero dándole al fondo un poco más de realismo, o, por mejor decir menos de convencional. Le he quitado la tiesura, la aridez, la entonación igual y uniforme; le ha dado variedad, flexibilidad. Observa y verás que en mi tragedia las gentes comen, duermen, se emborrachan, se dicen pullas.[2]

It was, however, seen at the time as an apology for dictatorship and an indirect compliment to Napoleon III. While it remains Vega's most ambitious work, its popularity and ultimate historical importance are far below those of *El hombre de mundo*.

In one respect this play closes an epoch: that of the Neo-classic comedy which, as we have seen, enjoyed an unbroken development right through the Romantic period. The story of a reformed rake and philanderer whose recent marriage is gravely threatened both by a still unrepentant companion and by his own hyperconsciousness of the ease with which a husband can be deceived, it conforms strictly to the unities of time, place, and action. Its theme belongs to the same social-moral convention as do those of *Indulgencia para todos* or *Marcela*. It ends inevitably with a marriage and an *escarmiento*. To this extent *El hombre de mundo* belongs with Zorrilla's *Don Juan Tenorio* performed the previous year. Both plays are end-products. They mark the middle 1840s as a critical moment in the modern Spanish theatre.

In another respect Vega's play represents a change to something new. For all its outward similarity to the drama of Moratinian inspiration, the spirit and atmosphere are strikingly different. Valera came close to defining the difference when, looking back on the play in 1881, he commented that it lacked the witty refinement and elegance, the detachment and *idealidad*, of the 'alta comedia', but could be excused on the grounds that 'el escritor pintó sólo, *con fiel realismo*, lo que en la clase media veía'.[3] What characterises *El hombre de mundo* in fact is that, in sharp contrast to Rivas's *El parador de Bailén* for example, in which the regular comedy approaches farce, Vega's play verges on high drama. In spite of the usual droll scenes of below-stairs lovemaking and drawing-room misunderstandings, we are conscious all the time of a potentially very serious matrimonial situation developing between Luis and Clara. The degree of tension and suspense which this generates alters the whole tone of the play and in particular affects the figure of Luis, whose role as the stock comedy-figure of the biter who is in turn bitten is gradually displaced by the much more dramatic and personal one of the jealous and vengeful husband. Don Juan too, cynically undertaking the seduction of his friend's newly married wife, is closer to villainy than to comedy.

There is nothing, therefore, in this play or in any of the rest of Ventura de la Vega's work which is suggestive of the 'eclecticism' postulated by Allison Peers. *El hombre de mundo* is in no sense equidistant from Neo-classicism and romanticism. Its combination of the old unities and comedy formula with a new middle-class setting, a new and wholly anti-Romantic emphasis on marriage rather than love, and the hint of new serious possibilities, makes Vega's play an obvious link between the old regular comedy and the *alta comedia* which was shortly to follow.

III. STAGNATION IN THE THEATRE

Between the end of romanticism and the appearance of Ibsen the fortunes of the theatre in Europe as a whole were at a low ebb. Spain was no exception. In fact the decline of the theatre was simply part of a general fall in the level of creative achievement in all branches of literature between the middle 1840s and the Revolution of 1868. The two earlier prevailing types of play, the post-Moratinian comedy and the Romantic drama proper, had both run their course. Vega's *El hombre de mundo* ought to have been the prelude to a large-scale renovation of drama. But, despite a confused awareness on the part of some critics that the time was ripe to 'libertar el drama antiguo de todo cuanto es incompatible con nuestras nuevas costumbres' (S. Bermúdez de Castro), no such renovation took place.

What happened instead was first of all an unnatural prolongation and progressive debasement of the historical drama brought into vogue by romanticism. How anachronistic this became is revealed by Palacio Valdés's apprehensive awareness when he came to review García Gutiérrez's *El grano de arena* in 1881 that he was in a sense measuring himself against Larra, who had reviewed *El trovador* fifty years earlier, long before Palacio himself was born! As we have just seen, the Romantic dramatists had regularly paid their debt to Moratín in the intervals of carrying through the renovation of the Spanish theatre. In the same way, during the decades which followed, the leading playwrights, in the midst of timidly developing the new *alta comedia*, whose setting was essentially contemporary and whose concern was with moral and social problems, continued sporadically to stage more or less old-style historical dramas. Avellaneda's theatre, which like Rubí's is transitional, illustrates the point perfectly. In the same way Tamayo's 'high comedy' period belongs between his play on the theme of Juana la loca, *La locura de amor*, which scored a success of major proportions in 1855, and his masterpiece, *Un drama nuevo* (1867), set in Elizabethan England. Ayala contributed *Un hombre de estado*, drawn from the death of Rodrigo Calderón, in 1851 and *Rioja* (1854), before turning to contemporary themes. Núñez de Arce's only significant play, *El haz de leña* (1872), is on the well-worn subject of Philip II's son Don Carlos. A host of minor dramatists including Florentino Sanz (*Don Francisco de Quevedo*, 1848), and Narciso Serra (*La boda de Quevedo*, 1854), the dramatic collaborators F. L. de Retes and F. Pérez Echevarría (*La Beltraneja*, 1871), Carlos Cuello (*La mujer propia*, 1873), M. Zapata (*El Castillo de Simancas*, 1873), and F. Sánchez de Castro (*La mayor venganza*, 1874) contributed to keep the genre alive until it received fresh impetus from the early work of Echegaray, who established his reputation in 1875 with *En el puño de la espada*, set in the sixteenth century. Thereafter, the historical drama survived irrepressibly in the work of Villaespesa, Ángel Guimerá, and Marquina, with whom it made its entrance into the twentieth century. The striking contrast between this flourishing tradition and the miserably small output of significant plays with a contemporary setting is one of the major features of Spanish nineteenth-century drama. With conspicuously few exceptions playwrights before the end of the century seem inexplicably unwilling to look their times in the face and when they do so, all too often they seem to be peeping timidly out upon exclusively middle- and upper-class society from behind a thick protective screen of morality and conformism. The Romantic legacy of *criticismo*, 'la tendencia' as it came to be called, which is so visible in the polemical novels of the 1870s, and in the poetry of writers as dissimilar as Núñez de Arce and Rosalía de Castro, is absent from the stage. The theatre, which had been the Romantics' battleground, turned its back not only on the ultimate problems of the human condition but even, until Dicenta's *Juan José* in 1895, closed its doors upon serious social protest. The choice it presented to its audiences was simply between the pseudo-Romantic *comedia* 'de asunto histórico, de expresión lírica y desenfrenada' and the pseudo-realist *comedia* 'de asunto presente, reflexiva, moral y más psicológica en situaciones y caracteres' (N. Alonso Cortés), neither of which, despite Echegaray's Nobel Prize, was destined to stand the test of time.

While Ventura de la Vega's *El hombre de mundo* is conventionally held to mark the beginning of a transition towards drama of contemporary social problems in an upper-bourgeois setting, the claims of Tomás Rodríguez y Rubí (1817-90) cannot be overlooked. Born in the same year as Zorrilla, he came to literature, like Ventura, via the *Liceo* and staged his first play in 1840. Within five years he was being described as the leading younger dramatist and three of his early plays, *La rueda de la fortuna* (1843), *Bandera negra* (1844), and *El arte de hacer fortuna* (1845) were by the standards of the time smash-hits. The first two of these belong inevitably to the category of historical dramas, but already they represent an evolution of the genre similar to that which is visible in the later historical novel. The past is increasingly exploited not for its own sake, as in mainstream romanticism, but as a disguise for allusions to the present, and in particular to the contemporary political scene. Thus there is a smooth transition from these plays to Rubí's true political *comedias*, firmly set in the present, such as *El arte de hacer fortuna*, its sequel *El hombre feliz* (1848), and (after an interval due to Rubí's political commitments) his masterly *El gran filón* (1874), a biting satire of political vindictiveness and *arrivisme*, of a piece with the central chapters of Pereda's *Los hombres de pro* (1872) but more comic. These plays represent a definite progress towards the *alta comedia* formula both in their setting and in their didactic and moral involvement with problems of the day. A third group of Rubí's plays comes even closer. These are his dramas not of public office, historical or contemporary, but of private family life, four of which—admittedly not the best—were staged before Vega's *El hombre de mundo*. It is these plays which substantiate Rodríguez y Rubí's claim to be regarded as the main writer of bourgeois social drama before Tamayo turned to it with *La bola de nieve* in 1856. Some fourteen of Rubí's plays belong in this category, which began with *Detrás de la cruz el diablo* (1842) and included among its best examples *La escala de la vida* (1857) and *Fiarse del porvenir* (1874). In both of these, as in López de Ayala's *Consuelo* and Tamayo's *Lo positivo*, the central theme is money and social position, seen from the standpoint of slightly conventionalised and sentimentalised middle-class morality, with honest work in the end financially rewarded but excessive materialism properly punished.

IV. TAMAYO Y BAUS

The pioneering work of Vega and Rubí bore fruit in the 1850s with the emergence of two recognised masters of *alta comedia*: Adelardo López de Ayala (1828-72) and Manuel Tamayo y Baus (1829-98). Between them they carried through a renovation of the theatre which, though on a much smaller scale and with far less creative results, was at least similar in direction to that which Ibsen was preparing to bring about in European drama as a whole. If Cánovas del Castillo could write in 1881 'Lo que más atrae ahora la atención de la sociedad culta es la exposición y resolución de *problemas de la vida*, ya individuales, ya sociales, y el estudio *psicológico* de las pasiones humanas en la escena', the credit is largely due to them. And when all has been said in their disfavour, it should be recalled that no such attempt at renovation was even begun in Britain until the time of Robertson and Pinero years later.

Tamayo came from a well-known family of actors and both his brothers had stage careers, though he himself spent most of his life as a minor employee in the civil service. From a very early age he translated and adapted foreign plays for his parents' company in Granada and before he was twelve had achieved a local success with *Genoveva de Brabant*, taken from a French original. In 1884 he moved to Madrid and during the next nine years staged in rapid succession some sixteen plays, including his first wholly original one in 1848, *El cinco de agosto*. For the most part translations or imitations, often written in collaboration with others, they reflect a lengthy apprenticeship to his craft.

Between 1853 and 1870 when Tamayo gave up writing for the theatre at the early age of forty-one, he staged a further eighteen plays. They include, in the very front rank of his production, three which no history of the Spanish theatre in the nineteenth century can overlook: *Virginia* (1853), *La locura de amor* (1855), and *Un drama nuevo* (1867). These were Tamayo's great successes. Strangely, considering that Tamayo is one of the two dramatists whom we chiefly associate with the *alta comedia*, not one of these three plays belonged to that genre. Flanking them, but rather below them in literary merit, stand Tamayo's major contributions to bourgeois high drama: *La bola de nieve* (1856); *Lo positivo* (1862); *Lances de honor* (1863); and *Los hombres de bien* (1870). *La ricahembra* (1854), another historical play written by Tamayo with a certain amount of assistance by the scholar and critic A. Fernández Guerra, because of its type and the element of collaboration, occupies an intermediate position.

In an assertive prologue to *Virginia*, to which may be compared Ventura de la Vega's letter to Romea on the subject of his own *La muerte de César* (1863), Tamayo sets out his ideas on what tragedy should be like in the Spain of 1853. Two principles, realism and moralism (both fatal to true tragedy), govern the outlook of this youthful lawgiver. Criticising French Classical tragedy for affectation and Italian Neo-classical tragedy for frigidity, Tamayo advocates on realistic grounds dropping both chorus and its modern equivalent, the confidant; avoiding the Greek idea of fate; varying the versification; and above all extending the plot to reveal the origins of the tragic events and not merely their climax. On moral grounds he asks '¿No resultaría una enseñanza profundamente saludable de hacer ver el extremo de angustia y degradación a que puede llegar el hombre impulsado por una pasión desordenada no reprimida a tiempo?'

The answer is to be seen in *Virginia* itself. It conveniently combines the traditional Spanish themes of liberty and honour. But while it contains potentially tragic elements, it is not a true tragedy, for the simple reason that there is no such thing as an overtly moral tragedy. Esquer Torres's confused arguments in its favour collapse the moment it is observed that the forces in conflict are not, and cannot be, equally balanced. Apio Claudio is a mere villain armed with a power against which Virginio and his daughter are powerless. The aim of the play is not to reveal a tragic evolution of character but the trivial *moraleja* that evil conduct recoils on the doer.

Fortunately, in *La locura de amor* and *Un drama nuevo* Tamayo succeeded in subordinating his moralistic preoccupations to the depiction of authentic human emotion. Doña Juana of *La locura de amor*, while stimulating strong admiration by her 'prudencia' in her public role as queen, moves the audience to deeper feelings of sympathy and compassion by the tender submissiveness and tormenting jealousy of her private role as a wife. In all but one respect *La locura de amor* deserves to join the great central group of Romantic dramas discussed in an earlier chapter. But that respect is fundamental. This is, like *Macías* or *Los amantes de Teruel,* a drama of love and death: but it is not a drama of *fate*. There is no symbolism, no deeper dimension of cosmic interrogation. The importance of *La locura de amor* in the history of Spanish drama derives less from what it contains than from what it lacks—authentic romanticism. *Un drama nuevo* has been

unanimously acclaimed as Tamayo's masterpiece since its first performance. It is a story of love, jealousy, and professional envy among
a group of actors in Elizabethan London, Shakespeare himself figuring prominently among the characters. The play as a whole owes
something both to *Hamlet* and *Othello*, and its similarities to plays
by Lope, Rotrou, and Dumas have been minutely analysed. Sugges-
tions that it compares in quality either with Shakespeare or Pirandello,
however, reveal a lack of critical perspective. What the play does
undoubtedly illustrate is two of Tamayo's basic traits. The first, in
contrast to the hasty improvisation characteristic of so much that was
written for the stage in nineteenth-century Spain, is the trouble which
Tamayo took with his best work. The second is his own and his
century's lack of moral detachment. Instead of an evenly-balanced set
of forces, Tamayo allows the main counterforce, Walton, like Apio
Claudio in *Virginia*, to be tainted with villainy, and what (in spite of
the overdrawn climax) might have come close to genuine tragedy
remains, sadly, near-melodrama.

La bola de nieve was written during a productive period of *cesantía*
in which Tamayo found himself after the Liberal triumph following
the battle of Vicálvaro in 1854 which led to the takeover of power by
the political generals O'Donnell and Espartero. It also saw the composition of *La locura de amor* and four other minor plays including
Hija y madre (1855), a tear-jerking melodrama on the theme of filial
ingratitude which was still played in the provinces until recently. *La
bola de nieve* illustrates, like Ventura de la Vega's *El hombre de
mundo*, the adaptation of the Bretonian light-*comedia* formula to the
exigences of a theatre audience which now demanded stronger sensations. Beginning as a satirical comedy of comic jealousy between two
sets of fiancés, it changes key in the last act and turns into a high
drama of vengeful passion and remorse. It was Tamayo's last comedy
in verse and clearly represents a transition in his development. This is
further emphasised by the gap in his production of major works
between 1856 and 1862. It is a curious fact too that after *La bola de
nieve* Tamayo consistently refused to acknowledge directly the author-
ship of his plays, all of which subsequently were produced under
pseudonyms.

Lo positivo, Tamayo's first real *alta comedia*, was staged scarcely
a year after the fantastic success of Ayala's *El tanto por ciento* on a
similar theme and the two plays are in many ways the central works
of the genre. Based on a French model, but largely original, *Lo*

positivo is a typical pre-realist play of ideas nicely calculated to censure but not to shock. Taking issue, in a note of bland and humorous remonstrance, with the tendency to subordinate the higher human incentives and emotions to mere monetary advantage, Tamayo contrasts the noble compassion and disinterestedness of Rafael with the selfish business principles of his prospective father-in-law, deliberately manipulating the plot in favour of the former. The result, though utterly unconvincing, has something of the sentimental charm which the Quintero brothers were later to exploit so successfully, and almost solves the difficult problem of making virtue interesting. *Lances de honor* and *Los hombres de bien*, on the other hand, are written in quite a different tone of moral indignation. In the latter case, Tamayo (having in the meantime gone over to Carlism like Pereda) found himself exposed as a result to bitter attack as a 'neo' and a reactionary. This may well have been a factor in his decision to stop writing for the stage.

Lances de honor is a highly emotional and exaggerated drama attacking the practice of duelling. *Los hombres de bien*, on the other hand, unwisely attempts to combine two levels of social criticism. One centres on the figure of Adelaida, the emancipated woman, who begins by losing her respect for her father—very justifiably as it happens—and ends as the mistress of a cruel and odious adventurer. The other involves the ignoble hypocrisy and cowardice of the three 'right-thinking men' who provide the play with its title. It is not clear in either case where the necessary connection is to be found between emancipation and self-degradation, or between respectability and cowardly hypocrisy; the play strikes the reader of today as arbitrary in conception and querulous in tone. The essential defect of Tamayo in all his *alta comedia* plays is that he merely defends one conventional pattern of behaviour—the traditional Catholic one—against another conventional one, without attempting, in the manner of the true dramatist of ideas, to lead his audience towards a newer, less conventional, outlook. It is this which explains why his dramas of passion and jealousy, *La locura de amor* and *Un drama nuevo*, have stood the test of time better. Both have been successfully filmed.

V. LÓPEZ DE AYALA

The career of López de Ayala illustrates one of the basic facts of literary life in nineteenth-century Spain. This was that a successful novel, play, or collection of poems was the best passport to public office and a career. Ayala's career was the classic one. In 1849 he arrived in Madrid from his home town in Guadalcanal near Badajoz without finishing his education, without friends or resources apart from his old family name and a newly-written play, *Un hombre de estado*. In an extant letter to Sartorius, the *Ministro de la Gobernación*, he peremptorily demanded its performance. It was staged by the *Teatro Español* in January 1851 and Ayala was at once given a post under Sartorius with an income of 12,000 *reales*. Following the pattern immortalised by Pereda in *Pedro Sánchez* he took up journalism, made his name, and in 1857 was in parliament. A decade later he was helping to prepare the rising of 1868 and when it came wrote its famous September Manifesto. His mediation at the battle of Alcolea which brought about the fall of Isabella II was rewarded by the governorship of Barcelona and he went on to be Foreign Minister under the victor, Serrano. He held the post three times more, the second time under Alfonso XII, whose restoration he had assisted in bringing about. In 1878 he was elected *Presidente del Congreso* and a year later, shortly before his death, was offered the Prime Ministership. He had been elected to the Academy in 1870.

Although his output consisted all told of some fourteen plays, his really significant works are no greater in number than Tamayo's and can be reduced in the same way to two groups: his historical dramas, notably *Un hombre de estado* (1851) and *Rioja* (1854); and his contributions to the *alta comedia*: *El tejado de vidrio* (1857), *El tanto por ciento* (1861), *El nuevo Don Juan* (1863), and *Consuelo* (1878).

Un hombre de estado, on the theme of Don Rodrigo Calderón, the unhappy favourite of Philip III, illustrates an important aspect of the evolution of the historical drama in the mid-century period. By contrast with Tamayo's *La locura de amor* which, as we have seen, is fully within the spirit of the Romantic drama but without its deeper dimension and symbolism, this first memorable play of Ayala is in all respects an example of the *alta comedia* in a historical setting. Like Consuelo a quarter of a century later, Don Rodrigo, far from making love the centre of his existence, deliberately rejects it. He marries from self-interest and, after reaching the peak of worldly ambition, falls from power and is sent to the scaffold. Unlike Consuelo, however, he is shown in repentance and undergoes something very like a tragic evolution of character in the last two acts. Though marred by inequalities of tone and by introduction of the melodramatic figure of

Doña Inés, the play has moments of real grandeur which, though never approaching the Shakespearian, inevitably call to mind the Wolsey-theme of *Henry VIII*. *Rioja*, Ayala's other notable historical drama, also contains a certain elevation of tone which sets it above the mere chronicles so frequently passed off as drama at the time. Its theme, that of renunciation of love and office for motives of gratitude, is nobly conceived. But in Ayala's choice of circumstances to express the theme we perceive an unfortunate discrepancy between the cause of Rioja's obligations to his friends and the inhuman self-sacrifice which is its effect. The result, which might have been tragic, is merely quixotic.

Unlike Tamayo, Ayala has left on record few of his opinions about the theatre. But from his famous eulogy of Calderón (1870) can be drawn three conclusions which serve as an introduction to his *comedias de salón*. The first concerns his times, which Ayala saw as 'un período en que la duda, contaminando todos los espíritus, debilita el alma y hace indecisa la forma de nuestra literatura'. The connection between religious doubt and literary form is not obvious, but the implication is clear. Ayala ranges himself with the partisans of *buenas ideas*. The second concerns the theatre of his time, which Ayala describes contemptuously as

una literatura dramática atolondrada y raquítica que unas veces frívola y sin ingenio, nos vola el tiempo, sin producir deleite ni enseñanza, y otras, al sentir la frialdad de su pobreza, se finge honrada y católica, y sermonea y lloriquea para conseguir la limosna del aplauso.

His position here is equally distant from trivial escapism and pious moralism. Thirdly, while insisting on the need for the dramatist to identify himself with the outlook of his audience, Ayala, in common with the majority of his fellow-writers and critics at the time, condemns realism as 'nocivo al arte' and praises instead Calderón's 'ardiente espiritualismo'. His, then, is a conventional position. His aim is to write plays which are moral without moralising, which are elevated without being out of reach of his audience, and which are artistic constructs and not mere copies of reality. Twenty years earlier his purpose ('desarrollar un pensamiento moral, profundo y consolador') had not been very different.

In both cases the emphasis is on morality. In his four major plays Ayala concentrated his criticism on two major human failings: greed for wealth and anti-social behaviour. Though a bachelor, Ayala appears not to have been a celibate. For many years he carried on an affair with the famous actress Teodora Lamadrid. But in two of his best-known plays, *El tejado de vidrio* (1857) and *El nuevo Don Juan* (1863), he satirises cynical and systematic *donjuanismo*. This was not new. Indeed, the earlier of the two plays has certain similarities with Ventura de la Vega's *El hombre de mundo* of twenty years before, a fact which emphasises that play's significance. The difference lies in the tone, which is noticeably more serious. The Conde is a rather different figure from Ventura's Don Luis. His guilt is not merely retrospective but actual. Secretly married, he undertakes the conquest of a friend's wife only to see his own on the verge of eloping with one of his disciples and admirers. What is mere appearance in *El hombre de mundo* is reality in *El tejado de vidrio* and the Conde only narrowly escapes the permanent dishonour with which his conduct threatens others. *El nuevo Don Juan* looks backwards also, to Zorrilla's masterpiece. But as we have already noticed, the *alta comedia*, in contrast to Romantic drama, lays the emphasis not on love as a spiritual force but on marriage as a social institution. The professional seducer is seen not as a sinner whose soul is at stake but as a threat to the basic nucleus of society: the family. His punishment is less in the hands of God than in those of the community whose rules he breaks. Its verdict is harsher than Zorrilla's. Ayala's Don Juan fails to redeem himself and is punished publicly by his own victims. Losing not only his intended mistress but also his future wife, he is baulked both of illegitimate and legitimate satisfaction and left despised, rejected, and, at his final ignominious exit, implicitly excluded from decent company. While neither of the two plays in question goes the length of exploring the extreme consequences of seduction, like Pereda's *El buey suelto*, they illustrate the tendency characteristic of literature at the time to rally to the defence of conventional middle-class values.

El tanto por ciento (1861) and *Consuelo* (1878) represent the peak of Ayala's dramatic production. Both were smash-hits and for the former Ayala received not only the congratulations of the entire literary world of Madrid, but also a gold crown worth more than 6,000 pesetas, paid for by public subscription. Though apparently similar in type to *El tejado de vidrio* and *El nuevo Don Juan*, their formula is really quite different, being a blend of direct social criticism and sentimentality. The comedy-elements which survive in the plays of frustrated seduction disappear. Their place is taken by a more developed love-interest; and it is this, not humour, which provides the contrast point to the selfish greed which is now the principal theme. *El tanto por ciento* is the story of a collective swindle involving the fortune of the hero and the honour of the heroine: both are seriously compromised by the middle of the play only to be triumphantly recovered at the end, with the discomfiture of the heartless clique who hatched the plot. Technically the play is Ayala's most complex production, with three suitors manoeuvring for the hand of the heroine, each at the same time being involved in the financial transaction, along with other false friends and even the servants. The distribution of the various resulting chains of events, so as to provide rapid alterations of fortune in each act and a climax of extreme suspense, is a remarkably skilful piece of dramatic construction. Unfortunately the behaviour of the characters is subordinated to the situation and remains rather mechanical.

Consuelo is much simpler, being closer, in Ayala's intention, to a comedy of character. It shows the unhappy consequences of marrying for money: a more serious treatment of Tamayo's similar theme in *Lo positivo*, with the positions reversed. As theatre it is once more splendidly effective, with a superb curtain-scene at the end of each act. But the rigidly didactic framework within which the action is confined renders it unduly linear. Consuelo makes her selfish decision in the first act almost without hesitation. She never fully regains the audience's sympathy and her fate lacks pathos as a result.

VI. ECHEGARAY

Already by the early 1870s it was clear that the *alta comedia* of Tamayo and Ayala had not succeeded in revivifying the Spanish theatre. It failed either to produce a clean break with the heritage of Romantic drama or to prevent the stage from being invaded by a regiment of didactic dramatists intent, not on challenging the traditional Catholic values to which audiences paid lip-service, but on serving them up stripped of every reasonable qualification which might offend against silly and ignorant prejudice. 'El teatro español', wrote Palacio Valdés, looking back in 1879,

merced a los trabajos de los Eguilaz, Larra, Rubí y otros, había
dado grandes pasos hacía el confesionario; se postraba a los pies del
coadjutor de la parroquia . . . rezaba el rosario todos los días.
Cuando adoptó otro género de vida, todas las gentes dijeron
'¡Echegaray es el que lo ha pervertido . . . !'[4]

That José Echegaray (1832-1916) should have been seen, even at
the beginning of his career, as a revolutionary and subversive
dramatist serves to remind us of the extraordinary aberration of taste
and judgement into which the Spanish theatregoing public had now
fallen. Initially a mathematician and engineer, later a Minister of
Finance and founder of the Bank of Spain, Echegaray turned to
drama during a short period of exile while in his early forties. The
success of his first play, the one-act *El libro talonario* (1874), was
followed by the staging in rapid succession of more than sixty other
plays. These tended to be either fantastic successes or total failures:
even his fortunes as a dramatist tended to extremes. Among the most
memorable successes were *En el puño de la espada* (1875), *O locura
o santidad* (1877), *El gran galeoto* (1881), *Dos fanatismos* (1887), *El
hijo de Don Juan* (1892), *Mariana* (1892), *Mancha que limpia* (1895),
La duda (1898), *El loco dios* (1900), and *A fuerza de arrastrarse*
(1905).

Although Echegaray began with the little *comedia de salón* mentioned above, in which a young wife ingeniously turns the tables on
her unfaithful husband, he made his name in the 1890s with a series
of historical verse-melodramas which have led to his being frequently
referred to as a 'Romantic' or 'neo-Romantic'. But it is necessary to
make a distinction here. What saves the small group of major
Romantic dramas from the oblivion into which Echegaray's other
plays have deservedly fallen is their theme: the struggle of man,
supported by love, against the hostility of life and fate. Deficient as
their expression of it sometimes is, that theme gives them grandeur
and literary significance. Echegaray's theatre, whether historical or
modern in setting, lacks such thematic importance. It has only situations. With one or two exceptions—not among his best-known plays
—everything in Echegaray is subordinated to situations. His essential
quality as a dramatist was his astonishing ability to invent and exploit
to the uttermost, with characteristic humourlessness, the most
grotesquely improbable theatrical situations. Psychological verisimili-
tude and significant commentary on human life and behaviour are

thus, for the most part, automatically ruled out. Suspense, and suspense alone, reigns supreme. We marvel that a middle-class theatre audience could applaud such a production as *En el puño de la espada*. In it a woman who years before has been raped, who has married a man ignorant of her experience, and who has had a son as a consequence of it, sees the culprit play rival to her (and his own) son for the hand of the heroine. The guilt of the mother being written in blood on the blade of a dagger, the son expunges it by plunging the weapon into his own breast! In *La última noche* (1875) we find a demonic banker (following the inevitable stage direction 'Ríe con risa satánica') proclaiming:

> Quiero vivir y gozar
> babilónicos placeres;
> quiero divinas mujeres;
> quiero, soberbio, eclipsar
> las glorias de Baltasar,
> y, moderno semidiós,
> siempre del placer en pos
> volar por el ancho mundo.
> ¡La muerte es sueño profundo;
> el oro, el único dios!

In *O locura o santidad* a father allows himself to be taken for a lunatic in order to ensure his daughter's marriage to the son of a duchess, a marriage which is threatened by certain unlikely circumstances connected with his own upbringing. In a small number of plays (*El gran galeoto, Dos fanatismos, El hijo de Don Juan*) Echegaray attempted to break away from melodrama and write social drama of ideas. The first of these three plays, Echegaray's greatest success, widely translated and played outside Spain, illustrates the tragic effects of malevolent gossip, in an exaggerated thesis drama which makes an interesting comparison with a similar type of play by Tamayo, such as *Lances de honor*. *El hijo de Don Juan* reveals the influence of Ibsen's *Ghosts* and demonstrates Echegaray's genuine desire to extend the range of his work. But he remains for us the maximum representative of Spain's theatrical decadence in the late nineteenth century. The award to him of the Nobel Prize in 1904 was the occasion of a spirited protest by several members of the Generation of 1898. How futile that protest was is shown by comparing the extremely successful *La muralla* of Calvo Sotelo in our own time with *O locura o santidad*. Despite the passage of more than seventy years we perceive an unmistakable similarity of manner.

Among the contemporaries of Echegaray may be mentioned briefly Leopoldo Cano (1844-1934), the author of similarly overwritten plays on social themes, such as *La trata de blancas* (1887) and his most important work, *La pasionaria* (1883), which hinted at conflict between the interests of the Church and the army. Eugenio Sellés (1844-1926) seemed to Clarín at the time to represent a hopeful possibility in the drama. But he never equalled the success of his first major play, *El nudo gordiano* (1878), which harking back to Calderón, and in contrast to Galdós's *Realidad*, perceived in the murder by the husband of the unfaithful wife the only possible solution to feminine adultery. José Feliu y Codina (1847-97) exploited the possibilities of regional rural settings for plays on the traditional theme of honour and revenge, notably *La Dolores* (1892), pointing the way to Benavente's rural plays in the next century. Enrique Gaspar (1842-1902), whose period of productivity lasted from 1867 to his death, wrote some twenty-six original plays. His chief contribution was to the drama of moral thesis. His best plays, *Las personas decentes* (1890) and *La huelga de hijos* (1893), attack the moral and sexual shortcomings of the middle class. He strongly defended the prose-medium against López de Ayala's use of verse, and his plays have some pretensions to realism. But apart from occasional audacities (which the theatregoing public was quick to reject) he remained on the whole close to the manner of Tamayo.

VII. GALDÓS

Once the main impact of Echegaray had been absorbed, the theatre seemed once more in a phase of decline. But just at this time a combination of financial difficulties and desire for public applause led Galdós to attempt to repeat on the stage the triumphs he had won with his novels (see below, pp. 131-45). In 1892 he staged a theatrical version of his dialogue-novel *Realidad* with María Guerrero as his leading lady. The play's moderate success encouraged Galdós and it was eventually followed by a score of other adaptations and original dramas. These fall chiefly into two periods: 1892-96, which saw, after *Realidad*, *La loca de la casa* (1893), *Gerona* (1893), *La de San Quintín* (Galdós's first original play, 1894), *Los condenados* (1894), *Voluntad* (1895), *Doña Perfecta* (1896), and *La fiera* (1896);

and 1901-05, which saw *Electra* (1901), *Alma y vida* (1902), *Mariucha* (1903), *El abuelo* (1904), *Bárbara* (1905), and *Amor y ciencia* (1905). After this, though Galdós staged seven more plays, his production declined both in quantity and quality.

Given the almost total absence of significant Spanish drama in the 1890s apart from his own productions, it is difficult to see Galdós's plays in perspective or to assess their contribution. They represented a sudden, unexpected, and at the time disconcerting contrast to the debased Romantic theatricality of Echegaray and his followers, to the translations from the French which abounded, and in general to what we now contemptuously think of as the *teatro de astracán*. They aimed at bringing life, vitality, observation, and above all *ideas* to a theatre which was in decay. But Galdós did not possess the technical ability to achieve his aims consistently and his audiences lacked the flexibility of outlook required to accept his innovations, whether of form or content. He had four striking successes. *La de San Quintín*, *Doña Perfecta*, *Electra*, and *El abuelo*, the last two being by any standards major works of modern Spanish drama. *Electra* created a furore, sold 20,000 copies in a matter of days, and helped to bring down the Conservative government of General Azcárraga, which was succeeded by a Liberal one under Sagasta. It was the only time in this century in Spain that a work of literary protest directly affected society. *El abuelo*, Galdós's last triumph, marks the end of a period in the history of the Spanish stage.

In retrospect we perceive that, from the rise of the *alta comedia* onwards, the problem in the theatre was that of conciliating some measure of truth and significance with the refusal of realism. The result was at best a compromise which could only be maintained sporadically in individual plays. It provided no basic formula and regularly collapsed into the convulsive striving after exaggerated effects of Echegaray and his followers in their worst moments. The advent of serious drama, of ideas and social protest, beginning with Galdós and Dicenta was delayed but inevitable. It is unfortunate that no dramatist of real creative power emerged to complete the work of these two pioneers.

NOTES

1. *Revista de Teatros*, XV. See *Obras completas*, II, 185.
2. A. López de Ayala, *Obras completas*, I (Madrid, 1965), xx.
3. *Obras completas*, II, 588.
4. 'Semblanza de Echegaray', *Obras completas* (Madrid, 1959), II, 1208.

Chapter 7

BÉCQUER, ROSALÍA DE CASTRO, AND PRE-*MODERNISMO*

I. THE RENOVATION OF LYRIC POETRY

FROM ABOUT THE MID-CENTURY new forces were incubating in Spanish lyric poetry. Their remoter origins inside Spain are lost in the welter of influences operating on romanticism. But Cossío, in his monumental work on the poetry of the second half of the nineteenth century, cogently indicates the rise of the *balada* as a factor of major importance. Related to the lyric by its brevity and to narrative poetry by its content, the *balada* formed an intermediate genre often dramatically conceived and containing a strong dialogue-element. As such, it was not sufficiently different from the *romance* (versification apart) to achieve really independent status and has not survived this period. In the fifties it enjoyed great popularity. Among its cultivators we have already noticed Ventura Ruiz Aguilera. His use of the *balada*, however, almost exclusively as a vehicle for reflections on events of the nation's past and for the discussion of contemporary social and political questions diminishes the importance of his role in popularising it. Credit for naturalising the *balada* into Spanish poetry, in a form recognisably like its northern European counterpart, falls to a lesser poet, Vicente Barrantes (1829-98), whose thirty *Baladas españolas* appeared in 1853. Barrantes's *baladas* are in themselves mediocre; they lack both genuine lyricism and real mastery of poetic technique; in many cases their theme is borrowed from a foreign source; but what is really innovatory and original about them in the Spanish context is the element of fantasy which Barrantes succeeded in taking over from the ballad-tradition of northern Europe. At a time when a new liberating influence in poetic imagination was needed Barrantes endeavoured to point one out.

Poetry of a very different kind was that of Antonio de Trueba (1819-89), in whom as a *cuentista* we have already seen a follower of Fernán Caballero. Barrantes was a man of broad European culture, acquainted with German and English poetry at a time when few Spanish writers looked beyond France. Trueba, a self-taught shop-assistant, was largely cut off from foreign influence. In compensation, however, he was close to the popular tradition, and like Fernán, was among the earliest systematic collectors of Spanish folk-poetry. With *El libro de los cantares* (1852) he scored an immense success. The work went into eight editions during the next twenty years, after which it was followed up with *El libro de las montañas* (1868) in identical vein. Trueba, like Bécquer, identified poetry with feeling. His personal manifestos—the article 'Lo que es poesía' of 1860 and the prologue to *El libro de las montañas*—are important chiefly for their insistence on this point at a time when Spanish poets were obsessed with ideas. A comparison between their contents and Bécquer's *Cartas literarias a una mujer* reveals marked similarities. A second persistent feature of Trueba's *credo* was the deliberate moralism which led him to publish, in collaboration with Carlos Pravia, a set of *Fábulas de la educación* (1850) for school purposes. Trueba's favourite method was to develop an anonymous *copla* which he had collected into a kind of *balada*, adding to it a brief and usually moral narrative element suggested by the original *copla* and told semi-dramatically, often in dialogue. His ability to project the genuinely popular tone of the *copla* is striking. Cossío, himself a collector of folk-poetry, testifies to having come across versions of Trueba's poems recited to him as *bona fide* examples of traditional *cantares* by peasants in the 1920s. The significance of Trueba's work is summed up by J. Frutos Gómez de las Cortinas as follows:

Tras la estruendosa trompetada del romanticismo retórico el autor de *El libro de los cantares* postula una poesía de temas simples, de sentimientos menos detonantes, de expresión más natural y sencilla. A pesar de los inevitables barquinazos prosaicos, con su obra consiguió un triple efecto; echar la última y definitiva paletada sobre la poesía hinchada y altisonante, despertar la afición poética de los lectores (hastiados de confusiones líricas y piro-técnicas verbales) y, lo más importante de todo, hacer ver a los nuevos poetas que el método directo para llegar a la verdadera poesía consiste en la expresión natural de los sentimientos íntimos. Trueba, revalorando la poesía popular, inaugura un nuevo período en nuestra poesía del siglo XIX.[1]

Among his sincerest admirers in the 1880s was the young Unamuno, no study of whose poetry is complete without reference to Trueba's influence. More gifted than either Barrantes or Trueba was José Selgas y Carrasco (1822-82). Of humble origins, he owed the opportunity of making his mark in Madrid, like Ayala, to the patronage of Sartorius. His first collection of verse, *La primavera* (1850), was remarkably successful and promptly imitated. *El estío*, which followed in 1853, consolidated his reputation and brought him temporarily to the leading place among younger poets. It is noteworthy that his name is expressly mentioned by Bécquer in 1860 in the complaint about the state of poetry at the time quoted below (p. 96). The affinities of Selgas's poetry with German *Lieder* were immediately recognised. They are combined with the sentimental moralising intention noticed in Trueba which, as the typical mid-century phenomenon, has its counterpart in the novel of Fernán Caballero and not a few of Tamayo's plays. Selgas's lyrics deal predominantly with flowers, birds, and trees, less for their own intrinsic beauty than as symbols of moral qualities. This feature links them to the poetic apologue or fable which, after a period of unpopularity during the Romantic period, revived under the influence of *buenas ideas* and was cultivated afresh in the 1840s by Hartzenbusch and Campoamor among others. The most famous example is 'El sauce y el ciprés'. Of greater merit is his descriptive poem in *octavas reales*, 'El estío', which gave the title to his second collection. Selgas's gentle melancholy tone, his subjectiveness, and his considerable technical talents earned him a special place among the poets of his period. Features of 'El estío' have been quoted as among the sources of inspiration for several of Bécquer's *Rimas*. Significantly, Barrantes, Trueba, and Selgas all wrote for the magazine *El Album de Señoritas y Correo de la Moda*, which favourably mentioned one of Bécquer's earliest poems, his contribution to the Quintana commemorative volume of 1855, as well as publishing his 'Anacreóntica' the same year.

In 1857 the 'favor germancista' associated with Barrantes and Selgas underwent a major development as a result of an event of decisive importance for Spanish post-Romantic poetry. This was the publication in *El Museo Universal* of fifteen poems by Heine translated into Spanish by Eulogio Florentino Sanz (1825-81), already known as a dramatist and a poet in his own right. The uprising of 1854, which has been said to close finally the period dominated by the surviving great Romantics (Rivas, García Gutiérrez) and which halted Selgas's poetic development in mid-career, ironically occasioned Sanz's being sent to a diplomatic post in Berlin (1854-56). This provided him with the opportunity to compose the translations which were to have an electrifying effect on younger poets after his return. They were followed in the same year by further translations of Heine in the *Correo de la Moda*, the work of Arnao, Ignacio Virto, Javier del Palacio, Ángel María Decarrete, and especially Bécquer's close friend Augusto Ferrán y Fornés (1836-80). With these it may be said that a new trend in Spanish poetry was already in being.

With the work of Ferrán we arrive at the very threshold of Bécquer's own work, not only because of the friendship which united the two poets, nor because of the immense documental importance of Bécquer's review of Ferrán's first book of poetry, *La soledad* (1861), but also because of the close similarity existing between some of Ferrán's work and some of Bécquer's, amounting in a couple of cases to unquestioned influence on the latter. Ferrán who, apart from Sanz, was the only poet of any significance in Madrid who knew German really well, in 1861 published (also in the *Museo Universal*) some sixteen poems translated or imitated from Heine; but with an important difference. Ferrán, a Sevillian, was deeply under the spell of Andalusian popular *cantares*, not expanding or adapting them as Trueba had done with examples from his own collection of popular poetry, but imitating them directly so as to preserve their brevity and distinctive southern flavour. The combination of both influences, Heine's *Lieder* and popular Andalusian folk-poetry, is the characteristic of Ferrán's verse—his second collection, *La Pereza*, was published, like the *Rimas*, in 1871. This is what, thanks to the influence he was able to exert on his friend because of his wealth, his familiarity with German, and his earlier emergence as an avant-garde poet, Ferrán transmitted to Bécquer.

A feature of criticism after the mid-century was the growing conviction that Spanish poetry was in a state of complete decadence. Its cause is easily traceable to the failure of poetry in the decades immediately following the Romantic triumph to maintain the level of creativity attained in the 1830s and early 1840s. Already in 1859 Francisco Zea had described his fellow-poets in a letter to Ruiz Aguilera as 'esos fingidos cisnes, esos reales y verdaderos grajos'. A year later Bécquer referred sadly to the few remaining possibilities of 'un género que abandonaron Tassara, Ayala y Selgas'. Valera in 1869 described his times as 'un período anti-poético hasta lo sumo'. Núñez de Arce's famous poem 'Las arpas mudas' (1873) is the culmination of this state of concern. But, though Darío was still a child and Martí (the oldest of the Latin American *modernistas*) was in his early twenties, still a decade away from *Ismaelillo*, the renovation had begun.

II BÉCQUER

The true point of departure for modern poetry in Spain is incontestably the *Rimas* of Gustavo Adolfo Bécquer (1836-70), published in 1871. Born in Seville, the son of a painter, Bécquer was left an orphan in 1847. After a brief period of training in the studio of one of his father's successful pupils, he abandoned painting and moved to Madrid (1854) in search of a literary career. Success, however, eluded him and for some years he lived in poverty writing for minor newspapers. The *zarzuela*, then in its heyday, provided the only lucrative outlet for poetic talent and between 1856 and 1863 Bécquer churned out a number of librettos in collaboration with others. His first serious work was a *Historia de los templos de España* (1857), probably suggested by Piferrer's *Recuerdos y bellezas de España* (1839). Though only a few instalments of it were published, it contributed to the formation of Bécquer's prose style and brought him into contact with the themes of some of his *leyendas*. The first of these, 'El caudillo de las manos rojas', appeared in 1858, and marks the beginning of Bécquer's main productive period, which lasted until 1866. It got off to a bad start. In mid-1858 Bécquer suffered a serious illness, probably tubercular or venereal in origin, from which he never fully recovered. Shortly afterwards he seems to have enjoyed—or suffered—the mysterious love-affair to which some critics have attempted to relate the composition of the *Rimas*. Thereafter his luck changed. In late 1860 he joined the staff of the newly founded *El Contemporáneo* (with which Valera and Galdós were also to be associated), and formed his important friendship with the poet Augusto Ferrán; in May 1861 he married. With these events coincided a year of intense creative activity. This included the publication of the *Cartas literarias a una mujer* and the important review of Ferrán's *La soledad* which are among Bécquer's main writings on poetry, together with seven of his twenty-two *leyendas* in prose. More journalism and *leyendas* followed. In 1864, during a summer at Veruela in northern Spain, Bécquer sent to *El Contemporáneo* the charming, intimate, and at times rather *costumbrista,* essays called *Cartas desde mi celda* and at the end of the year obtained the well-paid post of government censor of novels which provided his living during most of the next four years. During 1867-68 Bécquer, who had by now composed his famous *Rimas,* though only a handful had been published (chiefly in 1866), prepared a manuscript of them for publication. Unfortunately, during the panic of the Revolution of 1868, the manuscript was lost and the poet was forced to prepare a second one, partly from memory. It is this second manuscript which, with minor additions and variations, forms the basis for modern editions. Bécquer's marriage, though it produced three children, was not a happy one. It broke down in the summer of 1868, in the fatal seventh year, and Gustavo took two of his children to live with his brother Valeriano in Toledo. The latter died in September 1870 and his death was followed by that of the poet on 22 December. Like Espronceda, he died at the age of thirty-four.

It was seen earlier that the poetic renovation of which Bécquer and Rosalía de Castro came to be the leaders began in the late 1850s with the fusion between poetry of popular inspiration (Trueba) and the current which was influenced by German lyrics (Selgas), a fusion effected chiefly by E. Florentino Sanz. To this current of renovation Bécquer adhered from the publication in 1859 of the first of the *Rimas* (XIII, 'Tu pupila es azul'), despite the fact that this was an imitation of Byron. Earlier, the main formative influence on him had been F. Rodríguez Zapata (1813-89), a colleague and follower of the venerable Lista. The latter had spent his declining years teaching in Seville and forming there a fresh brood of poets, of whom perhaps the most famous was López de Ayala. Others worthy of mention among this group, the only nucleus of real eclecticism which might be credibly mentioned in support of Peers's theory, were J. Fernández Espino (1810-75); Juan José Bueno (1820-81); José Amador de los Ríos (1818-78); José Lamarque de Novoa (1828-1904); and Bécquer's friend and editor, Narciso Campillo (1835-1900). Though their poetry often reveals anachronistic survivals of pre-Romantic elements, their importance lies in their compactness as a body under accepted leadership and their conscious continuation of the traditions of poetry

associated with the earlier so-called 'escuela sevillana'. Zapata introduced Bécquer to Horace, to Golden Age lyric verse (Rioja, Cetina,
Villegas), and to such Romantic writers (Chateaubriand, Scott,
Lamartine, Zorrilla among them) as the followers of Lista (and hence
of Schlegel) allowed themselves to admire. But the handful of surviving poems written under such influences, including Bécquer's earliest
known work, an ode on Lista's death, and his contribution to the
homage-volume to Quintana (1855), belong to the mere pre-history
of his verse. Between then and 1859 Bécquer published no poetry
that we know of. When he broke his silence with what is now the
thirteenth *rima*, the combined influence of the *Correo de la Moda*
group of Germanising poets and his rediscovery of the popular
Andalusian *cantar* had decisively intervened.

The originality of Bécquer's poetic *credo*, expressed in the *Cartas
literarias*, the review of Ferrán, and the later *Introducción sinfónica*
can only be seen to proper advantage by comparing it with such
different pronouncements as, for example, Campoamor's *Poética* and
Núñez de Arce's Academy address. Here a brief summary of
Bécquer's statement about his art must suffice. An initial distinction
is that which he makes between poetry in the old rhetorical tradition
and his own lyrical ideal:

> Hay una poesía magnífica y sonora; una poesía hija de la medi-
> tación y el arte, que se engalana con todas las pompas de la lengua,
> que se mueve con una cadenciosa majestad . . . Hay otra natural,
> breve, seca, que brota del alma como una chispa eléctrica, que
> hiere el sentimiento con una palabra y huye, y desnuda de artificio,
> desembarazada dentro de una forma libre, despierta con una que
> las toca, las mil ideas que duermen en el océano sin fondo de la
> fantasía . . .

The first—'magnificent', 'sonorous', 'the daughter of thought'—is
poetry of *statement* saying, or trying to say, great things memorably.
Núñez de Arce was on the way to becoming its last High Priest. The
second, Bécquer's, is poetry of *suggestion*. It is born not of *ideas*, the
obsession of Bécquer's contemporaries, but of a mysterious creative
process more akin to vision favoured by a peculiar state of trance-
like reverie below the level of conscious thought and logical co-
ordination. Here images and impressions unconsciously stored in the
depths of the poet's mind:

Ideas sin palabras
palabras sin sentido
cadencias que no tienen
ni ritmo ni compás
Memorias y deseos
de cosas que no existen . . .

well up, fuse, and combine, in a manner which Bécquer, happily for
us, repeatedly struggles to describe, especially in the second of the
Cartas literarias. Conditioning this accumulation and selection of
poetic material is not conscious reflection but emotions, 'porque la
poesía es el sentimiento', and sensations. At the moment of creation,
which Bécquer almost always associates with light, the poet's previous
sense of nervous oppression suddenly gives way to illumination and
joy. The 'ardientes hijas de la sensación' and the 'memoria viva de lo
sentido' appear as a vision and the poet at last writes 'como el que
copia de una página ya escrita'.

We notice here not only the contrast with mid-century 'poetry of
ideas' but also with the poetic manner of romanticism. When Bécquer
reproduces his memories and sensations as lyrics, neither he nor they
are the same. The initial experience, which for the Romantics *was*
inspiration, for Bécquer is only the *fount* of inspiration. When he
writes, he is out of its grip; the experience itself, latent in the poet's
mind, has meanwhile undergone a process of depuration which turns
it into the stuff of poetry. But at this point, when the internal process
ends and the external one of creating verbal expression begins,
Bécquer is confronted with the poet's essential problem: the limitations of language. The thing of everyday use, 'the instrument of
objectivity' (Machado), resists the poet's attempt to force it to express
fine shades of subjective meaning. Hence the first *Rima*:

Yo sé un himno gigante y extraño
que anuncia en la noche del alma una aurora,
y estas páginas son de ese himno,
cadencias que el aire dilata en las sombras.

Yo quisiera escribirlo, del hombre
domando el rebelde, mezquino idïoma,
con palabras que fuesen a un tiempo
suspiros y risas, colores y notas.

> Pero en vano es luchar; que no hay cifra
> capaz de encerrarlo, y apenas, ¡oh hermosa!
> si, teniendo en mis manos las tuyas,
> pudiera al oído cantártelo a solas.

The *Rimas* themselves appear to have been grouped together by the poet's friends, who prepared the posthumous edition in an order not necessarily intended by the poet. Gerardo Diego has argued that it corresponds to four basic themes: I—XI concerned chiefly with poetry and the poet; XII—XXIX mainly expressing love in its ascendant, hopeful phase; XXX—LI dominated by misery and disillusionment; and LII—LXXIX basically on themes of solitude and despair. Rica Brown, Bécquer's best biographer, accepts the first category but suggests as basic themes for the rest of the *Rimas*: first woman, the joys and sorrows of love, and woman's role in poetic inspiration; and second the ultimate destiny of man, and related themes (including death, immortality, and faith). This last grouping, overlooked by Diego, is of great importance as linking Bécquer (along with Rosalía de Castro, as we shall see presently) with the Romantic legacy of spiritual unrest. While we must regretfully disagree with Rica Brown on the degree to which these themes (especially the last) are personal to Bécquer in his period, unquestionably the most original group is that dedicated to poetry and the poet himself. Here Bécquer resurrects the Romantic idea of the poet-seer, intuitively and emotionally tuned-in to a world-spirit, emanating ultimately from God ('origen de esos mil pensamientos desconocidos, que todos ellos son poesía, poesía verdadera')

> desconocida esencia,
> perfume misterioso
> de que es vaso el poeta.

With the spirit the poet, despite his yearning, cannot achieve total unity. It is the hidden force behind the poetic act, essential yet indefinable, to which he can respond, but which he cannot fully express. Thus all poetry remains 'esa aspiración melancólica y vaga que agita tu espíritu con el deseo de una perfección imposible'. Within this poetic mystique the role of woman and love is primordial. 'El amor es el manantial perenne de toda poesía', while woman, who is at once the source and object of love as well as possessing (in contra-distinction to masculine conceptual intelligence) special qualities of

feeling and intuitive response to beauty, is 'el verbo poético hecho
carne'. Genius has feminine attributes. Thus the themes of love,
poetry, and woman are ultimately inseparable. But a distinction can
be made between those *Rimas* in which love is seen semi-platonically
as the indefinable essence of all things—'. . . ley misteriosa por la
que todo se gobierna y rige'—and those which may bear direct
reference to the poet's own emotional experience. Thus in ix the kiss
becomes the symbol of universal cosmic harmony and union:

> Besa el aura que gime blandamente
> las leves ondas que jugando riza;
> el sol besa a la nube en Occidente,
> y de púrpura y oro la matiza;
> la llama en derredor del tronco ardiente
> por besar a otra llama se desliza.
> Y hasta el sauce, inclinándose a su peso,
> al río que lo besa, vuelve un beso.

In xi and xv woman ('vana fantasma de niebla y luz') is the ethereal
symbol of unfulfilled aspiration; while elsewhere the purely anecdotic
content of the poems allows us to conjecture at a direct connection
between them and Bécquer's mysterious love-affair or affairs prior to
his marriage. In general the latter are less satisfactory and at times
are not far from the manner of Campoamor's best *Doloras*. But when
Bécquer leaves the concrete human situation entirely behind, expressing his fulfilment or frustration in accumulations of pure metaphor
(xxiv, xli, liii), the result is once more outstandingly beautiful. The
last major group of Bécquer's poems, those which were prompted by
despair at the collapse of his love-ideal, contain conventional topics
inherited from the Romantics. They are probably Bécquer's least
original poems in theme. Their tone is plaintive rather than anguished.
But they contain a pathos which none of Bécquer's predecessors
achieved in the same measure—Arolas's famous 'Sé más feliz que yo'
perhaps comes nearest.

Bécquer's poetic technique has not been fully explored analytically.
We note his preference for expressions of discontinuous movement:
'tembloroso, ondea, errante' and the like; for those of the mistily
indefinite and impalpable; for light-imagery; for brevity of form, or
the cumulative repetition of stanzas on the same simple model rather
than complexity of structure; for simile rather than metaphor. But

the difficult simplicity, the apparent artlessness of his verse, resists
the attempt even of so sophisticated an analyst of form as Bousoño to
lay bare its secrets.[2]

III. BÉCQUER'S PROSE

Eighteen of Bécquer's twenty-two *leyendas* were published in
various Madrid newspapers between 1861 and 1863. We may thus
plausibly regard them as probably antedating most of the *Rimas*. The
genre, of course, was not in itself new. Its roots were partly popular
and local, in the oral traditions current about particular spots,
churches, sacred images, and the like; partly literary, stemming from
oriental religious literature, apologues, and stories of magical events.
The 'historical' wing of romanticism, and especially Zorrilla, had
delighted in the former, whose fanciful elements had led to a renewal
of interest in the latter, coinciding with a growing shift from verse
to prose as a medium. By the late 1850s, strengthened by the
traditionalistic tendency of *costumbrismo*, its nostalgic desire to
salvage charm from the past, prose *leyendas* had emerged as a highly
popular minor art form, which like the *cuadro de costumbres* itself
often tended to shade off into something resembling a short story.

Bécquer's *leyendas* possess great variety, ranging from the now
conventional equivalents of Zorrilla's *tradiciones* ('El Cristo de la
calavera', 'La promesa') which led to his being regarded in some
quarters as a neo-Catholic sympathiser, via the purely fantastic and
symbolical ('Los ojos verdes', 'El gnomo') to the exotic ('El caudillo
de las manos rojas', 'La Creación'), and finally the familiar *madrileño*
ambience of 'Es raro'. Similarly they vary greatly in quality from the
merely anecdotic ('Apólogo') and religious/moral ('Creed en Dios',
'La ajorca de oro') to those of more profound significance or personal
feeling ('Tres fechas'). Many reveal Bécquer's special ability to deflect
the reader's interest gradually from the real to the fantastic by means
of a deft personal introduction or the placing of a historical or topo-
graphical detail. Their combination of fantasy with humour, pathos,
and, more rarely, irony shows great technical ability. In general, however, the content and manner of the *leyendas* are less original than
their style, which occupies a unique place in the history of Spanish
nineteenth-century prose. 'Milagro aislado', Díaz Plaja calls it, and
goes on: 'No son demasiados los hallazgos estilísticos de Bécquer.

Con todo, se destacan luminosamente en la chata y gris prosa ocho-
centista española'.[3] The real renovatory impulse in Spanish prose
came in the end, as it did in poetry, from Latin America with
modernismo. Significant is the fact, too often overlooked, that
modernista elements appear in Latin American prose earlier than in
verse. Still, several of the features introduced by Montalvo, Martí,
and González Prada, and later superbly exploited by Darío, are
anticipated by Bécquer in the *leyendas*. With no prior stylistic tradition to develop, Bécquer created a type of lyrical prose which, in its
employment of semi-poetic rhythms and diction, its emphasis on
sensations (optical, tactile, and auditive) rather than ideas or feelings,
its colourful and pictorial descriptive approach, together with its
occasional audacious use of metaphor, portends the future 'poem in
prose'.

A final contribution by Bécquer to the development of Spanish
nineteenth-century prose was the virtual creation of the literary essay
in *Cartas desde mi celda* (1864). Though Larra's critical essays and a
number of *cuadros de costumbres* had led the way and suggested the
techniques of mingled observation and reflection, nothing quite like
these intensely personal, descriptive, thoughtful letters to the public
from the ruined monastery of Veruela had appeared previously. They
underline once more Bécquer's striking originality.

IV. ROSALÍA DE CASTRO

Side by side with the work of Bécquer and second only to it in
importance as portending the future path of Spanish poetry was that
of Rosalía de Castro (1837-85), the major poetess of the nineteenth
century and the only one whose work still commands critical attention. She was born in Compostela, the illegitimate daughter of a
woman of good family. The precise identity of her father is unknown.
Brought up in her native Galicia, she learned its dialect and popular
poetry from her nurse. In 1856 she moved, for family reasons, to
Madrid where she soon seems to have made the acquaintance of Ruiz
Aguilera, Sanz (the translator of Heine), and Bécquer, with others of
the latter's circle. Two years later she married the historian and art-
critic Manuel Murguía. Already she had published her first book of
verse, *La flor* (1857). It was followed by *Cantares gallegos* (1863) and
Follas novas (1880), both in Galician. Her masterpiece, *En las orillas*

del Sar, appeared in Spanish in 1884. Her marriage, though it produced six children, seems not to have been of the happiest. Though reportedly cheerful in family life, she was clearly a depressive, over-responsive to the minor trials of everyday existence. In addition, her health was delicate. In middle life it grew worse and she died of cancer at the age of forty-eight.

Unlike Bécquer, whose early evolution is only scantily illuminated by surviving poems, Rosalía's tragic story can be followed relatively easily. Her earliest poems attest the enormous influence which Espronceda continued to exercise after his death. The themes, the tone, and even the versification are mere imitations of his manner, as can be perceived from the following quotation from *Fragmentos*:

> Cuando, infeliz, me contemplé perdida
> y el árbol de mi fe se desgajó
> tuvieron, ¡ay!, para llorar mis ojos
> de amargura y de hiel tristes despojos.
> La nada contemplé que me cercaba,
> y . . ., al presentir mi aterrador quebranto,
> miré que, solitaria, me anegaba
> en un mar de dolores y de llanto.
> Nadie ni amor ni compasión cantaba,
> ni un ángel me cubrió bajo su manto;
> sólo la voz mi corazón oía
> de la última ilusión que se perdía. . . .

Cantares gallegos reveals quite a different influence, that of the *baladas*, in particular those of Trueba and to a lesser extent of Ruiz Aguilera. The introduction reveals the astonishing impact of Trueba's *El libro de los cantares*, published eleven years earlier, which Rosalía now professes to be imperfectly imitating. Her modesty was unnecessary. Though she stamps herself as Trueba's disciple by following his method of adapting folk-song lyrics, the creative level of her poetry is in every way superior. His ingenuous moralism is replaced by a deep and dolorous insight; his pedestrian technique by a virtuosity and metrical inventiveness whose results, as they became apparent, were at first disconcerting to critics and then widely imitated. The great novelty of the collection was, of course, its being written in Galician, a dialect whose relationship to Spanish is somewhat akin to that of Lallans with respect to English, and involves similar advantages and limitations. It created for Rosalía a small, but intensely devoted,

public in her home region, and to many Galicians abroad she became
a symbolic figure. It gave her a theme which held her deepest
allegiance and a diction which challenged her ability to revive it as a
poetic medium:

> Cantart' ei, Galicia,
> teus dulces cantares,
> qu' así mô pediron
> na veira do mare.
>
> Cantart' ei, Galicia,
> na lengua gallega,
> consolo dos males,
> alivio das penas . . .
>
> Qu'así mô pediron,
> qu'así mô mandaron,
> que cant'e que cante
> na lengua qu'eu falo.

All but four of the thirty-seven poems or groups of poems which
compose *Cantares gallegos* are in the form of glosses on popular
lyrics. Here Rosalía, like Trueba, meets the difficulty which confronts
the poet who deliberately forsakes conventional diction for the much
more limited poetic possibilities of popular or pseudo-popular
language. Important areas of vocabulary, of concepts, and of imagery
are denied her once she confines herself to imitating the plain speech
and unsophisticated outlook of folk-poetry. But her success is proved
by the same criterion that was applied to her model. Some of
Rosalía's *cantares* have, like Trueba's, been taken over by the people
of Galicia as authentic popular productions. Typical of Rosalía's
effective use of simple means (direct comparison and contrast) to
express a familiar human emotion is part of XIII:

> Unha muller sin home . . .,
> ¡santo bendito!,
> e corpiño sin alma,
> festa sin trigo.
>
> Pau viradoiro,
> qu'onda queira que vaya
> troncho que troncho.

Mais en tend' un homiño
¡Virxe do Carme!,
non hay mundo que chegue
para un folgarse.

Que zamb' ou trenco,
sempr' é bó ter un home
para un remedio.

Love-songs, mainly of a plaintive and tender kind, together with poems embodying popular wisdom, sometimes satirically, form the majority of the poems in this collection. But in these the imprint of Rosalía's personality is less than in the principal secondary group of poems in which the theme is not individual feeling, but the poetess's response to Galicia itself, its countryside, its folkways, its typical inhabitants, and especially its contemporary situation. Writing in Castile, Rosalía repeatedly expresses her intense longing for her homeland:

¡Ay!   ¡quén fora paxariño
        de leves alas lixeiras!
        ¡Ay, conque prisa voara
        foliña de tan contenta
        para cantar á alborada
        nos campos da miña terra!

and consoles herself with memories of its beauty and simplicity. But her identification is deeper than mere personal nostalgia. Her songs of farewell and absence mirror the feelings of generations of immigrants forced into exile by conditions which Rosalía attributes resentfully to Castilian predominance. Here her verse strikes a virile note of pride and reproach:

Premita Dios, castellanos,
castellanos que aborreço,
qu'antes os gallegos morran
qu'ir a pedirvos sustento

which found a deep echo in her native region. This first collection of poems by Rosalía in her native dialect led to a revival of Galician as a literary medium. The poems of *Follas novas* being for the most part to the late 1860s, and are therefore not so far separated in time from the *Cantares* as the date of publication of the volume suggests.

But in the interval a great change had overtaken Rosalía's work. Much of the popular inspiration of the *Cantares* has disappeared for ever, together with the occasional notes of lightheartedness and humour to which it had given rise. The poems of *Follas novas* are the fruit of a deeper and more sombre insight. To associate this simply with the Galician *modo de ser*, as critics have tended to do, is to ignore its close relationship with the extensive spiritual malaise which already affected the intellectual minority in Spain and elsewhere in Europe. This is the proper context of Rosalía's tragic vision of life. Her later poetry illustrates a stage of the on-going process by which Romantic world-weariness was gradually being transformed into the more intellectually consistent pessimism (with undertones of despair) which is characteristic of the Generation of 1898.

That Rosalía was aware of the ferment of unrest abroad in Spain is clear from the introduction and its references to a 'tristeza, musa d'os nosos tempos' and to the 'cousas graves' which 'N'o aire andan d'abondo'. Though she modestly disclaimed, as a woman, the capacity to handle profound thought in her poetry, there can be no doubt that the medular part of her last two collections is the numerous poems of dolorous meditation on existence. How consubstantial such meditation was with her own existence is revealed by her well-known

> Una-ha vez tiven un cravo
> cravado no coraçón . . .

which so clearly inspired Machado's 'Yo voy soñando caminos'. Rosalía's early nostalgia and sadness have now hardened into bitterness and intermittent hopelessness:

> Quién fora pedra . . .
> sin medo â vida, que da tormentos
> sin medo â morte, que espanto da.

Her hatred of Castile and its harsh landscape ('¡D'o deserto fiel imaxe') and longing for the humidity and greenness of Galicia survive intensified by time. In Books IV and V ('Da terra' and 'As viudas d'os vivos las viudas d'os mortos') Galicia's beauty, in ironic contrast to its poverty and hunger ('desdichada beldá'), is celebrated afresh, but Rosalía is the first to emphasise that this theme, which had earlier been the essence of her work, is now subordinate to 'à eterna layada queixa que hoxe eisalan todo-l-os los labios'.

5 * *

V. 'EN LAS ORILLAS DEL SAR'

En las orillas del Sar, though published in 1884, collects poems many of which, according to González Besada, had appeared in *El Progreso* of Pontevedra during the middle 1860s. If this is so, Rosalía's major creative period must have coincided with her early thirties. It is also clear, however, from internal evidence, that a fair number of the poems were written later. Certainly there are clear signs of an evolution of outlook in the collection. Basically, though Rosalía's few critics have tended to minimise this issue, the starting-point for many of the poems is a deeply rooted spiritual malaise. These are poems of insight: repeatedly Rosalía resorts to Espronceda's image—'caída la venda de los ojos'—of a sudden acquisition of clear-sightedness. There can be no doubt that, as in the case of the older poet, the key-element is the collapse of religious confidence. The poems in the early part of the collection, and sporadically almost to the end (though then a new note of religious hope appears), are explicit:

> Mi Dios cayó al abismo,
> y al buscarle anhelante, sólo encuentro
> la soledad inmensa del vacío.

Lacking this existential support (longed for, but not recovered, if at all, until later life) reality reveals itself to Rosalía as an intensity of desolation:

> Todo es sueño y mentira en la Tierra.
> ¡No existes, Verdad!

In the chopping-down of the oak-forests of Galicia Rosalía found not only another cause for protest at the treatment of her native province but also a symbol of life left desolate by the cutting-away of long-standing hopes, beliefs, and illusions. Among these were most of life's consolations, not merely religious certainty, but love, now bitterly presented in terms of insincerity; children, the source of some of her most deeply pathetic poems:

> ¿A dónde llevaros, mis pobres cautivos
> que no hayan de ataros las mismas cadenas?
> Del hombre, enemigo del hombre, no puede
> libraros, mis ángeles, la égida materna.

and even creativity itself, the poet's ultimate support:

> La palabra y la idea—Hay un abismo
> entre ambas cosas
> —Desventurada y muda,
> de tan hondos, tan íntimos secretos,
> la lengua humana, torpe, no traduce
> el velado misterio.

The result is a deep, brooding despair relieved only at intervals by hope or lonely resignation, though in a few poems Rosalía fleetingly recaptures enough confidence in art and faith to proclaim

> ¡Hay arte! ¡Hay poesía! ¡Debe haber cielo; hay Dios!

En las orillas del Sar stands as the most important single volume of verse, apart from Bécquer's *Rimas*, to be published in Spain during the interval between the collapse of romanticism and the advent, side by side, of *modernismo* and the poetry of the Generation of 1898 at the end of the century. In it, more than in any of the other numerous collections of verse dominated by pessimism and despair which came out during that period, we see the authentic legacy of Romantic insight being handed on from Espronceda to Unamuno and Antonio Machado. But while Rosalía thus stands unique in her period for her deeply felt and deeply moving comment on the human condition, her themes alone are not her only claim on the interest of posterity. She also played a not unimportant part in the gradual extension of Romantic experimentalism with lyric metres which culminated in the innovations of the *modernistas*. While most of the poems in *En las orillas del Sar* are in conventional seven-, eight-, and eleven-syllable lines, novel combinations of six-, eight-, and ten-syllable lines, of alexandrines, and of sixteen- and even eighteen-syllable lines, often with vigorous *enjambement*, frequently appear. But rhyme gives way largely to assonance, in line with the Bécquerian tendency away from verbally emphasised musicality towards a vaguer inner harmoniousness. Thus, with Rosalía and Bécquer Spanish lyric poetry once more achieved a fertile balance of genuine feeling and technical originality.

Bécquer's poetry was viewed with contempt by poets of the older generation and was slow to achieve the popularity it has now long enjoyed. Núñez de Arce dismissed it contemptuously as 'suspirillos germánicos'. Campoamor went even further and accused it of:

un cierto seudotrascendentalismo patológico que consiste en un histerismo soñador que crea un género nervioso, asexual y amorfo y que muchos llaman sugestivo y que no sugiere nada.[4]

Valera, in spite of the remarkable critical alertness which made him hail the appearance of Darío, did not recognise the importance of Bécquer until the appearance in 1878 of the second edition of the *Rimas*. Similarly, when he came to prepare his anthology of nineteenth-century verse in 1902 he inexplicably overlooked Rosalía de Castro: undoubtedly one of the greatest gaffes Spanish criticism records.

But among the minority of serious contemporary and younger poets Bécquer had numerous admirers and imitators. When Manuel Reina looked back to the early 1870s his thoughts were of

la plácida lectura
de Hugo, de Heine, Bécquer y Espronceda.

It is clear that from then on Bécquer's influence was highly active. We notice it in poets as different as Reina himself and Manuel del Palacio, to say nothing of the host of minor figures exhaustively listed by Cossío. But by far the most notable of Bécquer's imitators were Rosalía de Castro and Darío. Doubt has been cast on Rosalía's debt to Bécquer owing to the problem associated with the dates of her poems. Darío for his part maintained an ungenerous silence with regard to Bécquer in his autobiography.[5]

VI. PRE-*MODERNISMO*: REINA AND RICARDO GIL

Among the last important group of poets to emerge in the later nineteenth century are the pre-*modernistas* Manuel Reina (1856-1905) and Ricardo Gil (1855-1908). Reina, born in Puerto Genil (Córdoba) in wealthy circumstances, finished his university education in Madrid and at the age of twenty scored a success with the publication in *La Ilustración Española y Americana* of his poem 'La música'. This was followed in rapid succession by two collections of poems, *Andantes y allegros* (1877) and *Cromos y acuarelas* (1878), before Reina turned to politics, where he was a follower of Sagasta and later Maura. Elected to parliament in the same year (1886) as Galdós, Reina subsequently became a Senator (1893) and Civil Governor of Cadiz.

Between his early collections of poems and his relapse into silence

in the late 1880s intervenes his founding and editorship of *La Diana*
(1882-84) which, during its short life, was a literary magazine of
major importance. The list of its contributors includes the names of
practically every leading writer: Núñez de Arce, Selgas, Ruiz
Aguilera, Manuel del Palacio, and Salvador Rueda along with a
dozen other poets; Echegaray and Tamayo represented dramatists;
Pereda, Valera, Clarín, Cánovas, Castelar, Ortega Munilla, and
Galdós (to whom the April number of 1883 was probably the first
public *homenaje*) along with numerous others who contributed prose.
The foreign authors translated for *La Diana*'s columns—Gautier,
Baudelaire, as well as the usual Hugo, Dumas, De Musset and
Lamartine, Poe and Longfellow (instead of Byron, the vogue for
whom still persisted), and above all the Germans, not merely Goethe,
Schiller, Heine, but also Uhland and such lesser figures as Pfeffel,
Zedlitz, Kerner, and Hartmann—attest the shifting influences on
Spanish letters at the time. It should be noted that Reina is the first
to introduce the concept of the 'poète maudit' to Spain in one of a
group of poems, *La lira triste*, published in 1885. For a decade after
the closure of *La Diana* Reina published no collected verse and
appears to have undergone a personal crisis which produced a marked
change in his later work: *La vida inquieta* (1894), *Poemas paganos*
(1896), *El jardín de los poetas* (1899), and the posthumous *Robles de
la selva sagrada* (1906). These constitute his mature production.

Reina's first two collections of poems, written in his early twenties,
are undistinguished except for the extreme use of visual effects and
sensory appeal of the diction in a number of poems (reminiscent of
Arolas) and for Reina's remarkable gift for musicality, already
apparent. The themes, however, are conventional and second-hand:
liberty and liberalism, the poet's dream of the ideal woman and its
betrayal, and the pleasures of the senses. Once more the influence of
Espronceda is uppermost, together with those of Quintana, Zorrilla,
Byron, De Musset, and Hugo, tempered by acquaintance with
Schiller, Bécquer, and Heine. Such influences and choice of themes
in the late 1870s reveal the pathetic inability of all but a tiny minority
of Spanish poets in this period to emancipate themselves from a
Romantic heritage which was by now wholly debased.

During the interval of sixteen years between Reina's second and
third books of verse a mysterious alteration occurred within his poetic
personality, the causes of which are not wholly clear. 'A un poeta'
(1884) is a key poem. Its central affirmation:

> ¿Por qué los deleites y venturas
> no canto yo, como en la edad pasada?
> Porque el negro pesar, con mano fiera
> hundió en mi pecho su punzante daga

is repeated in 1890

> Ya no ostenta la púrpura y el oro
> mi musa como ayer: negros cendales
> viste, y derrama ensangrentado lloro
> ante los pavorosos funerales
> de lo bello, lo grande, lo elevado
> de todos los sublimes ideales.

We must conclude that Reina had awakened to the spiritual crisis which was spreading relentlessly through the Spanish intellectual minority. 'La ola negra' (1888) significantly denounces the advance of scepticism among the young (Reina was thirty-one). This new unhappy insight combined with apprehension at the moral and social decay of Spain, as in Núñez de Arce, is one of the keynotes of *La vida inquieta*. Art and sensual pleasure begin to take their place as the poet's refuge and consolation. One of the basic components of the *modernista* outlook which was now establishing itself in Latin America (Valera had already perceived—and denounced—the combination of *descreimiento* and *sensualidad voluptuosa* in *Azul . . .*)[6] is, then, present in Reina's later work. Significantly, when he was asked to contribute a flower-poem to a floral anthology in 1918, Reina chose the lilac, the flower whose delicate colour was a favourite with the *modernistas*, for which they were to be much satirised.

La vida inquieta is Reina's central work. His remaining collections see the disappearance of his earlier politico-social preoccupations and an increasingly exclusive dependence on purely literary inspiration (e.g. in *El jardín de los poetas* which is wholly given over to praise of the great poets of the past and calls to mind Darío's 'Medallones' in *Azul . . .*). In common with the majority of his fellow-poets Reina also cultivated the longer narrative *poema*, notably in *Poemas paganos*, which consists of two such works, one on an episode of Classical Greek history, the other—less successful—on the abjection of Rome under Nero, and a group of five linked sonnets on the theme of feminine heartlessness. This collection links Reina, though rather tenuously, with the pagan Classical element in *modernismo*, but not with Parnassianism, which had no appeal to his Andalusian temperament. From his posthumous collection may be quoted 'El bajel del arte', which illustrates both Reina's revaluation of the sonnet, his favourite verse-form, and the degree of his approach to the early *modernista* manner.

The historical importance of Reina as a poet arises from his position equidistant from romanticism (he was still writing in praise of Espronceda after the turn of the century) and *modernismo* (he was eulogised by Darío in a long poem in 1884). The passage from the expression of emotions to that of sensations, a feature of the later movement, is already apparent in Reina, especially in his intense if limited visuality and plasticity, as can be perceived in this description of dawn:

> Báñase, perfumada de azucena
> la aurora, en linfas de doradas mieles;
> y oculta flauta melodiosa suena
> entre flexibles palmas y laureles.
> Aves canoras, de luciente pluma,
> llenan el aire de vistosas galas
> y en lagos de zafir, rosa de espuma
> abren los blancos cisnes con sus alas.

Paganism, exoticism, sensualism, and the exaltation of Art are also present along with other call-signs of early *modernismo*, the swan, Venus, nymphs, ondines, satyrs, and the like. Symbolism, however (the important sphinx-symbol of life's enigma especially), is absent, as are synaesthesia, neologisms, and real audacity of metaphor or metrical innovation. Reina remains above all as a poet of light and colour who did much to prepare the atmosphere for the new movement.

Ricardo Gil, though an almost exact contemporary of Reina, came to poetry later, publishing his first collection, *De los quince a los treinta*, in 1885, when, as the title indicates, he was thirty. Its opening poem, 'Invitación', emphasises the modesty of the poet's aims, disclaiming exalted pretensions, and comparing his poetic flights to those of the swallow rather than the eagle. Like Reina's, Gil's literary importance lies in the way in which his work illustrates the transition to *modernismo*. Beginning under the influence of Selgas, Zorrilla, Campoamor, and Bécquer, Gil was, according to Onís, 'uno de los pocos que se acercan a la poesía francesa'.[7] Catulle Mendès, for example, is an influence he shares with Darío. The result was the intimate, delicate, and elegant verse of *La caja de música* (1898) for which Gil is chiefly remembered. Here, alongside poems still in the manner of Campoamor and Bécquer, and some rather didactic social poetry on the late nineteenth-century 'progressive' pattern, appear a number of poems whose tone and manner is even more unmistakably pre-*modernista* than Reina's. Characteristic of these is the fairy-tale poem 'Va de cuento':

> ¿Va de cuento? Vaya, será mi heroína
> la princesa rubia de los rancios cuentos. . . .

so intimately akin to Darío's famous 'Sonatina'. With Gil, therefore, we may close our survey of poetry before the great renovation initiated by *Azul* . . .

NOTES

1. art. cit., 79.

2. C. Bousoño, *Seis calas en la expresión literaria española* (Madrid, 1951), pp. 187-227.

3. G. Díaz Plaja, *El poema en prosa en España* (Barcelona, 1961), pp. 25-6.

4. R. de Campoamor, 'Poética', *Obras completas* (Madrid, 1901), III, 310.

5. But the contribution of I. L. McClelland to *Liverpool Studies in Spanish Literature*, I (Liverpool, 1940), to which the reader is referred, clinches the matter.

6. Valera's *carta-prólogo* to *Azul* . . . (22 October 1888).

7. F. de Onís, *Antología de la poesía española e hispanoamericana* (Madrid, 1934), p. 49.

Chapter 8

PEREDA, VALERA, AND PALACIO VALDÉS

IT IS VISIBLE THAT AFTER 1868, more accurately after *La fontana de oro* (1870), Galdós's first novel, a dramatic change overtook Spanish fiction. Suddenly it became the dominant literary genre, and its whole appearance altered; 'En rebote espectacular', writes López-Morillas, 'la novela pasa, de narcótica o evasiva, a ser inquietante y problemática'.[1] It was the heyday of the novel of thesis. The decade 1870-80 saw Alarcón's *El escándalo* (1875) and *El niño de la bola* (1880); Galdós's *Doña Perfecta* (1876), *Gloria* (1876-77), and *La familia de León Roch* (1878); as well as Pereda's *Los hombres de pro* (1872), *El buey suelto* (1877), *Don Gonzalo González de la Gonzalera* (1878), and *De tal palo, tal astilla* (1879).

I. PEREDA: EARLIER WORKS

José María de Pereda was among the novelists most deeply stirred by the Revolution of 1868. The twenty-first child of an old-established family of country gentry in Santander, he was brought up in an atmosphere of strict Catholicism and rigid class-distinctions, neither of which he ever seems to have questioned. They dominate his work. His earliest publications were would-be humorous and satirical articles followed in 1864 by *Escenas montañesas*, a collection of *cuadros de costumbres* which mark a transition in his work from set-piece description to story-line and strongly delineated characters.

The triumph of the Liberal revolution roused Pereda to combat. Like Alarcón and Clarín, Pereda saw in it a major upheaval not only in society but above all in ideas. Contrasting the upheaval associated with the battle of Vicálvaro in 1854 he wrote in *Pedro Sánchez*: 'El primero [i.e. that of 1854] transformó el aspecto exterior de los pueblos; el segundo [the Revolution of 1868] influyó grandemente en el modo de pensar de los hombres.' He himself lost no time in attempting to set matters right, and between November 1868 and July 1869 he published a series of violently intemperate political articles laying to the charge of the Liberals the whole range of national ills from the loss of the colonies to the bankruptcy of the Exchequer. He accused them of the grossest kind of financial and political corruption, of wilfully sullying the purity of Spanish Catholicism by encouraging the immigration into the country of Mohammedans, Jews, and Protestants, and of encouraging blasphemy in the *Cortes*. He also joined the Carlist Party. Henceforth his writings were dominated by the most intransigent traditionalism, which it is difficult to disassociate from his social allegiances and class situation. In his works can be found all the major beliefs, fears, and prejudices of the rural provincial gentry. Angry at the resurgence of power by the radical-minded urban middle class, jealous of its commercial and administrative predominance, shocked by its irreligion, and threatened by the unrest in the countryside which followed the Revolution, Pereda and his class clung blindly to belief in a closed paternalistic pattern of rural society which provided them with a social role, and to the traditional outlook, with religion in the foreground, which maintained its stability. Like Alarcón, who belonged to the same class of country gentry, and Fernán Caballero, who had married into a slightly higher one, Pereda hankered nostalgically after the good old days before 'dissolvent' progressive influences made themselves felt. Ultimately his idealising of the countryside is motivated by its resistance to these influences. But behind the idyll lurks the reality of a squirearchy defending its privileges.

Escenas montañesas was followed in 1871 by *Tipos y paisajes* and in 1881 by *Esbozos y rasguñas*, in both of which Pereda's nostalgic tendency to contrast the present of his 'terruño' unfavourably with the past of a few decades earlier is accentuated. But apart from the inclusion of valuable personal reminiscences in the last collection there is little real development. Although Pereda continued sporadically to produce *costumbrista* sketches until 1890, they are indistinguishable in manner from his earlier work.

Tipos y paisajes earned him the unqualified admiration of Galdós, who wrote eleven years later: 'La lectura de esta segunda colección de cuadros de costumbres impresionó mi ánimo de la manera más viva. Algunos de tales cuadros, principalmente el titulado "Blasones y Talegos", produjeron en mí verdadero estupor'.[2] The two novelists were fast friends, but their difference of outlook was irreconcilable. It was Galdós who first took advantage of the more liberal literary atmosphere after 1868. Pereda responded at once to his challenge, answering *La fontana de oro* (1870) with *Los hombres de pro* (1872), the first of four highly tendentious novels he was to produce in the 1870s.

Each of these four novels deals with a facet of social stability: *El buey suelto* (1877) and *De tal palo, tal astilla* (1879) with the basic nucleus of that stability—marriage; *Los hombres de pro* and *Don Gonzalo González de la Gonzalera* (1878) with its political dimension. *El buey suelto*, as Montesinos has shown, stands in an intermediate position between the satirical description of a 'type' (in this case 'the bachelor'), characteristic of *costumbrismo*, and a novel proper. It labours to prove that any marriage (except the kind dealt with in *De tal palo, tal astilla!*) is better than none, and that bachelorhood means squalid discomfort, furtive sexuality, expense, and misery. Everyday observation disproves both propositions. *De tal palo, tal astilla*, a reply to Galdós's *Gloria*, deals from the ultra-Catholic point of view with the specific case of marriages where one party is an infidel. Again Pereda's extreme outlook plays him false. Instead of exploring a painful conflict of love and religious allegiance, he presents a head-on collision of ideologies complicated by a melodramatic sub-plot with a religious hypocrite as the villain. Both elements are intended to throw into relief the fortitude of Águeda, the heroine, but in fact only succeed in underlining her inhuman inflexibility, at the expense of the hero, who is driven to suicide.

Los hombres de pro and *Don Gonzalo González de la Gonzalera* caricature the newly enriched provincial bourgeoisie of plebeian origin and its entry, disastrous in Pereda's view, on to the political stage. But the message of both books is in the end negative and confused. The first unwisely attempts to combine satire of Simón Cerrojo, alias Don Simón de los Peñascales, and his career in politics, with an exposure of Spanish parliamentary institutions. The result is self-contradictory. If the overt *moraleja* is that of its final sentence: 'La desgracia de España, la del mundo actual, consiste en que quieran ser ministros todos los taberneros y en que haya dado en llamarse verdadera *cultura* a la de una sociedad en que *dan el tono* los *caldistas* como yo'; there is nothing in the body of the novel to suggest that the system of cynical corruption and spoils distribution of which he is a victim is in any way his creation or that the old directing class, left to themselves by the Simón Cerrojos, would dismantle it. *Don Gonzalo González de la Gonzalera* examines the rural end of the situation. The *status quo* of a tiny village is overturned by the wealthy *parvenu* and a trio of 'Liberal' henchmen only marginally less nasty than their confrère in Alarcón's *El niño de la bola*, published the following year. How insecure the *status quo* was, is demonstrated by the speed of Don Gonzalo's triumph over the local squire and priest. The violence of oppression which Pereda attributes to the 'Liberal' upstart does not distract us from his inability to suggest a more convincing alternative than oligarchic paternalism resting on ignorance.

The main technical feature of this early group of doctrinal novels is the excessive influence of theme on plot-structure and characterisation. Instead of appearing to be an exploration of a human or social situation, they give the impression that the reality with which they deal has been forced to conform to a ready-made framework of ideas. But worthwhile works of fiction cannot be produced by the home-dressmaking method of placing a pattern on the material and cutting round the edges. A principle of selection there must be; but while it need not be exclusively aesthetic, it clearly should not lead to a presentation of life in terms which contradict our everyday experience.

El sabor de la tierruca (1881), in contrast, is of major importance both technically and because of the shift in Pereda's attitude towards rural society which emerges in it. Though written quite rapidly in the summer of 1881, following Pereda's usual habit of composition, it is carefully put together and complex in narrative structure. The episodes, though inevitably dictated by and developed in accordance with the theme, which is once more that of the defence of a rural community against political contamination, are faultlessly patterned. Four strands of narrative (two love-affairs illustrating Pereda's insistence on closed vertical class-structure, plus two chains of political events illustrating his benevolent conservatism, but for once doing some justice to Liberal idealism) are skilfully woven together so as to take full advantage of parallelism and contrast. They reach a narrative climax in Chapter 20. After this the novel, though changing course slightly like its predecessor *Don Gonzalo*, rises to a dramatic climax in the bloodless battle-scene between the two rival villages. Along with its improved craftsmanship we notice in the novel the emergence of that idyllic presentation of country life, which was to reach its peak in *Peñas arriba*, contrasting not only with the more convincing vision of Pardo Bazán, but even with Pereda's own earlier work.

II. PEREDA AND REALISM

At this point reference may usefully be made to the question of Pereda's realism. Nothing more aptly illustrates the negative aspect of the legacy of *costumbrismo* to public taste than the expectation, the demand even, that reality be suitably prettified before being presented to the average reader. Pereda at first responded to it by defending the extreme realist position. 'Esclavo de la verdad', he declared, 'al pintar las costumbres de la Montaña las copié del natural, y como éste no es perfecto, sus imperfecciones salieron en la copia'. But one feels that the remark which escaped him twelve years later in *Pedro Sánchez*, that 'hay mentiras necesarias y hasta indispensables, como son las del arte en cuanto tienden a embellecer la Naturaleza y dar mayor expansión y nobleza a los humanos sentimientos', is much closer to his real belief. The fact is that no satisfactory definition of realism which involves the work of Pereda can be evolved. Baudelaire's well-known statement that the aim of the realist is to present reality as it would be if he were not there, touches the essence of the movement. However unattainable objectivity is in actual fact, the realist author must convey the impression of writing objectively. This means not only presenting his material with apparent detachment, but also selecting it without undue prejudice. On both these counts Pereda fails, not only in his early sectarian novels, but even in his later masterpieces *Sotileza* and *Peñas arriba*. Whether his theme is political or moral, or merely drawn from the life of his *patria chica*, Pereda is always too close to it, too emotionally involved with it, too prone to relate it to his personal ideology. Secondly, Pereda's reality is always seen from the same viewpoint, that of the middle class. Only the squirearchy and bourgeois characters are seen from their own level. Pereda's 'interesantes patanes', as Galdós described them, are seen patronisingly from above. What finally cuts Pereda off from realism is that none of his novels, full of problems as they are, studies the real problem of the region, which is poverty, from the inside, as Galdós does with regard to his 'region'—Madrid. In that respect *La puchera* is a disappointment.

By the middle 1880s, Pereda was tired of 'problems' in any case and, like Galdós after the 'novelas de primera época', reached out towards a new phase in his work. Pereda defines his intention in writing *Sotileza* at the end of Chapter I as being that of offering to the consideration of later generations 'algo de pintoresco, sin dejar de ser castizo, en esta raza pejina que va desvaneciéndose entre la abigarrada e insulsa confusión de las costumbres modernas'. The sentence contains three of the classic elements of *costumbrismo*: *pintoresquismo*, *casticismo*, and rescue from oblivion of *lo periclitado*. Only moralism is lacking, and that is present in the prologue.

III. PEREDA'S MATURITY

Two of Pereda's major mature novels, *Sotileza* (1884) and *Peñas arriba* (1895), follow this pattern, with *La puchera* (1889) not quite at the same creative level. In contrast, *Pedro Sánchez* (1883) and *La Montálvez* (1888) develop Pereda's criticisms of the bourgeois society of Madrid, from which Marcelo in *Peñas arriba* is gradually detached by the pleasures and responsibilities of life in the highlands of Cantabria. *La Montálvez* need not detain us. It is the exact opposite of a novel of observation, and shows Pereda sadly out of his depth. *Pedro Sánchez*, on the other hand, is the outstanding novel of Pereda's middle period. Its theme is one of the classic themes of the nineteenth-century novel: that of the young provincial who sets out to conquer the great metropolis, only to lose his soul in the process. Montesinos compares the novel with the *Episodios nacionales* of Galdós.[3] But its real filiation is surely with Balzac. Told in the form of memoirs of a left-wing journalist turned revolutionary leader, the novel is set in the Madrid of the early 1850s with its dramatic climax in the Revolution of 1854. It follows a logical tripartite arrangement charting successfully Pedro's rapid rise to fame, his brief period of power and success, followed by his retirement and disillusion. Meanwhile his public career is gradually overshadowed by his erroneous marriage, and both collapse together. Wisely, Pereda devotes 70 per cent of the narrative to Pedro's early struggles against a background based on his own experiences in the capital from 1852 until 1855. The evocation of mid-century Madrid, and especially of its literary and cultural life in Chapters 11 to 16, is for those who are impatient of his earnest regionalism incomparably the best thing Pereda ever wrote.

With *Sotileza* and *Peñas arriba*, by many regarded as his masterpieces, Pereda, encouraged by Menéndez Pelayo, returned to describing the manners and customs of his native province. What both novels have in common is a markedly less well-developed plot—never

Pereda's strong point—and a consequent tendency to resolve themselves into a string of episodes held together by the presence of the
central characters. In *Sotileza* the story concerns the youth and
mutual attraction of two young people, Sotileza herself and Andrés
Solindres, in the old city of Santander, whose conversion into a
modern commercial centre and resort Pereda so much regretted.
Blinkered by the class-prejudices of his age as Pereda was, he was
necessarily obliged to bring the affair to nothing, given the difference
in social status between the two young people. Nevertheless, it is the
only love-affair he ever described in his novels which holds the
reader's interest, because of its very unconventionality. But the story-
line, with its problems arbitrarily resolved by the storm at sea, involving Andrés—a characteristic piece of Peredan dramatic description—
is a mere pretext for nostalgic description of the life and customs of
the fisherfolk of Santander. They are described with a wealth of
observed detail and scrupulously accurate technical language (which
one suspects Pereda mistook for realism), but, as ever, from the outside. The same, however, cannot be said of *Peñas arriba*. Here Pereda,
inverting the theme of *Pedro Sánchez*, depicts the unwilling conversion of a young idle *madrileño* man-about-town into a useful, indus-
trious, and philanthropic rural squire. Set in Pereda's own *terruño*
and written with all the force of his own total conviction, the novel
centres on the patriarchal figure of Don Celso. Succeeding where Don
Román of *Don Gonzalo González* failed, Celso is the model rural
proprietor: in him and his friends Neluco and el señor de Provedaño,
Pereda synthesises the ideals, narrowly and defensively conservative,
but not without nobility and sincerity, which he had consistently
defended. We cannot accept them; but in *Peñas arriba*, for perhaps
the only time in Pereda's work, we can respect them, because of the
attractive human context in which they operate. There is, characteristically, no force in the book which seriously conflicts with them.

Pereda's other works, *Nubes del estío* (1891), *Al primer vuelo*
(1891), and *Pachín González* (1895), are of minor interest.

In retrospect Pereda's work appears as a last strenuous attempt to
resist the forces of change which were sweeping over Spanish society
and, after 1868, were increasingly reflected in the novel, altering both
its content and its narrative-techniques. Although Pereda contributed
something, probably unconsciously and chiefly via his use of dialogue,
to the development of realism, his work is really an end-product
without significant influence later.

A pendant, in a sense, to Pereda's *La Montálvez* is, however, *Pequeñeces* (1890) by the Jesuit P. Luis Coloma (1851-1914). A sermon in fictional terms, the novel takes as its theme the corruption of Madrid high society which tolerates as mere *pequeñeces*—peccadilloes—what for the Church are mortal sins. The story-line centres on the immoral life of the heroine, Currita, and culminates inevitably with her conversion under Jesuit influence. It gives Coloma ample opportunity for scathing satire of moral indifference in the directing classes and for advocacy of a morality league among 'decent' people of both sexes to exclude the sinners from society. The enormous success of *Pequeñeces* was only partly due to its intrinsic merits. It coincided with a resurgence of religious influence during the Restoration and provided the novel spectacle of a cleric writing in a semi-naturalistic vein. It was also suspected of presenting real-life people and situations, though Coloma denied this; significantly, perhaps, it was followed in 1891 by a third attack on fashionable society, Palacio Valdés's *La espuma*.

IV. VALERA: THE CRITIC

Amid the acrimony and debate, the clashing hostility between the 'two Spains', progressive and traditionalist, one figure remained isolated and in the opinion of Montesinos[4] even anomalous—Valera.

Juan Valera y Alcalá Galiano (1824-1905) was born in Cabra (Andalusia), a younger son of an impoverished but well-connected family. In 1847 he entered the diplomatic service, in which he attained the rank of ambassador, and until his retirement in 1896 he was frequently abroad. But his absences from Madrid did not prevent him from contributing, from the middle 1850s onwards, to leading Spanish newspapers and journals the vast series of critical articles on literary and intellectual subjects which successively appeared as *Estudios críticos sobre literatura, política y costumbres de nuestros días* (1864), *Disertaciones y juicios literarios* (1878), *Nuevos estudios críticos* (1888), etc. For a number of critics these are his most important works. They constitute a mine of information and an unparalleled first-hand guide to personalities, movements, and currents of thought and taste in the last half of the nineteenth century. All historians of the period's literature are indebted to them. Valera's judgement was not infallible: as we have seen, he overlooked Rosalía de Castro and was slow to recognise the genius of

Bécquer. But against these defects must be set that perspicuousness, which not only made Valera the discoverer of Ruben Darío (and thereby godfather of *modernismo*), but set him among the first to recognise the talents of Benavente and Baroja. He was unquestionably the only Spanish figure before Unamuno to be genuinely familiar with, and fully attuned to, the progress of culture in the world outside.

Though Valera's creative writing included poetry, drama, and short stories, apart from his criticism only his novels survive. Valera came late to fiction, publishing his first full-length novel at the age of fifty. By this time his outlook was set. For the present purpose it can be reduced to three basic postulates. The first of these is the complete independence of art from considerations of truth or utility; art served no end outside itself. For Eugenio D'Ors, Valera was 'el primero, el único esteticista del siglo XIX'; for his own part Valera described himself conventionally as 'partidario del arte por el arte' and insisted that form and form alone provided the only valid criterion for judging a work of art. Before Darío was born he had already proclaimed that 'la religión de lo bello es una forma del amor de Dios'. The second postulate is the desirability of excluding from works of art (the essence of which was for him 'la creación de la belleza') as far as possible all that is ugly, worrying, or sad. Hence Valera's dislike both of romanticism and realism, which he accused of harbouring a 'predilección por lo feo y lo deforme'. He held tenaciously that the primary aim of art was not to explore and interpret human experience, still less to exert a social influence, but to please. In this he was understandably both opposing the silly moralism of Fernán Caballero and Trueba, and the doctrinaire aggressiveness of so much post-1868 fiction. But he was in fact over-reacting. While sympathising completely with his contempt for 'el arte docente', we cannot for a moment accept the two consequences which, in his opinion, followed directly from it. One of these was the rejection of all distasteful truth: '¿qué provecho nos trae el retratar la verdad si la verdad es siempre inmunda?', he wrote; '¿no sería mejor mentir para consuelo?' The other was the requirement that ordinary reality must be embellished—prettied up—before it can become material for art. 'Si la novela se limitase a narrar lo que comúnmente sucede', he wrote revealingly, 'no sería poesía, ni nos ofrecería un ideal, ni sería siquiera una historia digna, sino una historia sobre falsa, baja y rastrera'.

Valera further held that in literature theses of all kinds are deplorable. 'Repudio', he asserted categorically, 'esas obras doctas y profundas que tienden a demostrar alguna cosa y que nada demuestran al cabo sino la imposibilidad de demostrar nada por medio de una fábula'. About this, let neo-Catholic or communist writers say what they will, there can be no argument. But in its day such an attitude set Valera apart.

Underlying all three postulates is the subordination of observation to creative imagination: 'la inventiva, que trueca, sublima y hermosea [los datos de la experiencia y la observación] haciéndolos muy otros de lo que son en realidad'. Hence Montesinos's description of Valera's novels as neither realist nor idealist, since they are as open to the real as to the fantastic.

V. VALERA'S NOVELS

Chronologically they fall into two groups separated by an interval of sixteen years during which Valera, heavily occupied with his diplomatic career, wrote only criticism and in 1894 a few short stories. It is, however, impossible to see any signs of an evolution within or between the two groups, each of which begins with a masterpiece: the first, with *Pepita Jiménez* (1874), followed by *La ilusiones del doctor Faustino* (1875), *El Comendador Mendoza* (1876), *Pasarse de listo* (1877), and *Doña Luz* (1879); the second with *Juanita la larga* (1895), followed by *Genio y figura* (1897) and *Morsamor* (1899).

Pepita Jiménez was translated into at least ten languages in Valera's lifetime and sold more than a hundred thousand copies. As the only foreign publisher to pay him a royalty was Appletons of New York, he wrote a special preface for their 1887 edition which explained the circumstances of composition. In the early 1870s he resolved to intervene in the polemics surrounding Krausism (see below, pp. 179-80) and defend the orthodoxy of the movement by relating it to the Spanish mystical tradition, which he began to study. The result was very different from what was intended, for the novel describes, with great charm and gentle irony, the gradual conversion (there is no other word) of a young seminarist from naïve religious fervour to rivalry with his father for the love of Pepita. However much self-deception and over-confidence in his vocation go to make up Luis's initial outlook, the inference is clear. Here as elsewhere (cf. P. Enrique of *Doña Luz,* Doña Blanca of *El Comendador Mendoza,* and Doña Inés of *Juanita la larga*), Valera, without falling into the 'clerofobia progresista de bas étage' with which Menéndez Pelayo reproached Galdós, emphasises the human rather than the spiritual features of his ecclesiastics and their closer adherents. Though he explicitly denies that the book contains either thesis or *moraleja,* it is plain that Luis's evolution from seminarist to lover and 'mozo crudo y de arrestos' implies a value-judgement on Valera's part.

In contrast to the often loose and discursive structure of the novel in his time, which was presently to culminate in the sprawling and elephantine *Fortunata y Jacinta, Pepita Jiménez* is short and exceptionally well-made. The story unfolds in two rapid phases. The first, culminating in the lovers' kiss, is in epistolary form; not, as usually, in order to present the situation from different angles, since all the letters are written by Luis, but in order to exploit the delicious contrast between the seminarist's constant references to saintliness, mortification, and sacred literature and his complete inability to resist the fascination of Pepita. In the second part, an interval of suspense is used to present Pepita directly, preparing her character for the masterly scene which follows when Valera brings the couple together once more. The initiative passes to her, and Luis's final surrender is as much to her dialectical skill as to her physical charms. At this point a lesser novelist would have concluded his tale. But Valera, aware that Luis's passivity at the private emotional level subordinates him unduly to Pepita, dextrously balances it with a final development which publicly establishes the ex-seminarist as the heir to all his father's aggressiveness and *hombría.* The narrative ends in perfect equilibrium.

In contrast, *Las ilusiones del doctor Faustino,* Valera's longest and most ambitious novel, reveals his failure to bring into artistic harmony the two contrasting elements in its conception. The result is an unsatisfactory amalgam of folletinesque incidents and the analytic presentation of a weak and frustrated personality. Its chief interest lies in the curious similarities between Faustino's *abulia,* emotional frustration and spiritual unrest, and similar features in the fictional heroes of certain novels of the Generation of 1898. *Pasarse de listo* (published in *entregas* 1877-78), which Valera admitted to be his worst novel, written, without enthusiasm, for the money its publication would bring, is a tasteless and in the end cruel story of misalliance and malicious gossip in which the happy ending is contrived at the price of the heroine's elderly husband's suicide.

Meanwhile, in *El Comendador Mendoza*, Valera had returned to the rural Andalusia which is the setting for all his really successful novels. At the same time he returns to two motifs of *Pepita Jiménez* which re-emerge sporadically in the rest of his fictional work. One is the love of an elderly man for a much younger woman, which begins marginally with the courtship of Pepita by Luis's father, continues here as a sub-plot ending with the declaration of the Comendador to Lucía in the last chapter of the novel, and becomes the principal story-element in *Juanita la larga*. The other is the juxtaposition of love and religion, which Valera, for all his disdain of novels such as *El niño de la bola*, *Doña Perfecta*, or *De tal palo, tal astilla* (where the juxtaposition is distorted into a contrast), seems, perhaps unconsciously, to have found fascinating. In this case at the centre of the plot is the resolve of the harshly religious Doña Blanca to induce her adulterine daughter to marry the real heir to the family estate and thus avoid a grave injustice. This resolve is foiled by the heroic disinterestedness of the girl's true father, the Comendador, who is rewarded with a young wife. The novel opens brilliantly and is written throughout with great charm, but as the plot unfolds its unreality grows increasingly apparent.

In *Doña Luz* the principal characters are once more a priest and a young woman; Valera concludes the first cycle of his novels on the same theme of sacred and profane love, with which it had begun in *Pepita Jiménez*. But now the circumstances are altered. Don Enrique, prematurely aged and broken in health by his missionary work abroad, is very different from the inexpert seminarist of the earlier novel. Trapped unsuspectingly by human emotion, he has no choice but self-repression. The effort is too much for his frail constitution. Meanwhile, Doña Luz, who bears a suspicious likeness to Pepita, falls victim to a cynical adventurer. Though entirely different in tone and treatment from *La Regenta*, which contains a marginally comparable situation, *Doña Luz* is an equally serious novel. Its discreet and sympathetic treatment of the plot's scabrous possibilities illustrates the difference between Valera's approach to the novel and that of his contemporaries in the 1870s.

At seventy Valera returned to fiction, after a long absence, with his last important novel, *Juanita la larga*. It fulfils more than any of the others his ideal of pure narration, without reference to contemporary problems or conflicts. Though a local *cacique* figures prominently, Valera eludes even indirect comment on his social role; though Juanita, like Pepita and Doña Luz, is solicited by both sacred and profane love, the former is now merely the result of a foolish caprice on the part of her would-be patroness, Doña Inés. Like Alarcón's *El sombrero de tres picos,* with which it has much in common, *Juanita la larga* stands apart from other nineteenth-century Spanish novels as a skilfully contrived piece of literary entertainment written for its own sake.

In his last two novels, *Genio y figura* and *Morsamor,* Valera abandons Andalusia for wider settings and more ambitious themes. But in neither case is he fully successful. Rafaela, the heroine of *Genio y figura,* the least convincing of Valera's full-length feminine portraits, belongs also to the least convincing of literary conventions, that of the idealised prostitute. Intelligent and generous, she not only achieves respectability but even confers it on her coarse and avaricious husband. Valera pursues the paradox through the chronicle of her extra-marital relationships to the point where, at fifty, Rafaela's unselfishness crystallises into an authentic ideal of self-redemption through her daughter. But here, her aspirations ironically thwarted by the girl's religious vocation, Rafaela's life reaches an impasse and she commits suicide. In the epilogue to the second edition Valera tried to interpret the novel in strictly moral terms as a sort of companion work to Pereda's *La Montálvez.* The effort was unsuccessful, but it serves to remind us of the extraordinarily obtuse neo-Catholic criticism with which Valera and his contemporaries had to contend.

Morsamor, Valera's last novel, has been described not unjustly as his *Persiles y Sigismunda.* Its theme is the gradual *desengaño* of one Fray Miguel de Zuheros. By magic arts he is enabled to undergo a series of fantastic adventures (which include a journey round the world in reverse direction to that of Magellan) whose symbolism is plainly the result of Valera's reflections on the disaster of 1898. Like Ganivet's *Idearium español,* the book stresses the need to reject dreams of grandeur and to accept reality with nobility and dignity. Unfortunately, the loose structure and extraordinary content of the narrative have only a tenuous relation with its theme.

While Valera's outlook, which he called that of a 'pensador optimista, sereno observador de las cosas y razonable filósofo', allowed him to avoid the crudity of the ideological novel of the 1870s, it also led him to ignore deliberately the sadder features and more serious issues of the human condition. This was a wrong choice, which all his charm and artistry cannot disguise. It is not the proper role of literature to 'mentir para consuelo'.

VI. PALACIO VALDÉS

Not far removed from Valera in his attitude to the novel, but lacking his broad culture and creative ability, is Armando Palacio Valdés (1853-1938). An Asturian by birth, he studied in Oviedo along with Clarín before moving to the Law Faculty of Madrid University in 1870. Like Valera he began his literary career as critic with *Los oradores del Ateneo* (1878), *Los novelistas españoles* (1878), *Nuevo viaje al Parnaso* (1879), and *La literatura en 1881* (1882). Since by some fatality Palacio's novelists do not include Pereda, Clarín, Galdós, or Pardo Bazán, and his account of poetry contains no mention of the renovation set on foot by Bécquer and Rosalía de Castro, these collections of articles leave a strong impression of the general mediocrity of Spanish thought and culture under the Restoration. They also reveal Palacio as a flippant and superficial, but always entertaining, critic. His standpoint at this time is highly representative: he took up a middle position in the realist-'idealist' debate, welcoming realism in principle since it liberated literature from many of the taboos and conventions left intact by the Romantics. But in familiar fashion he criticised the French novel for its alleged scepticism, 'groseros excesos', and insistence on 'desnuda realidad'. For him, as for Valera, 'la novela es una obra de arte y como tal su fin primero es realizar belleza . . . despertar la emoción estética'. Observed reality must be gently poeticised and slightly touched up with sentiment. Not surprisingly, Galdós's *Marianela* is cited as a praiseworthy example.

With such conventional theories (restated in his inaugural address to the Royal Academy in 1920 and *Testamento literario* in 1929) it is surprising to find that in the first half of his literary career Palacio Valdés took an active part in the religious and social debate then going forward in the novel. His first full-length fictional work, *El Señorito Octavio*, had appeared in 1881 when Palacio was twenty-eight. But it was with *Marta y María* two years afterwards that his literary personality really began to assert itself. In María de Elorza he portrays a younger and more beautiful Doña Perfecta. Her morbid religiosity is shown not only as perverted in itself (when she shudders voluptuously while a servant flogs her) but as sterilising her normal affections for her fiancé and family, and as leading to potentially disastrous civil consequences through her Carlist sympathies. Unlike Galdós, however, Palacio, having built up the situation, characteristically ignores its implications and, brushing aside any serious possibilities, hastens on to a contrived happy ending. Herein lies the secret of his popular success, and at the same time of his second-rateness as a novelist: he knew how to construct a strong fictional situation, but lacked the tough-mindedness necessary to work it out. In this he is at the opposite pole from Blasco Ibáñez, whose initial situations are so often pushed to equally unsatisfactory revolutionary and destructive extremes.

This is not to say that Palacio could not be courageous at times. In *La espuma* (1891), already mentioned as belonging to the category of Pereda's *La Montálvez* and Coloma's *Pequeñeces*, he not only savages Madrid high society but presents in studied contrast the starved and brutalised mercury-miners of Riosa, working with their children in the poisonous atmosphere of the mine to finance the adulteries of the shareholders. The radical young doctor who champions the workers occupies a lonely position in the history of the Spanish novel, where the problems of the industrial and rural proletariat have remained of marginal interest, not least to the supposed social 'regenerators' of the Generation of 1898. *La fe* (1892), significantly omitted from the currently available edition of Palacio's *Obras*, is a direct attack on the dogmas and practices of the Church, from which the hero Gil seeks refuge unconvincingly in a vain and irrelevant mysticism.

But these novels are not really representative. The mainstream of Palacio's production flows from *El Señorito Octavio*, 'novela sin pensamiento trascendental', through *José* (1885), a novel of fisherfolk on the model popularised by Pereda, *Riverita* (1886) and its sequel *Maximina* (1887), to Palacio's most popular novel, *La hermana San Sulpicio* (1889), and *La alegría del capitán Ribot* (1899). A complacent comment in the preface to *La hermana San Sulpicio* reveals Palacio's conscious tendency away from the novel of ideas and towards that of mere entertainment: 'Mi aspiración única', he writes, 'consiste en conmover a mis lectores, evitándoles el pensamiento'! After his second marriage and reconversion to practising Catholicism,

Palacio's sentimental, humorous, on the whole optimistic, and comfortably idealised presentation of reality became rather saccharine and showed an increasing drift towards artificially contrasted situations and falsified emotional and ethical conflicts. Typical of the latter are *Tristán o el pesimismo* (1906), with its opposed conceptions of marital honour, and the later *Santa Rogelia* (1926), whose emphasis on religious perfection in difficult domestic circumstances reads strangely after *Marta y María* and *La fe*.

In all Palacio Valdés published some twenty-four full-length novels between 1881 and 1936, together with four collections of short stories, his memoirs of early life (*La novela de un novelista*, 1921), and a number of occasional works, including the anti-feminist historical tract *El gobierno de las mujeres* (1931) and a defence of the allies in the First World War, *La guerra injusta* (1917). At the turn of the century his reputation, especially in the rest of Europe and America, where his work was widely known in translation, was immense: he was even compared to Tolstoy. Nowadays, though a few of his novels are frequently reissued, he no longer receives serious critical attention.

NOTES

1. J. López Morillas, 'La revolución de Septiembre y la novela española', *RO*, 67 (1968), 94–115.
2. Prologue to Pereda's *El sabor de la tierruca* (1881).
3. *Pereda o la novela idilio* (Mexico, 1961), p. 150.
4. In the opening chapter of *Valera o la ficción libre* (Madrid, 1957).

Chapter 9

GALDÓS, CLARÍN, AND PARDO BAZÁN

BETWEEN 1861 AND 1869 SPANISH LITERATURE was almost destitute of fiction except for three novels and a few short stories by Fernán Caballero, two collections of tales by Trueba, and Pereda's *Escenas montañesas*; unless, that is, we include twenty-nine novels by Fernández y González! 'Así,' wrote Menéndez Pelayo, 'entre noñeces y monstruosidades, dormitaba la novela española por los años de 1870, fecha del primer libro del Sr. Pérez Galdós'.

I. GALDÓS

Benito Pérez Galdós (1843-1920) was born in Las Palmas (Canary Islands), the youngest son of a moderately prosperous ex-soldier of the War of Independence and an inflexible, domineering mother, some elements of whose personality survive in Doña Perfecta. He had already begun to write when in 1862 he was sent to study law at Madrid University. He never finished the course. Instead, journalism and an understanding aunt provided money for his early years as a writer at a time when novels, other than those published in instalments or serialised in the press, had to be issued at the author's expense. Once launched on his career, his life settled into a steady rhythm of production, varied principally by travel all over the length and breadth of Spain as well as abroad, and numerous but discreet love-affairs. These, which lasted well into his old age, must have contributed immensely to the fund of close observation and vital experience on which his novels drew, but also contributed to his recurrent financial embarrassments. Always a progressive, politically conscious writer he accepted a seat in parliament from Sagasta in 1886 and three years later, in spite of ultra-Catholic opposition which dogged him all his life, was elected to the Royal

Academy. After 1892 he undertook singlehandedly the reform of the theatre, as he had previously initiated that of the novel in 1870. Though less successful, he persisted stubbornly and with *Electra* (1901) he rocked the nation. Like Larra he grew more radical with age and returning to parliament in 1907 he became the titular head of the Republican-Socialist opposition. His extreme standpoint, which faltered only at the end of his life, cost him his chance of a Nobel Prize in 1912. When he died, blind, relatively poor, and pathetically senile, he was still scarcely accepted in official, conservative, and Catholic circles. Except for the work of Blasco Ibáñez and a few minor figures, the novel of authentic social analysis and protest in Spain died with him.

Little can be learned about Galdós's theory of the novel from his critical writings. The most important, and least accessible, of these (it is characteristically missing from the so-called *Obras completas*)[1] is an essay entitled 'Observaciones sobre la novel contemporánea en España' which Galdós published in the *Revista de España*, XV (Madrid, 1870). Lamenting the failure of the modern novel to gain a good foothold in Spain, he attributed it partly to the corruption of taste by foreign translations and partly to the inability of Spanish writers to observe closely the reality around them. Pereda and Fernán Caballero were politely excepted from this condemnation. The central assertion of the essay is that it is the spectacle of the middle-class and contemporary urban customs, 'la sociedad nacional y coetánea' and 'el maravilloso drama de la vida actual', which must provide the main source of inspiration to the novelist. The ideals, the aspirations, the public and domestic life of this protean class; its political and commercial activities; its problems (especially its spiritual and sexual problems); Galdós saw these as the great themes of a new novel of manners. In three later writings; his prologue to Pereda's *El sabor de la tierruca* (1881); his inaugural address to the Royal Academy (1897); and his prologue to the third edition of Clarín's *La Regenta* (1900), Galdós developed his ideas further, but the doctrines (of realism and naturalism especially) which emerge are disappointingly vague and commonplace. Two points from the Academy speech are noteworthy. One pointedly underlines the difference between Galdós and his principal adversary in the novel, Pereda, not as creative writers but in terms of outlook:

Pereda no duda, yo sí. . . . Él es un espíritu sereno; yo un espíritu turbado, inquieto. Él sabe adonde va, parte de una base fija. Los que dudamos mientras él afirma, buscamos la verdad y sin cesar corremos hacia donde creemos verla hermosa y fugitiva. Él permanece quieto y confiado, viéndonos pasar, y se recrea en su tesoro de ideas, mientras nosotros siempre descontentos de las que poseemos y ambicionándolas mejores, corremos tras otra, y otras, que una vez alcanzadas tampoco nos satisfacen.

Herein lies part of the essence of Galdós's literary personality, his open-mindedness, his dynamic concept of the evolution of ideas, his self-awareness, his relativism. In Pereda and Galdós, not only two conceptions of the novel, but two contrasting conceptions of life and truth confront each other: one closed and static, the other broad, open, tolerant, and progressive. The second point of importance in the Academy speech is Galdós's definition of the novel:

Imagen de la vida en la novela, y el arte de componerla estriba en reproducir . . . todo lo espiritual y física que nos constituye y nos rodea.

Galdós here classifies himself once more as a realist, and also as a microcosmic novelist: not as a specialist in one branch of human behaviour but as the would-be creator of a total fictional world drawn from direct observation of reality. Not for nothing were Balzac and Dickens (whose *Pickwick Papers* he translated—from the French— and published in 1868) his acknowledged masters.

We must, of course, enter certain qualifications. Only the most inclusive definition of realism will fit Galdós; one which allows for the partisanship of his early thesis-novels and the obsessive interest in out-of-the-way spiritual situations of his later work, to say nothing of the fantastic element of, for instance, *El caballero encantado*, the lyricism of *Marianela*, and the difficulty of fitting figures such as Torquemada, Cruz, and Victoria (*La loca de la casa*), or Benina (*Misericordia*) and Nazarín into a realist conception of character. In spite of Galdós's outspokenness, certain anti-realistic taboos remain, especially in the sexual field, along with Galdós's failure to do full justice to marriage, in the nineteenth century the most important of all middle-class social institutions. We must not overlook, either, the virtual absence from his work of industrial society, the agrarian problem, or interest in the Spanish educational pattern. At the micro-cosmic level, in comparison with Balzac's *Comédie humaine*, its model, Galdós's world seems less complete. It is like a building with two of its main supports (the religious question, together with social analysis and criticism) in place and connected to each other; many rooms and floors exist; but the construction is far less a finished whole and already shows signs of disproportion.

Several ingenious attempts have been made to classify Galdós's production, but none is entirely satisfactory. What is indisputable is that one turning-point is visible in his work between *La familia de León Roch* (1878) and *La desheredada* (1881), while another occurs between *Misericordia* (1897) and *Electra* (1901). He began with a novelette in the fantastic genre, *La sombra*, written perhaps in 1867. It indicates that the starting-point of Galdós (like that of Pardo Bazán a decade later in *Pascual López*) was almost pure fantasy: that triumph of imagination over reality which in his mature period he was to fustigate as a major national vice, but to which ironically he himself returned increasingly in the last phase of his work.

La fontana de oro (1870), Galdós's first full-length work, marks both the beginning of the serious modern novel in Spain and the opening of Galdós's 'historical' period, which was to lead him, through *El audaz* (1871) and *Trafalgar* (1873), to the five successive series of *Episodios nacionales*, which together make up approximately half of his entire production. Written as the Revolution of 1868 was being prepared and finished shortly after its outbreak, *La fontana de oro* introduces Galdós's purposive approach to the historical novel. His aim is not to reconstruct the distant past descriptively, but to *interpret* the recent past didactically, so as to lay bare the origins of the ideological, political, and social processes operating in the Spain of his day. In addition, Galdós underlined 'la semejanza que la crisis actual tiene con el memorable período de 1820-23', the years in which *La fontana de oro* is set. The novel describes the unequal conflict of the minority Liberal faction which includes the hero, Lázaro (an early example of Galdós's use of symbolic names), and the reactionary regime of Ferdinand VII represented by the baleful figures of Coletilla, the Porreño sisters, and the monarch himself. It is interesting that Galdós altered the ending of the novel in the second edition to a less happy one. But later he reverted to that which now appears, in which Lázaro abandons the struggle and retires to provincial domesticity. In *El audaz* Galdós pushes his analysis back to 1804 and the origins of Liberal ideology. Once more the hero, Martín Muriel, a Liberal of prematurely advanced ideas, is hopelessly unsuccessful and becomes insane. These two novels show Galdós feeling his way towards the *Episodios nacionales*.

II. THE 'EPISODIOS NACIONALES'

In these Galdós developed to the full the potential already latent in some of the more socially and historically conscious *folletines* by writers like Escosura and Ayguals de Izco (see above, p. 44) who had already used the events of their own century as a setting. For almost forty years, with a significant gap between 1879 and 1898 separating the second from the third series, Galdós continued to explore systematically the recent past of Spain from 1807 to the Restoration, always with the same basic intention of tracing the living forces still at work in his own day: the projection of the past into the future.

No clearly defined or consistent *a priori* theory presides over the creative process: Galdós's own historical ideas expanded and evolved as he wrote. There is an especially marked shift of outlook between the second and third series. In the last analysis, as Hinterhäuser argues in his book on the *Episodios,* the progress of Spain towards liberty and a more civilised society is taken for granted as part of a pattern of historical determinism governed ultimately by Providence. But struggling with this Liberal-progressive optimism, and in practice more prominent, is the growing sense of disillusionment and pessimism.[2] From the fifth *episodio, Napoleón en Chamartín* (1874), to the thirty-fourth, *La Revolución de julio* (1904), Galdós's assumption of a slow but inevitable progress struggles with his deeper vision of a Spain split in half by two opposing fanaticisms, betrayed by the wilful absenteeism of his own middle class from political decision-making, and left at the mercy of a corrupt and inept self-perpetuating governing élite. This deep division within Galdós's outlook has not been fully analysed.

The first ten *episodios,* written at astonishing speed between January 1873 and the spring of 1875, explore the re-emergence of a Spanish national and patriotic ideal in the struggle with Napoleon. In them Galdós first comes to terms with the technical difficulties inherent in the fulfilment of so vast a conception. Balance was the major problem. Balance between fact: the external historical events, which Galdós's intention compelled him to keep in the background; and fiction: the ordinary lives of his purely imaginary characters involved as they are in the events; balance between the opposing ideological forces, without the sacrifice of Galdós's Liberal sympathies; balance most of all between narrative and interpretation. Such balance Galdós could only aim at instinctively, given the speed at which he was writing. It is not consistently achieved.

In the second series, written between 1875 and the end of 1879, the emphasis necessarily shifts from patriotic national self-affirmation to the struggle between traditional and progressive ideas which followed. At the same time, Galdós's design to shape the *Episodios* so as to form a chronicle of the rise to power of the middle class in nineteenth-century Spain becomes more apparent. The figures of Araceli, the narrator, and Don Primitivo Cordero, whose simple values—patriotism, order and work—are the elemental basis of bourgeois ascendancy, provide the first *Episodios* with ideological unity. They are now replaced by the hostile half-brothers Monsalud and Navarro, who symbolise the conflict between the 'two Spains' already adumbrated in *Napoleón en Chamartín*. Between the two warring ideologies the figure of Don Benigno Cordero incarnates Galdós's ideal of peaceful moderation in politics and civic responsibility.

Galdós was now as close as he ever became to satisfaction with the state of Spain. In the high noon of his creative career he discontinued the *Episodios* and turned in the 1880s and early 1890s to the *Novelas españolas contemporáneas* and to the theatre. When his ruinous lawsuit with his business partner Miguel de la Cámara forced him to return to the old money-spinners in early 1898, he was a greatly changed man. But it was not the loss of Cuba which changed him; it was disillusionment with his own class who, corrupted by their sudden achievement of power in 1868, had betrayed under the Restoration the ideals of *La Gloriosa*. In the later *episodios* Galdós struggled painfully between the search for a new ideal, based on 'la distribución equitativa del bienestar humano', which led him to renewed political extremism and the bitter 'No espero nada; no creo en nada', quoted by Casalduero from the thirty-fourth *episodio*, *La Revolución de julio* (1904).

III. THE 'NOVELAS DE LA PRIMERA ÉPOCA'

While Galdós was busy with the first *episodios* of the second series in the mid-1870s, it became clear to him that the restoration of the

Bourbons to the throne in December 1874 threatened the achievements of the Revolution of 1868, with which he was broadly in
sympathy. Nowhere was this more evident than in the field of
religious toleration. And so, early in 1876, Galdós began to serialise
in the *Revista de España* the most aggressive of his *novelas de la
primera época, Doña Perfecta,* timing its appearance to coincide with
debates in parliament on the religious question. It is a head-on attack
on religious intolerance and fanaticism with all their negative social
and domestic manifestations. Galdós's own religious position, despite
two full-length investigations by Scatori and Correa, is still a matter
of discussion, and in any case, like his politico-social view, it evolved
as his work progressed. What is certain is that all his life Galdós was
obsessively interested in religion—Correa has shown that its symbolism is traceable in novels not directly concerned with religious
themes—though his personal position remained, from a strict Catholic
standpoint, consistently unorthodox. Galdós failed to appreciate
religion at its deepest spiritual level, and seems to have lacked a
genuine inner sense of divine transcendence.[3] León Roch's statement
'Yo creo en el alma inmortal, en la justicia eterna, en los fines de
perfección' and José María Bueno's acceptance in *Lo prohibido* that
without a religious basis there can be no true morality seem to sum
up Galdós's ultimate beliefs. For the rest he strove to present religion
as a social gospel inseparable from practical good works, not devoid
of social protest, free from dogmatic restrictions (Ricard has emphasised the religious syncretism which underlies the character of
Almudena in *Misericordia*),[4] and based on the law of love: natural,
not supernatural, religion. Meanwhile, in his treatment of the Catholic
Church he attacked institutional Christianity, dogmatism, the authori-
tarian influence of the clergy on public and domestic affairs, the
inquisitorial spirit, fanaticism, and support for reactionary traditionalism.

The story of a young Madrid engineer, Pepe Rey, and his
unsuccessful struggle, in the stagnant atmosphere of provincial
Orbajosa, against Doña Perfecta and her clerical and reactionary allies,
Doña Perfecta was written at great speed in two months. Nevertheless,
especially after its original ending had been modified, it is not a crude
pamphlet based on black and white characters and forced situations.
Structurally, it reveals a well-organised pattern of movement (Chapters
V to XV and countermovement (Chapters XX to XXVII), with a centre
of balance in the confrontation of Pepe and Perfecta in Chapter XIX.

In terms of character Galdós makes a noteworthy effort to defend Perfecta's outlook from her own religious standpoint and, by causing Pepe to resort to improper methods of furthering his cause, he establishes a balance of moral justification. *Doña Perfecta* was followed in 1876-77 by *Gloria* and in 1878 by *La familia de León Roch*. In both these novels the struggle of the morally superior individual against an immobile social system honeycombed with cruel religious intolerance is emphasised afresh. The thesis of *Gloria* is that of the tragic consequences of a conflict between two opposed and irreconcilable religious ideologies, that of the Jew Morton and that of the uncompromisingly Catholic Lantiguas. León Roch, on the other hand, is the victim of a misguided marriage. His wife's readiness, with encouragement from her family, to allow religious considerations to affect her marital relationship, ends with the wreck of their marriage and their happiness. Both these novels, like all those of Galdós's early phase, are novels of dramatic conflict rather than psychological studies. Though conscious of an excessive predominance of theme over plot-structure and character-development, we admire Galdós's struggle to avoid taking sides against his major characters, while criticising their outlook and actions, and his ability to illustrate from different angles the great theme of all his fictional presentation of religious situations: the new commandment suggested in *Gloria*—'No entenderás torcidamente el amor de mí'.

Between *Gloria* and *León Roch* Galdós published his own favourite novel, *Marianela* (1878). It is his only poetic novel, but there is a curious discrepancy between the melancholy lyrical tone of the work and its theme: that of the cold, inevitable triumph of reality and scientific progress (Pablo, Teodoro Golfín) over imagination (Marianela). Casalduero's interpretation of the novel in Comptian terms is very persuasive. At this point the two-year interval between *León Roch* and *La desheredada* marks the end of a phase in Galdós's production.

IV. THE CENTRAL NOVELS

The appearance of *La desheredada* in mid-1881 marks the opening of the central phase of Galdós's work, often referred to as his 'naturalistic' phase. The adjective is appropriate to the extent that he now began deliberately to incorporate some of the more sordid and ugly aspects of physical and psychological reality into his work, and here and there (as in *Lo prohibido*) to lean a little towards heredity and social determinism as conditioning factors in human behaviour. But though Galdós at times employed naturalistic procedures, his outlook and literary personality were not those of a naturalist. We associate with naturalism a systematic pessimism, an insistence on the ignobler aspects of human nature, a degree (not absolute) of humourlessness, which were foreign to Galdós. The ultimate harmony symbolised in the embrace of Fortunata and Jacinta, the magnanimity of Ángel Guerra on his deathbed, the charming contrast between the squalid surroundings of Ponte and Obdulia and their dream-world of High Society in *Misericordia*, are the creations of a mind with a wider vision of life than that of naturalism. Nor can we forget in this context Galdós's own measured statement at the end of *Fortunata y Jacinta* that 'la vulgaridad de la vida' must be converted into 'materia estética' by the novelist; not, that is, merely faithfully reproduced, as was the naturalist ideal.

Some general features of the new phase of Galdós's work merit notice. One is Galdós's abandonment of imaginary locations for his novels (Orbajosa, Ficóbriga, Socartes) and his emergence as the classic novelist of nineteenth-century Madrid. Along with this shift of location from the abstract to the concrete goes a change in his vision of society, which, ceasing to be closed and hierarchical, becomes fluid and ever-changing. Social mobility, later to be caricatured in Torquemada's acquisition of a title, now begins to play an important role in several novels. The presentation of characters by means of heavily slanted biographical introductions is replaced by a subtler technique of 'clues' rather than direct unequivocal statements. At the same time dialogue becomes much more realistic and increasingly includes the brilliant reproduction of popular speech and idiom. Another feature is his increasingly systematic use after this point of the return-of-characters technique, which, though on a smaller scale than in Balzac, gives a growing consistency to his fictional world. Thirdly, we notice a change of manner, tone, and theme from the earlier novels, though *León Roch* can be seen as transitional in this as in the other respects just mentioned. Galdós becomes more detached and discursive. Novels of thesis, based on dramatic conflict, ideologically motivated characters, and the predominance of the religious question, give way to novels which are more concerned with what Galdós, in his dedication of *La desheredada* to the schoolteachers of

6 * *

Spain, called the 'dolencias sociales nacidas de la falta de nutrición y del poco uso que se viene haciendo de los benéficos reconstituyentes llamados Aritmética, Lógica, Moral y Sentido Común'. The major *dolencia*, the national vice, is self-delusion: *La desheredada*, the story of Isidora, a poor girl convinced that she belongs to the aristocracy, begins significantly in the madhouse of Leganés. Both here and in the following novels—*El amigo Manso* (1882), *El doctor Centeno* (1883), *Tormento* (1884), *La de Bringas* (1884), and *Lo prohibido* (1884-85) —which form a group, Galdós is at great pains to emphasise the deeper meaning which lies beneath the surface of the different narratives. At this level the characters and events are arranged so as to constitute a symbolic commentary on the Spain of the Restoration. Galdós employs two techniques to achieve this effect. One is the use of symbolic names: Isidora is a family connection of one Santiago Quijano-Quijada; her delusion is thus linked with the nation via its patron saint and with Don Quixote. In *El doctor Centeno* and *Tormento* Amparo Sánchez Emperador—a transparent reference to Spain (the order of her surnames is of key significance)—is entrapped by Pedro Polo *Cortés*, a dissolute priest, from whom she is saved by a liaison (not marriage) with Don Agustín *Caballero*, a man of order and principle who has made his money by commerce. The attentive reader does not overlook the disappointment Amparo causes Caballero to feel, or the irregularity of their union. The second technique which Galdós uses is that of carefully interlacing the private history of his characters with the public history of the nation, so that the symbolic union of one with the other remains prominent. Thus at the end of *La de Bringas* the ignominious collapse of Rosalía Bringas's dream of a life of upper-class elegance (characterised by wasteful extravagance and immorality) coincides with the dethronement of Isabella II for much the same reasons.

The whole group of novels points a pitiful picture of Spanish society. Hollow, squalid, devoid of ideals, peopled by fools, rogues, and mediocrities, dominated by hypocrisy, immorality, materialism, self-deception, administrative inefficiency, and the cult of appearances, it provokes in Galdós alternate reactions of disgust (visible in repulsive characters such as Sánchez Botín in *Lo prohibido*) and humorous resignation (a classic example of which is his account of ubiquitous functionaries, the Peces, in *La desheredada* I, 12). Where Galdós's vision seems most disconsolate is perhaps in *El amigo Manso* and *Lo prohibido*. The former, a charming and subtly constructed novel which portends Unamuno's *nivola*-technique, exploits the contrast between Manso, the Krausist professor, whose ethical and intellectual principles fail to impress either the heroine Irene or the public, and his shallow, but slick and practical, pupil Peña, who triumphs with both. In the latter, the wealthy and self-indulgent young hero, José María Bueno, attempts to seduce his three married cousins. At the end, ruined by one of them, disgusted with the second, and humiliatingly repulsed by the third, he finds his reward in impotence, illness, dependence, and death. But the story is not, like *La desheredada*, a morality: Galdós, who was no celibate, could on occasion take a lenient view of sexual promiscuity. Rather, *Lo prohibido*, in which bourgeois society is seen through the eyes of one of its true representatives, leaves behind the impression of a writer faced with an interesting but disagreeable field of observation.

V. 'FORTUNATA Y JACINTA'

In contrast, *Fortunata y Jacinta* (1886-87), Galdós's outstanding novel, owes much of its appeal to his friendly and sympathetic treatment of the teeming characters. Set in the mid-1870s, its first half develops as a chronicle of two family-groups. The Santa Cruz and the Arnáiz, on the one hand, are linked together by the marriage of Jacinta Arnáiz to the spoilt and self-indulgent Juanito Santa Cruz. The Rubíns, on the other, are drawn into the plot by the marriage of Maxi—one of Galdós's most original characters, a caricaturesque prefiguration in some ways of the hero of the '98—to Juanito's mistress Fortunata. The reactions of these four characters to the situation produced by Juanito's continuing liaison create a parallelogram of forces, all of which are in their way justifiable. Meanwhile, Juanito's swinging emotional allegiances throw into contrast the attraction of the safe, conformist middle class (Jacinta) and the warm, spontaneous *pueblo* (Fortunata). This is the core of the book. Around it Galdós weaves an elaborate web of subordinate episodes which have led to *Fortunata y Jacinta*'s being called 'una selva de novelas entrecruzadas'. The theme, so far as there is one in this great frieze of Madrid life, arises from the contrast between the illicit relationship of Juanito and Fortunata and their respective legal marriages. The liaison crosses boundaries of social class and culture, to say nothing of conjugal loyalty and morality. But it is solidly based on insurmountable mutual attraction and—very significantly—produces children. Both marriages, on the other hand, though sanctified by the Church and society, are in different ways unsuitable and remain sterile.

Galdós wisely refuses to point up the contrast aggressively. He prefers to present it as a conflict of natural instincts with inevitable social pressures. At the end the fates of the major characters reveal Galdós's recognition of life's less pleasant possibilities. But that recognition, which is part of the essence of his realism, is balanced by calm acceptance and qualified hope. Nowhere else in his work does Galdós succeed in giving such serene fictional expression to his sporadic sense of 'la armonía total y este claroscuro en que consiste toda la gracia de la Humanidad y todo el chiste del vivir'. Forces so unequal elsewhere—we think of the isolation of Camila (*Lo prohibido*) and Orozco (*Realidad*) amid the triviality and immorality of the rest of society—are brought into equilibrium symbolised at the end by the redemption and vicarious acceptance into the middle-class 'family' of Fortunata as she gives up her child to the childless Jacinta.

Fortunata y Jacinta illustrates also the difficulty of generalising about Galdós's fictional technique. Elsewhere, in *El amigo Manso* for example, critics have been able to show that his extraordinary speed of production (eleven pages or more a day) did not preclude finesse and originality of construction. Some of his early novels of thesis show great dramatic skill, itself dependent on a fine sense of tempo and economy of method. On the other hand, while *Tormento* contains cunning satire of the *folletín*, Galdós did not hesitate on occasion to use folletinesque techniques of the most extreme kind, especially in the *Episodios nacionales*. Here in his finest production and in some of the very long novels which follow it, Galdós gave free rein to his instinctive discursiveness. *Fortunata y Jacinta* rambles. The plot, after a 20,000-word exposition, goes round corners as the emphasis shifts from one set of characters to another. Chapters tend to become episodes in their own right. Articulations, such as Fortunata's casual meeting with Juanito at the end of Book III, are sometimes clumsy. Details are magnified, characters proliferate, and the ending itself is, in retrospect, arbitrary. Yet we recognise in this novel, which belongs unquestionably to Henry James's category of 'loose baggy monsters', Galdós's masterpiece. A wise and benevolent Nature—'La Naturaleza, que es la gran madre y maestra que rectifica los errores de sus hijos extraviados'—presides reliably over human destinies. Galdós never fully recaptured this mood.

VI. LATER NOVELS

His evolution after this moment of plenitude is interesting. In *Miau* (1888), his next novel, Galdós wrote his farewell to the world of the Civil Administration which had served him so well in earlier works. The story concerns an unemployed civil servant, Villaamil, and his vain struggle to regain his post. But, as Eoff emphasises, 'His story is essentially one of maladjustment growing out of the circumstances of home and professional life'.[5] Conditioned to depend absolutely on his bureaucratic post and lacking support from his family when he loses it, Villaamil evolves through a series of neurotic reactions to a point of temporary insanity. Yet at last, when he makes a reasoned decision to commit suicide, his choice seems the culmination rather than the rock-bottom of his pathetic life. Indirectly the novel exposes the hardship and personal stress inflicted on older functionaries by the *cesantía*-system. But chiefly it is a character-study in the line of Balzac's Père Goriot and Cousin Pons. A further major feature of *Miau* is the bifurcation which occurs in the narrative when Villaamil's epileptic grandson begins to enjoy a series of imaginary conversations with God. These influence both the grandfather's behaviour and the reader's response to his situation, and are very much an integral part of the book's structure. But they have the effect of introducing a strangely suggestive and audacious note of contrast to the realism of the work, which alters its whole tone. In addition they indicate that the note of religious preoccupation, never far below the surface in Galdós, has begun to flow strongly once more, though in a different direction from that of his early ideological novels.

In *La incógnita* (1888-89) and *Realidad* (1889) we return to the world of *Lo prohibido* to examine from separate angles another case of adultery: that of Federico Viera and Augusta Orozco. The key-figure is, however, Orozco himself, Augusta's husband, who represents the loneliness of ethical superiority and detachment. It is as though Galdós had wished to explore this alternative outlook before turning to the more familiar world of Ángel Guerra and Benina (of *Misericordia*) in which spiritual superiority is seen in more conventional religious terms. Needless to say, Orozco was and has remained an enigmatic and unique figure, beyond the range of Galdós's Spanish audience.

The bifurcation portended in *Miau* is seen fully developed in the contrast between Ángel Guerra and Torquemada (*Ángel Guerra,*

1890-91; *Torquemada en la hoguera*, 1889; *Torquemada en la cruz*, 1893; *Torquemada en el Purgatorio*, 1894; *Torquemada y San Pedro*, 1895). Both lose a beloved child; both subsequently fall under the influence of a new set of values represented by a woman (Léré, Cruz); both undergo a very marked evolution of personality. But there the parallel ends. Torquemada's evolution is outward, social, and negative; Ángel's is inward, spiritual, and positive. In Torquemada Galdós explores satirically the incompatibility of materialist acquisitive values (in relation to which his own views had hitherto been ambivalent) with spiritual progress. In *Ángel Guerra* he depicts the gradual subordination of the hero's politico-social principles and private passions to the law of Love. Torquemada dies symbolically of a surfeit of food, Ángel ends his life on an impressive note of almost superhuman forgiveness.

Galdós's interest in saintliness and his curiously ambiguous attitude to it, already visible in Léré, whose family shows gross abnormality, are at the basis of his next three novels: *Nazarín* (1895); its disappointing sequel, *Halma* (1895); and *Misericordia* (1897). In the last of these Galdós created his most memorable heroine and most heroic figure, Benina, a supreme example of practical Christian charity, though founded on small-scale fraud. In the same ironic way, both Christ and Don Quixote serve as models for the creation of Nazarín. Galdós's last major novel, *El abuelo* (1897), proposes a dilemma at once personal and symbolic. The union of age and youth, tradition and renovation, at the end of the novel, was to reveal its relevance in the rescrutiny of Spanish values which followed 1898. *Casandra* (1905), a final attack on misinterpreted religion; *El caballero encantado* (1909), on the theme of national regeneration; and a feeble 'fábula teatral', *La razón de la sinrazón* (1915), closed Galdós's fictional career.

His influence, in spite of a certain hostility on the part of some of the Generation of 1898, was enormous. It can readily be traced in the work of Baroja, and is not absent from that of Unamuno and Ganivet. Pérez de Ayala in *Las máscaras* confesses it most eloquently. Much of the mistaken obsession of the Generation of 1898 as a whole with the regeneration of Spain by means of a renovation of values at the individual level, instead of by collective economico-social reforms, can be attributed to Galdós's ideological legacy. In Latin America his influence is clearly visible in the work of Gallegos and as recent a novelist as Carlos Fuentes began by borrowing from *Fortunata y*

Jacinta. The current spate of critical interest in Galdós since the early 1960s probably portends a major revival of popular interest in his work.

VII. CLARÍN: THE CRITIC

When Galdós's *La desheredada*, then regarded as audaciously 'naturalistic', came out in 1881, one of the only two critics who risked publishing a review of it was Leopoldo Alas (Clarín, 1852-1901). Brought up in Oviedo, where he became a close friend of Palacio Valdés, Clarín studied law at the local university before taking his doctorate in Madrid in 1878. After 1883 he held a Chair of Law in Oviedo until his death at the tragically early age of forty-nine. By that time he had become Spain's most feared and courted literary critic, an outstanding short-story writer, and the author of two works, *La Regenta* (1884-85) and *Su único hijo* (1890), which placed him alongside Galdós and Pardo Bazán as one of the major novelists to emerge in Spain after 1868. The most provincial of the three, he was also the least serene. His spiritual and intellectual unrest has been seen by critics as prefiguring that of the Generation of 1898.

Clarín's literary criticism was, as usual, first published in the press and then collected into volumes. The major collections, *Solos de Clarín* (1881), *Sermon perdido* (1885), *Mezclilla* (1889), *Ensayos y revistas* (1892), *Palique* (1893), and *Siglo pasado* (1901), are still useful to students of later nineteenth-century Spanish literature, not only, as is often the case with Valera's articles, merely because of the information they convey about contemporary conditions and attitudes, but also because of the genuine criticism of major works which they contain. By choice Clarín would have preferred to be a detached analytic critic; his definition of his ideal of criticism in the famous prologue to *Palique* leaves no doubt on that score. True literary criticism, he asserts, is

> 1°, crítica, es decir, juicio, comparación de algo con algo, de hechos con leyes, cópula racional entre términos homogéneos, y 2° *literaria* es decir, de arte, estética, atenta a la habilidad técnica, a sus reglas (absolutas o relativas).

But the situation in which Spanish literature found itself in the last quarter of the nineteenth century (and perhaps also his target-

audience of newspaper readers), to say nothing of his own aggressiveness, forced him to adopt a different ideal, that of 'crítica higiénica y
policíaca': implacable, destructive, chiefly satirical criticism designed
to counteract the prevailing *compañerismo* which presented mediocrities as writers of genius and encouraged their noxious proliferation
and public acceptance. Many of Clarín's articles are in consequence
now of minor interest: flagellations of writers whose work has been
forgotten.

In his drama and poetry criticism we perceive the absence of a
clearly thought-out theoretical position. Though (unlike Pardo Bazán)
he allowed himself to be carried away by the vogue of Echegaray, and
respected the work of Campoamor and Núñez de Arce, Clarín was
dissatisfied with what was being produced. He wanted to see innovation. But he had no positive doctrine to expound. His criticism in
these fields stands out only in contrast to the general complacency. In
regard to the novel, however, the situation was quite different: Clarín
knew very well what was wrong with Spanish fiction in his time and
where the responsibility for it lay. He had a defined doctrine. He
could point to a specific line of development: the French novel from
Balzac, through Flaubert, whom he revered, to Zola, whom he
courageously and consistently defended; and he had a shining
example in Galdós. In contrast to the reigning 'idealism' of Valera
and Cañete, and to the equivocal position of Pardo Bazán, Clarín
emerges as the champion of the Liberal conscience in fiction and the
most forward-looking and open-minded exponent of the realist-
tending-to-naturalist mode in the Spanish novel after 1868. Articles
such as 'El libre examen y la literatura presente'; those in praise of
Galdós; those which contain his contemptuous exposure of the later
Alarcón and the early Pereda, and not least those which document his
changing attitude to Pardo Bazán, are crucial.

VIII. THE NOVELIST

Comparing Clarín with Galdós as novelists we are conscious of a
major difference. Clarín lacked Galdós's spontaneous and almost
inexhaustible creativity, his continuous outflow of inventiveness and
observation not always perfectly combined. Trained in a precise
academic discipline which he taught for the rest of his life, Clarín
had a more synthetic and deliberative mind. This is perceptible in his

fictional work. He wrote only one outstanding full-length novel, *La Regenta*, but that novel is widely regarded as the supreme masterpiece of Spanish nineteenth-century fiction. Similarly, while Galdós frequently broke fresh ground not only in subject-matter but also in technique, Clarín remained broadly attached to established narrative-methods, consolidating in a masterly fashion the achievements of realism, rather than extending them.

La Regenta is the story of a young provincial woman, Ana Ozores, traditionally compared to Flaubert's Madame Bovary, married to a kind but elderly husband. Becoming gradually aware of her emotional and physical frustration, she wavers between her confessor Fermín, who falls passionately in love with her, and Álvaro, a more accomplished and experienced seducer who finally triumphs. F. Durand, in a cogent analysis of the novel,[6] emphasises also the central role of Vetusta (Oviedo) itself, the city in which the action takes place. What interests Clarín much more than Ana's eventual surrender, which occurs off-stage between two chapters, and at least as much as her inner vacillation, is the struggle for her bodily possession by Fermín and Álvaro as almost symbolic representatives of their native city. Fermín is in Chapter I 'el mismo que ahora mandaba a su manera en Vetusta': the spiritual lord of the town; Álvaro the incarnation of its discreetly veiled ideal of secular self-gratification. Both are corrupt, both become ultimately abject. Behind them stands a corrupt and abject society, the provincial equivalent of the squalid metropolitan society of Galdós's *Lo prohibido*. But honeycombed as it is with complicity in the adulterous situation, its hypocritical gossip forming part of Clarín's ironical commentary on the events, its presence (as public opinion) forcing Ana's husband to bring about the catastrophe, society plays an incomparably more active fictional role in *La Regenta* than it ever does in Galdós.

The novel falls into two major parts. Each is of fifteen massive chapters, the second part being somewhat longer and covering three years, in contrast to the three days described in the first. An analysis of the chapters, which vary in length from less than 6,000 words to nearly 16,000, reveals that each is carefully tailored to fit the incidents. Significantly short chapters, e.g. X and XXIII and XXIV, coincide with events of particular dramatic importance. Others, e.g. XII and XIII, and especially XXIX and XXX, the two extremely long concluding chapters (something like 30,000 words between them), combine incidents and descriptions in superbly organised sequences. Each chapter is conceived as a unit, a complete structural component of a fully unified artistic whole. Thus *La Regenta*, though huge, does not sprawl. When its generally slow tempo, the result of a predominantly scenic technique with a minimum of summary, limits the dramatic intensity of the Fermín-Álvaro conflict, this is a sacrifice imposed on Clarín by his will to present Vetusta both as a microcosm of life, and as a negative force conditioning the events of the narrative, a role not unlike that of Nature in Pardo Bazán's *La madre naturaleza*.

It has been argued that Clarín carried his critique too far, notably, for example, in his description of the amoral atmosphere of the Marquesa's house, so intrinsically unlikely within the oppressive ambience of a clerically dominated provincial town, and also in the obscene alliance of Fermín with Petra, Ana's maid. Certainly we are aware of an element of implacability in *La Regenta*, which is softened in Clarín's later work. At the root of this implacability is Clarín's moral preoccupation, undoubtedly a major feature of his literary personality, which must have been strengthened by his contact with Krausism as a doctoral student in Madrid. Ana, as Gullón has written,[7] succumbs in the last analysis 'por falta de densidad moral': she has no clearly defined ethical values. In their absence she is at the mercy of trivial religiosity on the one hand in conflict with a debased romantic dream of *amor-pasión* on the other. Thus she falls alternatively under the influence of Fermín and Álvaro, for whom religious or romantic phraseology is or becomes a mere instrument for the achievement of their desire. All three characters evolve in a downward spiral of humiliation. In the case of Álvaro, whose waning sexual capacity contrasts with his role and whose cowardly flight after his duel with Ana's husband reveals the man behind the reputation, the process is ironic. In those of Ana and Fermín it is sadder: Ana's illusions end with the viscid kiss of the effeminate Celedonio; Fermín's masterful ambition and vanity dissolve into utter moral degradation.

Su único hijo differs radically from *La Regenta*. Here the gentle humanity which is, along with his intellectualism and moral sense, a major characteristic of Clarín's personality, emerges in the treatment of the dreamy, ineffectual, and long-suffering husband, Bonis. His trivial affair with a passing actress is delicately portrayed as a liberation and a fulfilment of a pathetic, but not ignoble, love-ideal. Later, disillusioned with his mistress, betrayed by his wife, and swindled by her relatives, Bonis is revealed in full moral evolution. At the end of the novel he emerges ennobled, rejecting the (justified) insinuation that he is not the father of his wife's child, he finds in 'eso de ser padre' the achievement of his inmost aspiration.

IX. CLARÍN'S SHORTER FICTION

This gentle, even tender, treatment of humble unassuming figures, the world's victims, is an equally prominent feature of Clarín's short novels and stories. These appeared in various publications between 1876 and 1899 and were later issued in four collections during his lifetime. *Pipá* (1886); *Doña Berta, Cuervo, Superchería* (1892); *El Señor y lo demás son cuentos* (1892); and the significantly entitled *Cuentos morales* (1896). The least that may be said of them is that they rank Clarín with Alarcón, Palacio Valdés, and Pardo Bazán as the four outstanding figures in the history of the short story in nineteenth-century Spain. On the other hand, while none of them equals the verve and success of *El sombrero de tres picos*, Clarín's shorter fictional works are more often republished and have aroused more critical comment than those of any of his contemporaries.

Altogether Clarín wrote five short novels and some sixty short stories. Of the former the most often mentioned are 'Pipá' (1879) and 'Doña Berta' (1891). Pipá, the story of a street-urchin's day of glory and tragedy, is a small masterpiece of economic narrative method, superbly constructed and rising to a memorable, and for once fully naturalistic, climax in the horrible death of the child. 'Doña Berta' in contrast, is Clarín's most poetic story. Concerned with the search by a provincial spinster in Madrid for a picture of her lost love, it holds a place in Clarín's work similar to that of *Marianela* in Galdós's or *Le Rêve* in Clarín's admired Zola. No consideration of naturalism is complete without mention of these exceptional works. Equally unique is the profound and moving, yet utterly simple, 'Adiós, Cordera', surely Spain's finest nineteenth-century short story. Clarín's humour, in contrast, is a little dated, and his satirical short stories, especially those on quasi-religious subjects, are perhaps his least successful. The exception is 'Zurita', a delicious caricature of the Krausist ideal. Clarín's serious short stories on the religious theme (e.g. 'El señor', 'Cambio de luz', 'El sombrero del cura') illustrate his approach to the preoccupations of the Generation of 1898 rather than to the tenden-

tiousness of his own time. Memorable, finally, in the same sense, are
stories connected with the national problems (e.g. 'El Rana', 'Un
repatriado') which complete the picture of a literary personality to
which only the present day has begun to give a full measure of
appreciation.

X. REALISM AND IDEALISM

Before turning from the work of the realists proper to the timid
naturalism of Pardo Bazán we must consider briefly the transforma-
tion of literary outlook which their work ultimately represents and
the confusion of terminology which accompanied it. Even before the
1850s and 1860s the question of realism in the novel and on the
stage was very much a live issue. It underlies much of Larra's critical
work. We find it prominent in Piferrer's discussion of Avellaneda's
play *Alfonso Munio* in 1842. We have seen that Tamayo made it the
theme of his inaugural address to the Academy in 1859, and that
Ventura de la Vega claimed to have introduced it at last into tragedy
with *La muerte de César* a few years later. But it was sadly misunder-
stood. Tamayo spoke for the entire period when he asserted that not
all of what is true in the world has a place in the theatre. The general
view was that the presentation of unembellished reality would be
depressing, unartistic, and probably immoral. Such is the argument,
for example, of a characteristic article by Alarcón written in 1857
à propos of Ortiz de Piñedo's play *Los pobres de Madrid*. It was, the
horrified Alarcón thundered, an aspect of truth 'tomado en crudo,
presentado al natural sin darse el trabajo de componerlo, de agregarle
algún aliño, de cumplir con la obligación de todo arte'. Art, he
insisted, must be something more than simply 'una ventana con vistas
a la calle'. The same problem beset Palacio Valdés in 1871 when
writing his *semblanza* of Castro y Serrano. Nothing is more revealing
than to compare the article with Alarcón's of twelve years earlier.
Since then, Palacio notes, the battle has raged between *realistas* and
idealistas. He resolutely defends the former, albeit with a rather
curious choice of representative works (Campoamor's *Tren expreso*,
Núñez de Arce's *Idilio*, and Galdós's *Marianela*). But hardly do we
turn the page before encountering the old, threadbare distinction
between 'el realismo de la vida' and 'el realismo del arte', and find
ourselves back almost where we started. Valera, for all his naïve

description of *Juanita la larga* as a 'reproducción fotográfica de hombres y de cosas de la provincia en que yo he nacido', took exactly the same view as Palacio. Pereda, in his turn, defined realism as 'la afición a presentar en el libro pasiones y caracteres humanos y cuadros de la naturaleza, dentro del *decoro* del arte'. It is clear, then, that before and perhaps during the seventies the idea of depicting reality as objectively as possible without either moral or aesthetic embellishments (what the 'idealist' or, as they preferred to call themselves, 'spiritualist' critics referred to as 'poesía') had hardly been granted serious consideration. When it was not dismissed as unartistic, it was attacked as immoral. With the advent of the mature work of Galdós and Clarín, this ideal, without perhaps prevailing completely, came appreciably closer to realisation. We ought perhaps to mention at the same time that without the constant pressure on the reading public from the French realist novel (revealed by the regularity with which its influence was attacked) the task of these writers would certainly have been much harder.

The realist-idealist debate of the 1860s and 1870s overlapped with the polemic about naturalism. This is shown by the fact that the first use of the term *naturalista* referred to Pereda's *De tal palo, tal astilla*. But what really set off the second stage of the argument was the publication in 1883 of *La cuestión palpitante* by Emilia Pardo Bazán (1851-1921).

XI. PARDO BAZÁN AND 'LA CUESTIÓN PALPITANTE'

Born in Corunna, the only child of wealthy upper middle-class parents on whom in 1871 Pius IX conferred a Papal title, Pardo Bazán acquired in early youth habits of voracious reading together with wide intellectual interests and ambitions. In 1868, at the age of seventeen, she married and moved to Madrid, determined to devote herself to study and writing. Feijoo[8] was at this time her personality ideal; her first success came with a prize essay and poem on this eighteenth-century intellectual propagandist and early feminist. Articles popularising new scientific ideas, a book of poems inspired by the birth of her first child, and a biography of St Francis followed. It was not until 1879 that she published her first novel, *Pascual López*. The story of a young student in Compostela whose acquisition of a process for making industrial diamonds from his professor of chemistry loses him his sweetheart, the novel, though interesting, is important only as Pardo Bazán's point of departure. The mingling of conventional and fantastic elements and characters stamps it as belonging, if anywhere, to Alarconian pre-realism. It ran into three editions and encouraged Pardo Bazán to follow it up with *Un viaje de novios* (1881), another curiously hybrid production. In it elements of the novel of thesis—the plot concerns an unwise marriage undertaken by an over-young bride—combine with the profuse descriptions which Pardo Bazán at that time took to be an essential part of realism and with a sub-plot in which the heroine's naïve religiosity comes into painful conflict with the atheistic pessimism of her would-be lover, whom she eventually rejects.

Meanwhile Pardo Bazán's theoretical outlook had been changing rapidly. In the preface to *Pascual López* she had aligned herself with Valera: rejecting the neo-Catholic ideal of *arte docente*, she had echoed the view that 'toda obra bella eleva y enseña de por sí'. Introducing *Un viaje de novios*, she went a stage further, praising the French novel and placing realist observation and analysis before creative imagination. Here, for the first time, she broke her allegiance to the idealist novel with the blunt statements that 'la novela es traslado de la vida' and that 'lo único que el autor pone en ella, es su modo peculiar de ver las cosas reales', a paraphrase of Zola's famous reference to 'reality seen by a particular temperament'.

In 1882, just after the first translation of Zola into Spanish, Pardo Bazán developed her ideas in a series of articles published the following year as a book, *La cuestión palpitante*, with a preface by Clarín. The book caused a tremendous sensation, being popularly regarded as an outrageous manifesto by a young, wealthy, and aristocratic woman (a wife and mother to boot) in favour of French pornographic and atheistic literature. In actual fact it is nothing of the kind. Its importance lies in four features. The first is Pardo Bazán's attack on idealism. Her memorable description of it as 'la teoría simpática por excelencia, la que invocan poetas de caramelo y escritores amerengados' and of its products as 'libros anodinos y mucilaginosos', and pap for an infantile audience, marked the end of the movement's near monopoly of respectability in Spanish literary criticism. The second is her explanation and critique of naturalism. At once the crux of the book's argument and its weakest part, this section contains the clue to Pardo Bazán's entire literary personality and to her subsequent evolution as a novelist. Nothing more clearly indicates her real position with regard to the movement she is supposed to represent than the haste with which she passes from the most brief and superficial account of Zola's ideas to criticism of them. Indeed it would be truer to say that her account of them is simply in terms of their defects. Ignoring the sociological and philosophical features of naturalism, she exaggerates, in order to condemn them, the elements of 'scientific' accuracy and impersonality of observation which Zola had seen as the movement's original contribution to the novel, and defends Zola himself on the very grounds of literary talent which Zola—taking them for granted—wished to minimise.

For Pardo Bazán naturalism is a pretentiously pseudo-scientific movement based on the application to human behaviour of a narrow concept of determinism, with a deplorable tendency to overemphasise the sordid, the ugly, and the proletarian. Though vaguely aware of it as a liberating influence, she recoiled at the thought of a really all-out attack on social and sexual taboos. Hence the third important feature of *La cuestión palpitante*: its defence of realism as 'una teoría más ancha, completa y perfecta que el naturalismo'. Here she saw with relief the possibility of striking a balance between the indecorous excesses of naturalism and the prettified artificiality of idealism. Her ideal was the combination of this rather facile *juste-milieu* sort of 'realism' with respect for artistic form and what she called 'refinement'. It is a measure of the quality of her opponents that they saw in such an ideal a scandalous literary innovation. Finally, in *La cuestión palpitante* Pardo Bazán came to the defence of Spanish literature, whose 'carácter castizo y propio' she declared was 'más realista que otra cosa', and specifically championed the realism 'a la española' of Galdós (after his early period of thesis novels) and Pereda. Not surprisingly Zola dissociated himself at once from Pardo Bazán's position. He was right. When four years later he published *La terre*, Pardo Bazán showed how shallow her naturalist sympathies were by being dreadfully shocked.

La cuestión palpitante produced counterblasts from Campoamor, Alarcón, and eventually Menéndez Pelayo, with contributions from a number of minor critics. But the leader of the opposition was Valera, in his *Sobre el arte de escribir novelas* (1886-87), one of the best books ever written on the wrong side of an argument of which the author, by his own admission, was largely ignorant. Not having read any naturalistic novels, Valera argued from first principles that literature is and must be essentially pleasant and diverting. Truth is a secondary consideration: 'es extravío abominable' Valera asserted, summing up the idealists' case in one phrase, 'decirnos siempre cosas que, aunque fuesen ciertas, nos habían de amargar y atosigar'. By the eighth article, however, he had wisely taken in his sails and retreated to a second line of defence: that offences to religion and morality can never be artistic, a point so obviously false (where the writer's intentions are sincere and the religion or morality in question as conventionalised as those of nineteenth-century Spain) as to require no comment. Pardo Bazán's husband was among those greatly scandalised and the marriage collapsed into an amicable separation. Henceforth Pardo Bazán was free to follow her literary and intellectual interests without hindrance. These presently included not only literary polemics, but also intervention in political journalism and a fierce but hopeless struggle for feminine intellectual and social emancipation.

XII. THE CENTRAL NOVELS

Pardo Bazán's next novel, *La tribuna* (1883), occupies a modest but significant place in the history of Spanish literature as the first serious novel to deal with genuine urban working-class life. Set in a thinly-disguised Corunna it was the result of two months' intensive observation by Pardo Bazán, notebook in hand, at a tobacco factory there. It exemplifies, much more than Pardo Bazán's later work, her personal conception of naturalism as involving close and detailed observation of proletarian life, with a small measure of implicit social criticism, but without obtrusive determinism or pessimism. The story of a vaguely revolutionary working girl seduced and abandoned by a young officer, it centres on the upheavals following the 1868 Revolution, in which Pardo Bazán correctly perceived 'una vieja España impotente para triunfar, una nueva España incapaz de aprovechar el triunfo'. She herself, formerly a Carlist, now joined Cánovas's party. *La tribuna* also depicts, rather patronisingly, the mentality of working people who, Pardo Bazán had convinced herself, 'a Dios gracias, se diferencian bastante de los que pintan los Goncourt y Zola'. The novel was attacked by (among others) Luis Alfonso, the leading 'idealist' critic, as nauseating, atheistic, and full of low expressions! Possibly intimidated, Pardo Bazán published in 1885

El Cisne de Villamorta. It was her first big popular success, perhaps because of its more conventional plot and setting. In retrospect one wishes that the authoress had studied the main feminine figure, a plain middle-aged schoolteacher, rather than the addleheaded poet who is the hero.

1886 and 1887 saw the appearance successively of Pardo Bazán's two most memorable novels, *Los pazos de Ulloa* and its sequel *La madre naturaleza*. The former, which is regarded as her masterpiece, is best seen in perspective by contrasting it with Pereda's *El sabor de la tierruca* written about five years earlier. Pereda, mourning the paternalistic social ideas of the provincial landowning class from which he sprang, had painted a picture of harmony between enlightened landowners and contented peasants. Pardo Bazán tells a grimmer story of an upper class which has outlived its social role and retains only negative characteristics: idleness, violence, and irresponsibility in the Marqués de Ulloa, pathetic shabby-gentility in his neighbours. Usurping the Marqués's power and influence, Primitivo, his steward, exploits the estate and, together with a group of greedy and ignorant village priests, runs the political life of the area. His daughter, Sabel, is the Marqués's mistress. The semi-animal existence of their son Perucho completes the pattern of decay and degradation which Pardo Bazán depicts. The key-sentence, which the rest of the book expands, is spoken by the Marqués's uncle in Chapter II: 'La aldea, cuando se cría uno en ella y no sale de ella jamás, envilece, empobrece y embrutece'. Of this world the young priest, Don Julián, and the Marqués's wife, Nucha, are the victims, their gentleness and delicacy crushed by its brutality. If *La tribuna* contains Pardo Bazán's most naturalistic setting for a novel, *Los pazos de Ulloa* comes closer to the movement in its unrelieved pessimism. More than any of her other works it shows, too, her mastery of dramatic fictional technique. From a highly effective opening scene, the exposition (Chapters I to VI) develops through a series of revealing incidents to Don Julián's discovery of Sabel's position. Thereafter the novel is symmetrical around its centre of balance in Chapters XVI and XVII. An upward, hopeful, movement culminates in the birth of Nucha's daughter, Manolita; thereafter the narrative slips down towards the triumph of ignominy and barbarism at the end, underlined by the epilogue after an interval of ten years.

In the sequel the emphasis shifts. *Los pazos* is ultimately a study of a *social* process: the disintegration of a class; *La madre naturaleza* is a study of a *natural* process, albeit one which society condemns: the discovery of love by Perucho and his half-sister Manolita. The idyll of the two young people is set against a lush, vital, even sensual, natural background, in the vivid description of which Pardo Bazán reached her peak as a *paisajista*. But the symbolism of the central episode of the book (borrowed from Genesis by way of Zola's *La faute de l'abbé Mouret*) reveals nature's cold impassiveness behind its invitation to self-fulfilment via instinct. Perucho and Manolita consummate their love in all 'natural' innocence, under a symbolic 'tree of knowledge', only to find themselves cast out from an Eden unmoved by their human tragedy. But if nature is, innocently or ironically, to blame for their plight, society compounds the crime, condemning Manolita to expiate her 'fault' in a convent and Perucho to despair.

The central decade of Pardo Bazán's fictional production, that of the 1880s, ends with two short, intense, novels: *Insolación* and *Morriña* (1889). In these, while the theme remains that of human sexual behaviour, the scene shifts for the first time to Madrid. But, in spite of Galdós's attempts to introduce Doña Emilia to working-class life (which bore fruit in some of her short stories), the settings are both discreetly bourgeois. Perhaps for this reason especially *Insolación* was greeted with the usual loud accusations of pornography. The first part, in which a rich young widow, Asís de Taboada, indiscreetly accepts an invitation from a man-about-town to the Feria de San Isidro, is a *tour de force* of fast-moving dramatic description and stands with the very best of Pardo Bazán's work. Here two social worlds, that of the people and that of the upper-middle class, meet and fuse as Asís, under the influence of sunshine, alcohol, and the festive atmosphere, gravely compromises herself. Unfortunately Pardo Bazán baulks the consequences of the incident, and after a brief interval of tension and amorous intrigue, unconvincingly forces a morally decorous ending on to the novel. *Morriña* deals with the unequal struggle of a Galician servant-girl (symbolically named Esclavitud), against the circumstances of her birth—she is the child of a priest—and against class convention— she is in love with her employer's son. The novel ends with a suicide which, as R. E. Osborne points out,[9] is not by any means unique in Pardo Bazán's work.

With the arrival of the 1890s her outlook began to undergo a change. Her defiant feminism and militant intellectualism became

further invigorated by her growing sense of the imminence of the
catastrophe of 1898. From 1891 to 1893 she published single-handed
a monthly magazine, *Nuevo Teatro Crítico*, in which creative writing,
literary criticism, and essays on some of the major intellectual topics
of the period appear impressively side by side. Now too, having
established herself as a major novelist, she emerged as the most
prolific and probably the greatest Spanish short-story writer of her
times. Between 1892 and her death she published more than five
hundred short stories, in an astonishing variety of styles ranging
from some of her most audaciously naturalistic writings, through
humour, sentimentality, and more or less obvious *costumbrismo*, to
the symbolic *regeneracionismo* of 'El palacio frío', 'La armadura', and
'El mandil de cuero'. Both the short stories and the *Nuevo Teatro
Crítico* deserve a renewal of critical attention; in particular the
'Despedida', appended to the final issue of the latter, is a major
neglected document of the pre-1898 period.

XIII. THE LAST PHASE

In the last phase of Pardo Bazán's fictional work, which includes
Una cristiana and its sequel *La prueba* (1890); *La piedra angular*
(1891); *Doña Milagros* (1894); *Memorias de un solterón* (1896); *La
quimera* (1905); and *La sirena negra* (1908), we perceive her
conscious ideological intentions tending to get the better of her
creative ability. At the same time, perhaps under the influence,
among others, of the Russian novel, which she was the first to
publicise in Spain, her religious convictions began to obtrude into
her novels. Her two outstanding works of this period are *La quimera*
and *La sirena negra*. Both of them are of exceptional interest to the
historian of literature as having elements in common with the novel
of the Generation of 1898 and as illustrating attempts by a writer
of the older generation to come to terms with the emerging sensibility of the younger group. Thus *La quimera* caught Unamuno's
attention for its study of an artist in search of immortality. Gaspar
de Montenegro of *La sirena negra*, in whom Pardo Bazán develops
traits interestingly foreshadowed by Gabriel de la Lange of *La madre
naturaleza*, similarly reveals a temperament superficially like those of
Baroja's Fernando Ossorio or Azorín's Antonio Azorín. But Pardo
Bazán, like Galdós, possessed a vital confidence and serenity, based

Chapter 10

THE NOVEL IN THE GENERATION OF 1898

THE FORTUNES OF REALISM, it has sometimes been suggested, were closely connected to those of the middle class and Liberalism. When at the end of the nineteenth century middle-class hegemony and Liberal ideas began to be threatened by the rise of the proletariat and its extreme ideologies (socialism, communism, anarchism), realism was overtaken by crisis. Later a new form of realism, socialist realism, emerged as the literary expression of the organised working class. The theory is plausible and fits some of the facts, even in Spain where the middle class never really wrested control of political decision-making from an élitist minority, and where the threat from the proletariat developed late. Certainly, with the appearance of the Generation of 1898 crisis overtook realism in fiction; but the real origins of that crisis lie deeper than sociological considerations can fully explain.

With the Generation of 1898[1] we reach the climax of the process of enforced retreat from vital confidence, based on an orderly and purposive concept of existence guaranteed by reason and divine Providence. This retreat, initiated by the Romantics, continues well into the twentieth century. Certain aspects of the early twentieth-century novel clearly represent the culmination of this nineteenth-century process, and must therefore be considered at this stage. The unity of a generation is determined, not by adventitious factors of birth, leadership, or the half-dozen other influences which critics have tried to isolate, but by an *identity of sensibility,* that is, a common outlook on life. The outlook of the Generation is dominated by their collective recognition of the inability of the mind to make sense of human existence. Along with this recognition goes an increasingly desperate search for *ideas madres,* for a satisfying pattern of ideas, ideals, and beliefs with which to solve the threefold problem of truth, duty, and finality which they found confronting them. The problem of national regeneration, which had gained additional urgency from the disaster of 1898, posed this difficulty afresh. For one of the major legacies of the men of 1868 (Galdós and Clarín especially) to the Generation was the notion that in the spiritual and ideological regeneration of the individual lay the key to the regeneration of the nation.

The novel of the Generation of 1898 represents the response in fictional terms to this dual imperative: to explore and if possible resolve the crisis of ideals and beliefs at the individual level, while at the same time keeping in sight of the national problem. The characteristic novel of the Generation is one in which an ideologically conceived central character, reflecting the preoccupations already mentioned, faces a series of test-situations and carefully selected interlocutors, designed to explore and if possible solve his difficulties. In practice the effort fails. The diagnosis of the individual and national malady is commonly convincing, but there is no adequate therapy.

The type of fiction which emerged necessarily diverged from the older realist tradition. It represented a variant of the *Bildungsroman*, somewhere between the novel of ideas and the psychological novel. Among its major characteristics may be mentioned: abandonment of the balanced deployment of characters in favour of the preponderance of a single central figure; the subordination of plot and replacement of incidents by conversations and discussions; the minor role allotted to love-interest which never develops into an emotional solution to the hero's problems; and the conscious renovation of narrative style.

I. GANIVET

The first important novelist to explore the possibilities of the new formula was Ángel Ganivet (1865-98) in his novels *La conquista del reino de Maya* (1897) and *Los trabajos del infatigable creador Pío Cid* (1898). The two works are of very unequal merit and the second remained incomplete. Nevertheless, their importance, particularly in the case of *Los trabajos,* is outstanding not only intrinsically but also because in them we make contact for the first time with the fictional hero of the '98.

La conquista del reino de Maya is a politico-moral satire. In it Ganivet causes Pío Cid to appear to the Mayas, a savage African tribe, in the guise of a prophet-ruler. Once in command, he takes stock of their system and proceeds to bring in modifications designed to set the Mayas on the high road to civilisation. By arranging his narrative in this way Ganivet fulfils a dual aim: to satirise the existing state of politics and society in Spain; and to ridicule the prevailing belief in social perfectibility. In the early part of the narrative there is a review of the Mayas' customs, with particular reference to their kings, politicians, and military organisation. Here Ganivet attacks effectively the vices of the Spanish Monarchy, the corruption of the government, and the army's delusions of grandeur. The rest of the novel sees the imposition of positivistic 'reforms': the introduction of money, gunpowder, slavery, and other improvements. As in Orwell's *Animal Farm,* the emphasis is on change without progress, on the egotism, apathy, and folly of the people and the cynical opportunism of the rulers.

Pío Cid emerges from all this rather unsatisfactorily. It is clear that Ganivet at this time had no clear idea of the character of his hero. He is presented now as a cynic, now as an idealist, now as a melancholy intellectual. At the basis of his personality are 'sentimientos de benevolencia mezclados, bien es cierto, con no pequeña dosis de amargo pesimismo'. This evident duality arises from the conflict between Ganivet's will to believe in the regenerative force of ideas (of which Pío Cid's here are a sort of bitter travesty) and his realisation that human nature defeats attempts to put them into effect. Thus the book's doctrinal content remains negative and Pío Cid's character as yet undeveloped. In the sequel, *Los trabajos del infatigable creador Pío Cid,* we are on firmer ground. Here Pío Cid is presented in the guise of the individual reformer, striving for what he significantly calls 'el renacimiento *espiritual* de España', by bringing the force of his magnetic personality to bear on selected individuals from different levels of society, who are intended to represent in a semi-symbolic way aspects of the Spanish problem. Thus Purilla, the servant-girl, is taught to read and becomes a hospital-nun; del Valle is found a place in society and enabled to marry; Gandarias achieves a truer conception of poetry; the *maestro rural* Ciruela is persuaded to stay at his post; even the aristocracy, in the persons of the Duquesa and her son, undergoes Pío Cid's influence. To all of them Pío Cid preaches his doctrine of love, work, and ethical behaviour.

We gather from the main ideological section of the work, the conversation at the Fuente del Avellano, that progress in general is produced exclusively by an élite minority of directing intellectuals endowed with *energía espiritual* and a stock of (undefined) *ideas madres*. This minority, to whom Pío Cid implicitly belongs, are seen as leading the country (in particular its work-orientated middle class, Ganivet's target audience) towards regeneration, via 'un nuevo concepto de la vida'. The heritage of this curious mystique (we cannot call it a theory) is visible both in the work of J. E. Rodó, the influential Latin American thinker, and in Ortega's sinister invention of 'los mejores'.

How fragile Ganivet's inner confidence was in minority leadership, spiritual self-help, and *idées-forces*, is visible from an examination of Pío Cid. Two features of his complex personality are noteworthy. One is the obtrusive fact that Pío Cid's private life is markedly inconsistent with his doctrines. While exhorting others to work, he has no regular activity; while arranging the marriages of del Valle and Rosarico, he refuses to marry his mistress Martina; while proclaiming the need to regenerate Spain, he rejects political activity and refuses social integration. Closely related is the other important feature: the pessimistic scepticism which underlies all Pío Cid's philanthropic actions and idealist slogans. Not only is he presented as 'un hombre inteligente, pero desilusionado e incapaz de hacer nada', but in the vitally important dialogue with Consuelo in the third *trabajo* Ganivet underlines in a key-paragraph the duality of his hero:

'Debe [usted] tener en su alma un vacío inmenso que asusta . . . me parece ver en usted el hombre de menos fe que existe en el mundo. . . . Quizás la pena que usted tiene por vivir sin creencias le inspire ese deseo de fortificarlas en los demás'.

Pío Cid's reply to this incisive and accurate charge is a tissue of sophistries.

This duality in Pío Cid reveals Ganivet's own extreme ambivalence of outlook both in regard to the optimistic possibilities of life in general and the regeneration of Spain. It also underlines a further significant difference between the novel of the '98 and that of the previous generation. The typical pre-1898 novel is commonly concerned with conflict between two or more characters (Pepe Rey-Doña Perfecta), or between characters and exterior forces (Ana Ozores–Vetusta). The typical novel of the Generation of 1898, on the other hand, is essentially an account of one character in conflict with himself and his insight.

Technically *Los trabajos de Pío Cid* illustrates the '98 manner. The six *trabajos* constitute a single biographical story-line with no economy of incidents or characters and no organic development or dramatic action. Virtually the whole of the novel is deliberately centred on the personality of Pío Cid, to whom all the other characters are subordinated, and on his ideology. Love-interest is extremely slight and dramatic interest (in the absence of conflict of character) minor. The novel progresses instead from conversation to conversation, with dialogue occupying some sixty per cent of the text.

The basic flaw in the novel is the dissociation of Pío Cid himself, the demoralised *dirigente,* from his collective ideal, and his tendency to shy away into paradoxes and contradictions when confronted with the fact. We may assume that Ganivet's failure to complete the work was as much due to his inability to resolve this problem in fictional terms, as to the onset of the acute phase of his illness and his subsequent suicide.

In the preface to *La nave de los locos,* a key-document both to his own work and to the novel of the '98, Baroja wrote:

Toda la gran literatura moderna está hecha a base de perturbaciones mentales. Esto ya lo veía Galdós, pero no basta verlo para ir por ahí y acertar; se necesita tener una fuerza espiritual que él no tenía y probablemente se necesita también ser un perturbado; él era un hombre normal, casi demasiado normal.

The distinction is interesting for two reasons. First, it provides a clue to the central feature of the fictional hero of the '98; second, it reveals the shift of sensibility between Galdós's generation and Baroja's. It is noteworthy that Baroja does not attribute Galdós's inability to follow the line of development of which he was aware to age or prejudice, but to *normality.* The implication is plain: the novel of the '98 explores 'abnormal' states of mind different from those of Maxi Rubín or Nazarín; and further, the creators of the fictional heroes of the '98 are identified with these figures to an 'abnormal' degree.

The pertinence of Baroja's remarks is already illustrated in *Los trabajos de Pío Cid,* the first major novel of the '98. Pío Cid is nothing if not a *perturbado* and his state of mind directly reflects that of Ganivet, the novel being written with anything but detachment.

Precisely the same is true of what deserves to be counted as the second great novel of the Generation, though it appeared in the same year as Baroja's *Camino de perfección* and Unamuno's *Amor y pedagogía: La voluntad* (1902) by José Martínez Ruiz, Azorín (1873-1967).

II. AZORÍN

Azorín, as the invaluable research of Inman Fox[2] has shown, began his life's work as a deeply socially-committed writer with leanings, like those of Unamuno, Baroja, and Maeztu, towards sentimental anarchism. He was dismissed from his post on *El Imparcial* for his fiery denunciations of hunger and oppression in Andalusia. But by the turn of the century he was becoming disillusioned with the Left and with *engagement. Diario de un enfermo* (1901) marks the appearance of a phase of crisis which is further documented in three autobiographical novels: *La voluntad* (1902), *Antonio Azorín* (1903), and *Las confesiones de un pequeño filósofo* (1904). These constitute the first and most important phase of his work as a novelist.

Antonio Azorín, the hero of the trilogy, and the figure from whom Azorín took his pen name, is the first fully developed '98 hero. Like Pío Cid he is a *perturbado,* a man of 'hondas y trascendentales cavilaciones'. But there is a marked difference: 'Azorín no cree en nada'. Pío Cid can be seen at intervals poised on the brink of the abyss; Azorín has fallen over the edge. This the mark of the true '98 hero: he has no positive beliefs; his intelligence is purely corrosive. 'La inteligencia es el mal', Antonio Azorín laments in *La voluntad,*

> comprender es entristecerse. Observar es sentirse vivir. Y sentirse vivir es la muerte, es sentir la inexorable marcha de todo nuestro ser y de las cosas que nos rodean hacia el océano misterioso de la nada.

This is, of course, pure Schopenhauer. It attests, as we shall see confirmed with respect to Baroja, not only that the Generation of 1898 read more philosophy than any literary generation in Spain before or since—a fact of vital significance—but also that the major influence was that of systematic pessimism.

The consequence of Antonio's typically '98 compulsive intellectual analysis is anguish, based on the recognition that 'no hay nada estable, ni cierto ni inconmovible' and that human life is simply part of 'la dolorosa, inútil y estùpida evolución de los mundos hacia la nada'. Azorín (the author) embodies in the clerics Lasalde and Puche, as well as in Antonio's mystical *novia* Justina, his recognition that only faith can provide the answer to the problem here explored: but, unhappily, Antonio and his older friend Yuste have lost their faith. In 'El abuelo', the old peasant, we meet that serene ignorance of the problem which Azorín, like Baroja, half envied and half despised. In Chapter 14 of Part I, an important excursion on literary topics, the sublimation of the problem through art—a principal feature of *modernismo*—is bluntly dismissed. Later Antonio toys with action, a solution which was to fascinate Baroja, but also rejects it. At the end of the novel we find him in a state of complete moral collapse, vegetating in Yecla, and what is worse, married to a harpy. He is now sunk in that *abulia,* originally Ganivet's discovery, which, it is important to emphasise, is not just lack of willpower, but the natural debilitation of the will in the absence of those vital convictions (religious, nationalistic, humanitarian, or other) which stimulate its activity and give it a purposive orientation.

Once more the novel has very little real plot (cf. Azorín's own statement in the novel, 'Ante todo, no debe haber fábula'). It is dominated by the central character, from whose evolution it takes its shape and tempo, and in Part I especially is another example of 'discussion-fiction', crammed with dialogue.

In the two remaining parts of the trilogy Azorín abandons any attempt to present a story-line, whether as a series of episodes or as a description of an evolving personality. *Antonio Azorín* and *Las confesiones . . .* are merely a succession of descriptive *estampas* based on memories of Azorín's childhood and early manhood, his friends, his teachers, his excursions in Spain, his impressions. They owe their readability and charm to their simplicity and immediacy, achieved almost exclusively by mastery of style, and to a certain tone of gentle melancholy and delicate near-pathos which has a curious appeal.

The state of mind portrayed in Azorín's *La voluntad* was not intended to be taken as merely that of an individual. Describing his hero as almost a symbol, the author writes of him: 'Su caso es el de toda la juventud española'. The claim is exaggerated; but it serves as a reminder that the '98 writers were consciously interpreting in fictional terms what Pérez de Ayala in his turn was to call 'the Spanish crisis of conscience'.

III. BAROJA

No one was more aware of this than Azorín's close friend, the Oláran of *La voluntad*, Pío Baroja y Nessi (1872-1956). All his work was published in the twentieth century[3]; but his close identification with the outlook of the Generation of 1898 demands attention in the present context. A Basque like Unamuno and Maeztu, Baroja was born in San Sebastian. He trained as a doctor in Madrid and Valencia, but abandoned a medical career after a short period of general practice near his home town. He never married or seems to have had a significant love-affair, a fact which perhaps limits the range of his human experience. For most of his life he lived with his family in Madrid, growing gradually more of a recluse after middle age.

Baroja's theory of the novel can be easily reconstructed from his many writings on the subject. These include the preface to his *Páginas escogidas*; his essays 'Sobre la técnica de la novela' and 'Sobre la manera de escribir novelas'; several chapters of *La caverna del humorismo*; and above all the preface to *La nave de los locos*. The outstanding feature of his attitude is his hostility to conscious formal technique. Knowing how to write novels, Baroja believed, was a natural ability, which could not be developed or learned where it did not already exist: 'lo único que sabemos es que para hacer novelas se necesita ser novelista, y aun esto no basta'. Provided one had the knack, any kind of material or narrative-method could be used: 'la novela es un saco en que cabe todo'. His own novels, he asserted, were written without conscious planning (though they often reveal an instinctive sense of shape) and were based essentially on 'observation of life'. This last comment reveals the second main plank of Baroja's platform: his distrust of creative imagination. The two basic ingredients of his writing are thus: his own experience, especially that which he acquired in adolescence and early manhood, when his outlook crystallised; and what he called *reportaje*—direct observation of reality. Art came to be for him the representation of reality in a perspective which he had acquired through prior contact with it during his formative years.

That perspective was bitterly pessimistic and sceptical. The chief feature of Baroja's personality is his inability to accept the comfortable pattern of ideas and beliefs on which the mass of people uncritically base their lives. He and the central characters of his novels are dominated by compulsive intellectual analysis which erodes away their vital confidence. Thus the typical Barojan novel is one in which the hero or heroine undergoes, as a result of the experiences and conversations which the novel describes, a development of consciousness. The end of it is the acquisition of a deeper level of insight, almost always negative. Apart from the small group of figures closest to the central character, who act chiefly as foils and conversational partners, the mass of other personages in Baroja's novels represent the general body of mankind, for the most part selfish, superficial, and conformist, but above all unconsciously dependent on some sort of *mentira vital*.

Among the influences which chiefly affected the formation of Baroja's outlook, the most important were, as always in the Generation of 1898, philosophic. Three figures stand out: above all Schopenhauer, whom Baroja read regularly all his life and in whose work he found confirmation of his own pessimism, of his love-hate relationship with analysis, and especially of his growing tendency after about 1912 to retreat into abstention. Next in importance is Kant, in whom Baroja perceived chiefly the destructive thinker, the force which destroyed confidence in rationalism and in the power of the mind to understand ultimate reality. But Kant's categorical imperative also appealed powerfully to the one principle which Baroja never seriously questioned, and which ennobles so much of his work: the ethical principle. Finally in Nietzsche, during the first decade of this century, Baroja found a temporary source of positive affirmation and an intellectual support for the first major phase of his fictional work, which goes from *Camino de perfección* (1902) to *César o nada* (1910).

There are in fact three such phases in Baroja's evolution. The first, or 'Vitalist' phase just mentioned, is that in which Baroja explores the possibility of seeking life's finality, not in the after-life (in which he never believed) but in life itself, in living as the ultimate absolute, and in action as its real manifestation. The second phase is that of the *Memorias de un hombre de acción*, the long series of historical novels concerned chiefly with the nineteenth-century spy and adventurer Aviraneta, a distant relation of Baroja himself. Two-thirds of this series was written in the interval between *El mundo es ansí* (1912) and *La sensualidad pervertida* (1920), during which Baroja wrote no novels in a modern setting. The final phase, that of the search for *ataraxia*, serenity through self-limitation, continues from *La sensualidad pervertida* to the end of Baroja's production.

Baroja's first published book, *Vidas sombrías* (1900), marks the beginning of the twentieth-century short story in Spain. It also reveals, in characteristic pieces such as 'Nihil' and 'El amo de la jaula', his already deep disenchantment with life. The growth of this disenchantment can be followed in the opening section of *El àrbol de la ciencia* (1911), in *Juventud, egolatría* (1917) and *La formación psicológica de un escritor* (1936), all of which are autobiographical. The effects of his experiences and reflections as a medical student and doctor, his reading, his social and sexual frustration, and possibly features of his upbringing, combined with his depressive temperament to produce a state of mind very similar to that portrayed by Azorín in *La voluntad*. He sought anxiously for something to believe in, which would make sense of life. But in vain. 'De joven y sin cultura', he wrote, 'no iba a formarme un concepto, una significación y un fin de la vida cuando flotaba y flota en el ambiente la sospecha de si la vida no tendrá significación ni objeto'.

After a false start in *La casa de Aizgorri* (1900) Baroja produced his first really characteristic novel, *Camino de perfección*. Written as a companion work to *La voluntad* after Baroja and Azorín had made together the trip to Toledo which figures in both novels, it shows Baroja adopting the normal '98 technique of charting the development of personality in a dominant central character. Fernando Ossorio is Baroja's first important fictional hero. The book evolves in two main phases with an interlude in Toledo in between. The opening phase describes the onset of Fernando's spiritual malaise, at this stage seen as at bottom a religious crisis, accentuated by hereditary and environmental factors which Baroja was later to discard. After a brief and unsuccessful attempt to find relief through sexual activity, Fernando tries the effect of a walking tour through central Spain only to arrive at Toledo physically ill and psychologically crushed. But in Toledo the ethical impulse suddenly reasserts itself. Henceforth Fernando gradually recovers his balance, vanquishes *abulia*, and, brushing aside a powerful rival, marries. There are three other points of interest. One is the appearance of the Castilian countryside in all its austere beauty. This was an authentic discovery of the Generation of 1898. Earlier, as we see in Pereda's *Pedro Sánchez*, Castilian scenery had been synonymous with ugliness and squalor. The second point is the insertion into the narrative of sequences designed to express Baroja's savagely destructive criticisms of Spanish life, out-look, and national character. The third is the enigmatic ending, which implies the resurgence, to torment Fernando's son, of the negative influences which he himself has overcome.

From now to *César o nada* Baroja's novels present a gallery of figures united by their desire to cope with life energetically and to find exhilaration and meaning in the struggle for existence. 'Yo creía de joven', Baroja wrote in 1936, 'que el vivir, si no alegre, sería siempre digno del esfuerzo, si se hallaba animado por la acción y hasta por la violencia'. Broadly speaking, the criterion for distinguish-ing among this group of characters is their approach to morality, always the bed-rock of Baroja's outlook. On the one side Ramiro de Labraz (*El Mayorazgo de Labraz*, 1903) and Quintín Roelas (*La feria de los discretos*, 1905) sacrifice morality on the altar of success. On the other side stand Juan Alcázar and Hastings, of Baroja's first trilogy, *La lucha por la vida* (1904); Yarza, of *Los últimos román-ticos* (1906) and its sequel; María Aracil (*La dama errante*, 1908, and *La ciudad de la niebla*, 1909); and in the end César Moncada. All of these in different ways tend to illustrate Baroja's growing recognition that wholehearted participation in the Struggle for Life involved moral concessions which he was not prepared to advocate. The key-structure here is Iturríoz's warning to María Aracil, Baroja's emancipation-seeking feminist heroine: '¿Tú quieres ser libre? tienes que ser inmoral'. César Moncada comes closest to resolving the con-flict between vitalism and ethical behaviour, since his actions (like Pío Cid's) are aimed at social regeneration. But suddenly, while the novel is in full stride, César is shot down.

The defeat of César symbolises the failure of the action-ideal. In 1917 Baroja wrote categorically:

Yo también he preconizado un remedio para el mal de vivir: la acción. Es un remedio viejo como el mundo, tan útil a veces como cualquier otro y tan inútil como todos los demás. Es decir que no es un remedio.

Meanwhile, in the Basque adventure stories *Zalacaín el aventurero* (1909)—his best seller—and *Las inquietudes de Shanti Andía* (1911), followed by the *Memorias de un hombre de acción* (1913-28), he had transferred the ideal of action to a nineteenth-century setting where in the period of the Carlist Wars and the Slave Trade it could still carry conviction, though no longer relevant to the modern dilemma.

The centre of Baroja's work is marked by his masterpiece, *El árbol de la ciencia*, and his most deeply pessimistic novel, *El mundo es ansí*. Along with Pío Cid and Antonio Azorín, Andrés Hurtado, the hero of *El árbol de la ciencia*, is the third representative fictional hero of the Generation of 1898. In his search for 'una verdad espiritual y práctica al mismo tiempo' his changes of outlook oscillate from short-lived *ataraxia* to total despair. Meanwhile, the spectacle of Spanish society, rural and urban, moves him only to passive indignation, for Baroja, though fiercely critical, had no ready-made solution to propose. Crushed by a series of demoralising events, culminating in his wife's death, Hurtado takes his own life.

Baroja's later novels explore the possibility of achieving serenity by attempting to contract out of active life in society, by cutting down its possibilities, by retreat into self-limitation: the passive, negative ideal he sought in his own private life. But again an insuperable obstacle presents itself: the need for an emotional and sexual outlet. The significant later central characters—Murguía (in *La sensualidad pervertida*, 1920); Larrañaga (in the last great trilogy, *Agonías de nuestro tiempo*, 1926); Salazar (in *Susana*, 1938); Laura (in *Laura*, 1939); and Caravajal (in *El cantor vagabundo*, 1950)—struggle pathetically to conciliate insight and lack of capacity for illusion with the necessity for a sexual solution both physical and emotional. The exception is Javier Olarán, the priest of *El cura de Monleón* (1938), in which Baroja considers the alternative of religious asceticism. But his complete lack of sympathy with religion disqualifies him here in advance.

Baroja ended by asking himself courageously in *El cantor vagabundo* what Unamuno never appears to have had the courage to discuss: whether his lifelong malaise was not the result of a 'neurosis de angustia'. Certainly his outlook was unduly coloured by depression and pessimism; but along with these his work also expressed much of the *Weltanschauung* of our time. He wrote too rapidly and too much—more than sixty novels—and his reliance on spontaneity often led him into clumsy construction and unprepared effects; but his immense influence on fiction both in Spain and Latin America indicates that the force and sincerity of his literary personality were not adversely affected. While Cela's assertion in 1956 that 'de Baroja sale toda la novela española a él posterior'[4] is perhaps an overstatement, Baroja

remains, as Guillermo de Torre wrote,[5] 'el más poderoso tempera-
mento novelesco con que después de Galdós cuentan las letras his-
pánicas'.

IV. UNAMUNO

'¿Qué es la vida? ¿Qué fin tiene la vida? ¿Qué hacemos aquí
abajo? ¿Para qué vivimos? No lo sé . . . siento la *angustia metafísica*.'
So, in typical '98 manner, Azorín began *Diario de un enfermo* in
1898. It was a moment, for him of spiritual crisis, a crisis which was
not fully resolved until his return to religion years later. In 1897
another major writer of the Generation had undergone a similar
experience, from which he was never fully to recover. This was
Miguel de Unamuno y Jugo (1864-1936). Born in Bilbao, his arrival
in Madrid as an undergraduate in 1880 coincided with the last stage
of the collapse of *Krausismo* and its fallacious promise of a
harmonious synthesis between faith and reason. He himself was
desperately seeking to evolve an intellectual framework which would
support his childhood faith. He failed. Much of the rest of his life
was spent trying to find a way round rational obstacles back to faith,
above all back to faith in his own immortality. There were several
intermediate positions between acute anguish and the temporary
reacquisition of religious confidence, which Unamuno at different
times occupied. The most important of these was 'feliz incerti-
dumbre', an attempt to bend *angst* back on itself and see in it a
positive instead of a negative spiritual state. There were also sundry
avenues of escape from the problem which Unamuno explored. These
included survival through creative activity, through fame with posterity, through children, through trust in the non-rational evidence of
lo biótico, and finally evasion into pure activity. Practically all
Unamuno's novels and short stories in the end centre on this interior
problemática. Like the fiction of the '98 in general, they are essentially concerned with self-exploration and self-confession.

His first novel, *Paz en la guerra* (1897), was the result of twelve
years of gestation. It is an old-style realist novel of observation concerned with the rather desultory and tedious manoeuvres which
together with the abortive siege of Bilbao constituted the Second
Carlist War. As such it stands apart from the rest of Unamuno's
fictional work except for one figure: Pachico Zabalbide, who is

7 • •

largely a self-portrait by the author with details of his early spiritual malaise.

During much of his early manhood Unamuno was publicly committed to the extreme Left in politics and to the end remained true to his own peculiar brand of socialism. One might have expected, therefore, an element of social protest in his fiction once the context of the Second Carlist War had been left behind. But this—very significantly—was not the case. Like Baroja, Unamuno in a sense eluded one of the most interesting possibilities of literature in early twentieth-century Spain: that of popularising the rationale of social reform, by concentrating on the individual spiritual problem while at the same time proclaiming the need for national regeneration. Thus, when the basic problems of Spain were poverty, rural suppression, and stagnation, and Unamuno as a socialist recognised them, hardly a reference to them is found in his work.

Instead he turned now from what he later called 'el engañoso realismo de lo aparencial' to what he saw as *true* realism: 'la realidad íntima', the inner, noumenal, reality of his personages. This led him to the idea of the *nivola* and to a marked change of fictional technique.[6]

Unamuno's general outlook also changed radically during the next three decades. Losing faith in Spain's *tradición eterna* as a basis for national regeneration, he came to question at the same time his long-professed aim of stirring his readers out of their spiritual sloth. The result, in 1930, was the creation of the last great fictional figure of the Generation of 1898, Don Manuel of *San Manuel Bueno, mártir*. This short novel is the story of a rural priest who has lost his faith, but continues his ministry. The core of the narrative is inevitably Don Manuel's inner conviction that all our beliefs, all our values, rest on air: at the centre of things there is nothingness. 'La verdad, Lázaro, es acaso algo terrible, algo intolerable, algo mortal; la gente sencilla no podrá vivir con ella'. This is *the* truth for the Generation of 1898, the product of Ganivet's *escepticismo científico*, the source of Azorín's *angustia*, the basis of Baroja's equally explicit assertion that 'la verdad en bloque es mala para la vida'. What is a priest to make of it? In Baroja's *El cura de Monleón* we see one possibility: to leave the priesthood. In Don Manuel we see the other: heroic duplicity. His task is to hide the bitter truth from the simple minds of his flock and spare them fruitless misery. His reward, like Pío Cid's, is distraction from his own contemplation of the abyss by helping others; but also that of possibly earning his own salvation through the faith of his congregation. As in *La voluntad*, the final answer is seen as that of faith. But unlike Azorin Unamuno could never shake off the suspicion that religious belief was not just another *mentira vital*. Hence the ambivalence throughout *San Manuel Bueno, mártir* and the final desperate mental pirouette: 'creo que don Manuel Bueno, que mi San Manuel y que mi hermano Lázaro se murieron creyendo no creer lo que más nos interesa, pero sin creer creerlo, creyéndolo. . . .' We are left, in any case, with the uneasy feeling, voiced by Blanco Aguinaga, that Unamuno was here advocating the imposition on the collective mind of a limitation which he would never have accepted himself as an individual.

Unamuno's novels are at once an integral part of the fiction of the Generation of 1898 and yet in a basic respect separate. Their theme is the familiar theme of development of personality (seen as insight into a tragic reality); their characters reveal familiar oscillations of *abulia* and *voluntarismo,* and many belong to the same *perturbado* class as Pío Cid, Antonio Azorín, and Andrés Hurtado. Technically Unamuno's novels also conform to type, being hero-dominated and full of discussion. Indeed, Unamuno's shift from 'oviparous' to 'viviparous' technique is the classic example of a '98 novelist breaking out of old-style realism. But the direction in which Unamuno moves away (towards the novel of pure creative imagination, of infra-*realidad*), and his obsessive concern with finality as distinct from the here and now, set him apart from the mainstream.

V. PÉREZ DE AYALA

If the test of belonging to the Generation of 1898 is that of sharing its general outlook, and its preoccupations both at the personal and at the national levels, Ramón Pérez de Ayala (1881-1962) undoubtedly qualifies for membership, before 1914, during the first phase of his work. Born and educated in Oviedo, he was a friend and protégé of Clarín and Galdós. Later, with Ortega, he emerged as a prominent Liberal (left-wing) intellectual and eventually was ambassador to London during the Republic: an appointment which led subsequently to many years of exile. Although, in conversation with the present writer, he asserted that it was this which cut short his creative activities, he in fact published nothing significant after 1926.

From childhood he was terrified by the idea of death, which, he wrote, 'me producía terrible preocupación y una tristeza prematura impropia de mi edad'. We perceive at once a similarity with evocations of their childhood by Unamuno and Azorín. In later adolescence, as with Baroja and the rest of the Generation, his confidence in existence was further undermined by the influence of Schopenhauer. A definite spiritual crisis can be traced in his early poetry and clearly underlies his first novel, *Tinieblas en las cumbres* (1907). Its hero, Alberto Díaz de Guzmán, is also the dominating central character of *A.M.D.G.* (1910) and *La pata de la raposa* (1912), as well as figuring prominently in *Troteras y danzaderas* (1913) which completes the sequence. Guzmán takes his place beside Pío Cid, Antonio Azorín, Andrés Hurtado, and Augusto Pérez (in Unamuno's *Niebla*) as a major '98 fictional hero, and in some respects is the clearest example of what we mean by this term.

He is introduced, in typical fashion, as a *perturbado*: 'Guzmán, que era pintor novicio y traía entre ceja y ceja no se qué cosquilleos trascendentales [cf. Antonio Azorín's 'hondas y transcendentales preocupaciones'] sobre arte y hasta teología'. In the revealing 1942 prologue to *Troteras . . .* Ayala explains why, in terms which remind the reader forcibly both of Baroja and Unamuno. The purpose of the whole cycle of novels, he asserts, is to 'reflejar y analizar la crisis de conciencia hispánica'. Taking the ideological basis of characterisation for granted, he emphasises that the lesser characters represent individual vital attitudes and are designed to 'provocar o estimular en el protagonista reacciones de conciencia': the Barojan interlocutor-technique. The aim is clearly to stir up the reader's existential awareness.

Alberto, then, a quasi-symbolic figure like his companion in *La voluntad* whose evolution is so similar at first, represents 'la conciencia criticista y disolvente' of the *fin-de-siglo* intellectual about to be plunged into 'la tiniebla absoluta y fatal'. The eclipse of faith and vital confidence is symbolised in the novel by the eclipse of the sun. This event produces one of the clearest descriptions of the existential pessimism of the Generation of 1898 which we possess (Alberto is unburdening himself to an interlocutor):

'Yo tenía en el alma cumbres cristalinas y puras; la obscuridad ha penetrado dentro de mí, lo ha anegado todo, todo lo ha aniquilado. Ya no veré nunca la luz'.

Yiddy se ríe jovialmente.

'No se ría Vd. El que no seamos nada; el que no sepamos nada; el que sospechemos que el universo es una cosa ciega, estúpida y fatal; el que pasemos por la vida como la sombra ha pasado sobre las montañas sin dejar nada detrás de sí; todo eso no es cosa de risa.'

The familiar problems of death, truth, and human finality are all present here. The only missing reference is to the ethical principle, in which all the Generation found support. Consciousness of this comes later in Guzmán's evolution, as was also the case with Fernando Ossorio of Baroja's *Camino de perfección*.

For the moment Guzmán remains at the foot of the abyss, while Ayala in *A.M.D.G.*, a savage attack on Jesuit education, retraces his steps to sketch the origins of his hero's malaise. When we meet Guzmán again as an adult in the central novel of the sequence, *La pata de la raposa*, he is still 'un mozo a quien el azacaneo de la vida había despojado una por una de todas las mentiras vitales, de todas las ilusiones normativas'. Now, having fled, again like Ossorio, from familiar surroundings into the countryside, he begins to examine a series of avenues of escape from the 'terrible morbo de la moderna patología: la enfermedad de lo incognoscible' (another lapidary definition of the malaise of the Generation, which may be compared to Ganivet's description of it as 'un estado patológico intelectual'). These escape-mechanisms are represented by a group of symbolic animals; Guzmán's examination of them is the novel's ideological core.

Guzmán is now firmly on the road back to what Ayala, in the 1942 preface, was to call 'las normas eternas', i.e. the *ideas madres*, in the recovery of which the Generation of 1898 tended to see the answer to both individual and the national problems. A series of experiences, including imprisonment and the loss of his private fortune, stimulate in him a more positive outlook. His preoccupation with death and transcendence gives way to a more serene consideration of the means whereby life can be invested with purely immanent significance. 'Nuestra vida . . . es como una caja vacía cuyas paredes son la muerte . . . ¿Con qué hemos de llenar la caja?' Instead of trying, like Unamuno, to break out of the box, he now accepts life itself as the absolute, and gradually regains confidence. He has, like the vixen alluded to in the book's title, 'escaped from the trap', although at the price of suffering. With the section 'el alba' (in contrast to 'tinieblas' of the opening novel) Guzmán shakes off *angustia*. This is now seen merely as a phase which prepares the way for active inner reconstruction ('angustia mensajera del mañana'), a stage only in the process of reacquiring understanding of what Ayala calls 'el sentido común cósmico', the force which rules our destinies. Henceforth Ayala affirms a principle of cosmic equilibrium (postulated in his book of essays, *Las máscaras*, 1917) which manifests itself in life as the interplay of equally justified forces of good and evil. Within this pattern of ultimate harmony the individual achieves vital fulfilment by conformity to an archetypal personality which is gradually revealed to him by experience and reflection. Guzmán's decision, followed out in *Troteras y danzaderas*, to dedicate himself to literature with the aim of regenerating national sensibility through art, indicates the discovery of his own archetypal personality and the solution to his problem. In the 1942 preface to *Troteras y danzaderas*, already mentioned, Ayala makes an effort to link this solution even more closely to the problems of national regeneration, in order to give the early part of his work the appearance of complete conformity with the Generation of 1898 fictional pattern. But it remains unconvincing, like all such attempts to weld together the problem of the individual, the core of which was spiritual and intellectual, and that of the collectivity whose essence was economico-social.

In *Principios y fines de la novela* (1958) Ayala wrote: 'En la primera mitad de la vida el hombre se rebela animoso contra los valores establecidos . . . Esta experiencia analítica le sirve para que al llegar a la edad madura reconozca los valores eternos'. The reaffirmation by Ayala after 1914 of positive values ends the first phase of his fictional work and he was not to write another major novel until 1921. It is an appropriate point at which to conclude this consideration of the novel in the Generation of 1898.

NOTES

1. It should be noted that the existence of a 'Generation of 1898' as a coherent group has been denied by some, including Baroja.
2. 'José Martínez Ruiz, sobre el anarquismo del futuro Azorín', *RO*, *35* (1966).
3. See G. G. Brown, *A Literary History of Spain: The Twentieth Century*, pp. 31 ff.
4. C. J. Cela, *Don Pío Baroja* (Mexico, 1958), p. 75.
5. *Del 98 al barroco* (Madrid, 1969), p. 117.
6. See G. G. Brown, op. cit., pp. 14 ff.

Chapter 11

IDEOLOGIES AND ERUDITION

IN 1559 PHILIP II MADE UNAUTHORISED STUDY ABROAD, except in Italy and Portugal, a capital offence for Spaniards. In 1843 a young scholar, Julián Sanz del Río (1814-69), received a government scholarship to pursue in Heidelberg studies of German philosophy which were to transform Spanish intellectual life. Thus almost three centuries of relative isolation drew to a close.

Foreign intellectual influences were, of course, already operating in Spain before 1843. Most important was French encyclopaedic thought, materialist in tendency and critical of received ideas, especially in the fields of religion and politics. According to Schramm,[1] Salamanca University was a centre of encyclopaedic ideas and there Donoso Cortés, for example, developed in the 1820s a taste for Rousseau, Voltaire, Pauw, and Helvétius. British influence was also present. Monguió[2] cites besides Condillac and Destutt de Tracy, Locke, Hume, and Bentham as influential on José Joaquín de Mora's intellectual formation. Alcalá Galiano was also something of a Benthamite. But more important still was the Scottish 'common sense' school of philosophy led by Alexander Hamilton. Expounded in the University of Barcelona above all, by an exceptional trio of Catalan professors, Ramón Martí de Eixala, Francisco Llorens y Barba, and Manuel Milá y Fontanals, its influence extended from Mora, who published in 1832 *Cursos de lógica y etica según la escuela de Edimburgo*, as far as Balmes and Menéndez Pelayo.

A major intellectual event of the 1840s was the popularisation by Tomás García Luna of Victor Cousin's eclecticism. Its easy *armonismo* helped to calm the ferment of the 1830s and came close to being the official philosophy of the *moderado* Party under Martínez de la Rosa.

The contributions of Balmes and Donoso Cortés, the only Spanish thinkers of the mid-century with any claims to originality, have already been mentioned. The dogmatic and traditionalist tinge of their ideas was shared by Zeferino González, who undertook the restoration of Thomism in Spain, and Gumersindo Laverde Ruiz (1840-90), whose essays on philosophy, literature, and education from 1855 on prepared the way for the defence of traditional Spanish culture soon to be undertaken by Marcelino Menéndez Pelayo (1856-1912).

I. MENÉNDEZ PELAYO

Menéndez Pelayo was born in Santander and educated in the University of Barcelona. His precocious brilliance was such that a special decree was issued in order to allow him to take up a Chair of Spanish Literature in Madrid at twenty-two. Already, in *Polémicas de la ciencia española* (1876), he had sprung to the defence of Spain's contribution to philosophy and scientific thought which Azcárate, Revilla, and Perojo, three leading anti-traditionalist intellectuals, had described as existing only in imagination. At twenty-three he published two massive volumes of his *Historia de los heterodoxos españoles* (1880), followed by a third in 1882. *Horacio en España*, another vast survey, had already appeared in 1877.

Between 1883 and 1891 Menéndez Pelayo completed his five-volume *Historia de las ideas estéticas* as well as beginning his major work as a literary critic (*Estudios de crítica literaria*, 1885-1908). This was to be followed by the heavily documented *Orígenes de la novela* (1905-10), In addition we owe to his indefatigable scholarship an edition of Lope de Vega in twelve volumes, the *Antología de poetas líricos* (1890-1908), the *Antología de poetas hispanoamericanos* (1892-95), and his bibliographical works. These brilliant compilations crown a pattern of erudition which stretches back at least as far as the work of Bartolomé José Gallardo (1776-1852), to whose papers Menéndez Pelayo had access. Other intermediary figures include Böhl von Faber, Durán, Ochoa, and the team of scholars who edited the *Biblioteca de Autores Españoles* begun in 1846. Mention must also be made of José Amador de los Ríos (1818-78), the first native Spaniard to write a full-scale *Historia crítica de la literatura española* (1861-65) on genuinely scholarly lines.

Menéndez Pelayo's work has two aspects. The first is his achievement as Spain's greatest nineteenth-century scholar. For the first time the history of ideas in Spain was systematically investigated. Meanwhile, by a parallel process of research, literary criticism was established on a real basis of erudition. Here the two keynotes of Menéndez

Pelayo's work are historicism and balance. His defence of Spanish Renaissance scholasticism against the narrow Thomism of his own day did not exclude objective recognition of the revolutionary importance of later critical philosophy, especially Kant's, and a distinct Hegelian tinge to his own thought. Though essentially aesthetic in his approach to literature, he nonetheless recognised explicity what Valera and others never perceived: that beauty alone was not all. The aim of all his scholarship at its best was, as Laín Entralgo asserts, to overcome the deep mental schism which existed in his day between liberal and traditionalist intellectuals: 'la cruenta e inútil antinomia de la España del Siglo XIX'.

But apart from the intrinsic value of his scholarship stands its symbolic value. Menéndez Pelayo's defence of Spain's contribution to universal culture, his longing for a restoration of its distinctively national Catholic humanism, made him the great guardian and comforter of the Spanish spirit in the 1880s and 1890s. Then in 1898 his comfort failed, his national cultural ideal was discredited. He came to be seen, except among a narrow circle of scholars, as what Maeztu memorably called 'un triste coleccionador de naderías muertas'. Since the Civil War a deliberate attempt had been made to present him as the great example of a successful fusion of intellectual innovation and the national Catholic tradition.

II. KRAUSISM: SANZ DEL RÍO AND GINER

In retrospect, however, the main renovation of ideas must be attributed to Krausism, which enjoyed a whirlwind success after the publication in 1860 by Sanz del Río of his *Metafísica* and especially his *Ideal de la Humanidad para la vida*. Those who criticise Sanz's infatuation with a third-rate philosopher must first explain the popularity of his system of thought. The fact is that Krausism seemed able to fulfil the deepest needs of Spain's cultured minority. Its *racionalismo armónico*, which seemed to fuse Divine Providence with determinism and moral effort with Grace, offered to serious-minded men the possibility of retaining some religious ties without sacrificing their rationalistic allegiances. Its ethical imperative found an immediate response among those whose consciences were repelled by conventional religious sanctions. Its social standpoint accorded well with moderate liberal-progressivism. It even had an aesthetic doctrine. At last non-traditionalist Spaniards had found a system of belief which was also a way of life. The influence of Krausism on literature up to the Generation of 1898 cannot be disputed. Clarín's essay on his Krausist professor, Camus, and his short story 'Zurita', together with Galdós's *La familia de León Roch* and *El amigo Manso*, are only the most obvious examples of it. Its influence on Unamuno has not been fully explored, but is frequently mentioned by critics. Nor can we explain either the tenacious adherence of the Generation of 1898 to ethical absolutes—the only ones they accepted—or their avid interest in philosophy without mentioning Krausism.

Sanz del Río's major disciple was Francisco Giner de los Ríos (1839-1915), the founder in 1876 of the *Institución Libre de Enseñanza*. His personal influence and that of his exemplary life extended over two generations, from that of Pardo Bazán (whose first book of poems he financed) to that of Antonio Machado, who wrote one of his most memorable poems on the death of the Master. Among the founders and teachers of the *Institución* were the poet Ruiz Aguilera, the novelist and critic Valera, the dramatist Echegaray, and the publicist Joaquín Costa. Together with other famous collaborators they brought about a new climate of thought in Spanish intellectual circles which was a major factor conditioning the formation of the younger generation of writers.

III. POSITIVISM

Side by side with Krausism, and destined to succeed it as a major force in Spanish nineteenth-century intellectual life, came a really tough-minded philosophy, Positivism, equally opposed to theological and metaphysical speculation. Though his formal ties were more with Krausism itself, the emphasis laid by Positivism on material progress is visible in the work of Joaquín Costa (1844-1911). The historical significance of Costa's work in relation to literature lies in the fact that he above all perceived in the late nineteenth century that what Spain needed was not *moral* regeneration—the general level of virtue being much the same from age to age—but politico-social and economic renovation. His major works in this respect are *Reconstitución y europeización de España* (1910) and *Oligarquía y caciquismo como la forma actual de gobierno en España* (1902). His tragedy was two-fold. First, he failed to perceive that only a progressive mass movement could impose his programme of *escuela y despensa* on an unwilling oligarchy: his call for an iron dictator (which Baroja echoed as a young man) was a counsel of despair. Second, he failed to carry the younger generation of intellectuals with him except in his negative criticisms of Spanish political organisation (cf. Azorín's *El chirriato de los políticos* as late as 1927). After a short and ineffectual period in which Baroja, Azorín, and Maeztu ('Los Tres') accepted the idea of the writers' social mission and published a manifesto following Costa's lines of thought, the Generation of 1898 as a whole lost interest in practical *regeneración*. Two writers who seconded Costa's efforts and deserve mention for doing so are Mallada and Macías Picavea, the authors respectively of *Los males de la patria y la futura revolución española* (1890) and *El problema nacional* (1899).

IV. OTHER INFLUENCES:
'LA REVISTA CONTEMPORANEA'

Close behind Positivism came Darwinism (which Núñez de Arce unhappily tried to ridicule) and Herbert Spencer's pseudo-scientific sociology on the biological model. From Germany, hard on the heels of Krause, came Hegel (whose influence extends from Menéndez Pelayo to Unamuno) and Schopenhauer, of whose influence in *fin-de-siglo* Spain enough has already been said. Never was Clarín wider of the mark than in his statement in 1882 that Schopenhauer's popularity had passed its peak. A central role in the dissemination of these new philosophic and scientific influences was played by José de Perojo (1852-1908) in his too-little-studied magazine *La Revista Contemporánea*, founded in 1875.

With Schopenhauer, Darwin (as interpreted and applied by Haekel, whom Baroja recognised as one of the two main discoveries of his student days), and Spencer we reach the threshold of our own times. With mention of anarchist thought, so influential on the young Unamuno, Baroja, and Maeztu as well as on Azorín (who translated some Kropotkin), Marxism, which attracted Unamuno briefly, and the Nietzschean ideas in which Baroja found temporary comfort, we pass into the twentieth century.

NOTES

1. E. Schramm, *Donoso Cortés* (Madrid, 1936), p. 21.
2. L. Monguió, *Don José-Joaquín de Mora en el Perú del 800* (Madrid, 1967), Ch. 1.

BIBLIOGRAPHY

Historical Introduction

T. Aronson, *The Crown of Spain* (London, 1968)
G. Brenan, *The Spanish Labyrinth* (2nd edn., Cambridge, 1950)
R. Carr, *Spain 1808-1939* (Oxford, 1966)
H. Butler Clarke, *Modern Spain 1815-1898* (Cambridge, 1906)
E. Holt, *The Carlist Wars in Spain* (London, 1968)
S. de Madariaga, *Spain* (New York, 1958)
A. Ramos Oliveira, *Politics, Economics and Men of Modern Spain* (London, 1946)
J. B. Trend, *The Origins of Modern Spain* (Cambridge, 1934)

Chapter 1

Eichner, H. (ed.), *Romanticism, The History of a Word* (Toronto, 1972)
Juretschke, H., *Origen doctrinal y génesis del romanticismo español* (Madrid, 1954)
——, *Vida, obra y pensamiento de Alberto Lista* (Madrid, 1951)
Peers, E. A., *A History of the Romantic Movement in Spain* (Cambridge, 1940)
Díaz Plaja, G., *Introducción al estudio del romanticismo español* (Madrid, 1936)
García Mercadal, J., *Historia del romanticismo en España* (Barcelona, 1943)
Llorens, V., *Liberales y románticos* (Mexico, 1954)
——, *Literatura, historia, política. Ensayos* (Madrid, 1967)
Kromer, W., *Zur Weltanschauung Asthetik und Poetik des Neoklassizismus und Romantik in Spanien* (Münster, 1968)
Río, A. del, 'Present Trends in the Conception and Criticism of Spanish Romanticism', *RR*, XXXIX (1948), 229-48

Shaw, D. L., 'Towards the Understanding of Spanish Romanticism', *MLR*, LVIII (1963), 190-95

Martínez de la Rosa, F., *Obras completas, BAE* (Madrid, 1962)

Sarrailh, J., *Un Homme d'Etat Espagnol: Martínez de la Rosa* (Bordeaux and Paris, 1930)

Sosa, L. de, *Martínez de la Rosa, político y poeta* (Madrid, 1930)

Schearer, J. F., *The 'Poética' and 'Apendices' of Martínez de la Rosa* (Princeton, 1941)

Boussagol, G., *Angel de Saavedra, duc de Rivas* (Toulouse, 1927)

González Ruiz, N., *El Duque de Rivas* (Madrid, 1944)

Chapter 2

Salinas, P., *Reality and the Poet in Spanish Poetry* (Baltimore, 1940)

Cascales Muñoz, J., *Don José de Espronceda* (Madrid, 1924)

Alonso Cortés, N., *Espronceda* (Valladolid, 1942)

Pujals, E., *Espronceda y Lord Byron* (Madrid, 1951)

Casalduero, J., *Forma y visión de 'El diablo mundo' de Espronceda* (Madrid, 1951)

——, *Espronceda* (Madrid, 1961)

Pattison, W., 'On Espronceda's Personality', *PMLA*, LXI (1946), 1126-45

Larra, M. J. de, *Obras completas, BAE* (Madrid, 1960)

Nombela Campos, J., *Larra* (Madrid, 1909)

Burgos, C. de, *Fígaro* (Madrid, 1918)

Lomba y Pedraja, J. R., *Mariano José de Larra* (Madrid, 1936)

Moreno, R. B., *Larra* (Madrid, 1951)

Gómez Santos, M., *Larra* (Madrid, 1956)

Tarr, F. C., 'More Light on Larra', *HR*, IV (1936), 89-110

——, 'A Decisive Period in Larra's Life', *HR*, V (1937), 11-24

Revista de Occidente, 50 (1967; Memorial Number)

Chapter 3

Valbuena Prat, A., *Historia del teatro español* (Barcelona, 1956)

Peers, E. A. (ed.), *Liverpool Studies in Spanish Literature.* First Series (Liverpool, 1940)

Corbière, A. S., *J. E. Hartzenbusch and the French Theatre* (Philadelphia, 1927)

Adams, N. B., *The Romantic Dramas of García Gutiérrez* (New York, 1922)
Chao Espina, E., *Pastor Díaz dentro del romanticismo* (Madrid, 1949)
Lomba y Pedraja, J. R., *El Padre Arolas* (Madrid, 1898)
Méndez Bejarano, R., *Tassara, nueva biografía crítica* (Madrid, 1928)
Cotarelo, E., *La Avellaneda y sus obras* (Madrid, 1930)
Williams, E. B., *The Life and Dramatic Works of G. Gómez de Avellaneda* (University Park, Pa., 1924)
Figarola-Canedo, D., *Gertrudis Gómez de Avellaneda* (Madrid, 1929)
Bravo Villasante, C., *Una vida romántica: La Avellaneda* (Madrid and Barcelona, 1967)
Sandoval, A. de, *Catalina Coronado y su época* (Saragossa, 1944)
Carnicer, R., *Vida y obra de Pablo Piferrer* (Madrid, 1963)
Alonso Cortés, N., *Zorrilla, su vida y sus obras* (Valladolid, 1916)

Chapter 4

García, S., *Las ideas literarias en España entre 1840 y 1850* (Berkeley, 1971)
Shaw, D. L., 'The Anti-Romantic Reaction In Spain', *MLR*, LXIII (1968), 606-11
Castro y Calvo, J. M., *Balmes* (Vic, 1951)
Schmitt, C., *Interpretación europea de Donoso Cortés* (Madrid, 1952)
Larraz, J., *Balmes y Donoso Cortés* (Madrid, 1965)
Brown, R. F., *La novela española 1700-1850* (Madrid, 1953)
Montesinos, J. F., *Introducción a una historia de la novela en España en el siglo XIX*, 2nd edn. (Madrid, 1966)
——, *Costumbrismo y novela*, 2nd edn. (Madrid, 1960)
Zellers, W., *La novela histórica en España, 1828-1850* (New York, 1938)
Eoff, S. H., *The Modern Spanish Novel* (New York, 1962)
——, 'The Spanish Novel of "Ideas": Critical Opinion', *PMLA*, LV (1940), 531-58
Montesinos, J. F., *Fernán Caballero, ensayo de justificación* (Mexico, 1961)
Herrero, J., *Fernán Caballero: un nuevo planteamiento* (Madrid, 1963)
Zavala, I. M., 'Socialismo y literatura: Ayguals de Izco y la novela', *RO*, 80 (1969), 167-88
Samuels, D. G., *Enrique Gil y Carrasco* (New York, 1939)
Montesinos, J. F., *Pedro Antonio de Alarcón* (Saragossa, 1955)
Martínez Kleiser, L., *Don Pedro Antonio de Alarcón* (Madrid, 1943)
Ocaño, A., *Alarcón* (Madrid, 1970)

Chapter 5

Cossío, J. M. de, *Cincuenta años de poesía española (1850-1900)* (Madrid, 1960)
Cernuda, L., *Estudios sobre poesía española contemporánea* (Madrid, 1957)
Cano, J. L., *Poesía española del siglo XX* [*sic*] (Madrid, 1960)
González Blanco, A., *Campoamor* (Madrid, 1912)
Hilton, R., *Campoamor, Spain and the World* (Toronto, 1940)
Gaos, V., *La poética de Campoamor* (Madrid, 1955)
Murciano, C., 'Campoamor en el tapete', *CHA*, 151 (1962), 107-21
Somo Arregui, J., *Vida, poesía y estilo de don Gaspar Núñez de Arce* (Madrid, 1946)

Chapter 6

Valbuena Prat, A., *Historia del teatro español* (Barcelona, 1956)
Ruiz Ramón, F., *Historia del teatro español* (Madrid, 1967)
Cook, J. A., *Neoclassic Drama in Spain* (Dallas, 1959)
Peers, E. A. (ed.), *Liverpool Studies in Spanish Literature*. First Series (Liverpool, 1940)
Smith, W. F., 'Contributions of Rodríguez Rubí to the development of the *alta comedia*', *HR*, X (1942), 53-63
Tayler, N. H., *Las fuentes del teatro de Tamayo y Baus* (Madrid, 1959)
Esquer Torres, R., *El teatro de Tamayo y Baus* (Madrid, 1965)
Poyán Díez, D., *Enrique Gaspar. Medio Siglo de teatro español* (Madrid, 1957)
Mérimée, E., 'J. Echegaray et son oeuvre dramatique', *BH*, XVIII (1916), 247-78
Mathías, J., *Echegaray* (Madrid, 1970)
Grau, J., 'El teatro de Galdós', in *Cursos y conferencias* (Buenos Aires, 1943)
Peake, J. H., *Social Drama in Nineteenth Century Spain* (Chapel Hill, 1964)
Gregersen, H., *Ibsen in Spain* (Cambridge, Mass., 1936)

Chapter 7

Cossío, J. M. de, *Cincuenta años de poesía española (1850-1900)* (Madrid, 1960)

Ferrán, A., *Obras completas* (Madrid, 1970)

Frutos Gómez de las Cortinas, J., 'La formación literaria de Bécquer', *Revista bibliográfica y documental*, IV (1950), 77-99

Díaz, J. P., *Gustavo Adolfo Bécquer. Vida y poesía* (Madrid, 1958)

King, E. L., *Gustavo Adolfo Bécquer. From Painter to Poet* (Mexico, 1953)

Brown, R., *Bécquer* (Barcelona, 1963)

Díez Taboada, J. M., *La mujer ideal. Aspectos y fuentes de las Rimas de G. A. Bécquer* (Madrid, 1965)

Barbáchano, C., *Bécquer* (Madrid, 1970)

Benítez, R., *Ensayo de bibliografía razonada de G. A. Bécquer* (Buenos Aires, 1961)

Alonso, D., 'La originalidad de Bécquer', in *Poetas españoles contemporáneos* (Madrid, 1958)

——, *Bécquer tradicionalista* (Madrid, 1971)

Guillén, J., 'La poética de Bécquer', *RHM*, VII (1942)

Balbín, R. de, *Poética becqueriana* (Madrid, 1969)

González-Gerth, M., 'The Poetics of Gustavo Adolfo Bécquer', *MLN*, LXXX (1965), 185-201

Hartsook, J. H., 'Bécquer and the Creative Imagination', *HR*, XXXV (1967), 252-69

Berenger Carismo, A., *La prosa de Bécquer* (Buenos Aires, 1947)

Cuadernos Hispanoamericanos, 248/9 (1970; a *homenaje*)

Murias Santaella, A., *Rosalía de Castro: su vida y su obra* (Buenos Aires, 1942)

Tirrell, M. P., *La mística de la saudade. Estudio de la poesía de Rosalía de Castro* (Madrid, 1951)

Costa Clavell, J., *Rosalía de Castro* (Barcelona, 1966)

Nogales de Muñiz, M. A., *Irradiación de Rosalía de Castro* (Barcelona, 1966)

Aguilar Piñal, F., *La obra poética de Manuel Reina* (Madrid, 1968)

Chapter 8

Balseiro, J. A., *Novelistas españoles modernos* (New York, 1933)

Pérez Minik, D., *Novelistas españoles en los siglos XIX y XX* (Madrid, 1957)

Cossío, J. M. de, *La vida literaria de Pereda, su historia y su crítica* (Santander, 1934)

Gullón, R., *Vida de Pereda* (Madrid, 1944)

Montesinos, J. F., *Pereda o la novela idilio* (Mexico, 1961)

Clarke, A. H., *Pereda paisajista* (Santander, 1969)

Romero de Mendoza, P., *Don Juan Valera* (Madrid, 1940)

Krynen, J., *L'esthetisme de Juan Valera* (Salamanca, 1946)
Jiménez, A., *Juan Valera y la Generación de 1868* (Oxford, 1955)
Montesinos, J. F., *Valera o la ficción libre* (Madrid, 1957)
Merino, J., *Valera desde hoy* (Madrid, 1968)
Smith, P. C., *Juan Valera* (Buenos Aires, 1969)
Roca Franquesa, J. M., 'La novela de Palacio Valdés, clasificación y análisis', *Boletín del Instituto de Estudios Asturianos*, VII (1953), 426-58
Colangeli, M. R., *Armando Palacio Valdés: romanziere* (Lecce, 1962)
López Morillas, J., 'La Revolución de Septiembre y la novela española', *RO*, 67 (1968), 94-115

Chapter 9

Baquero Goyanes, M., *El cuento español en el siglo XIX* (Madrid, 1949)
Pattison, W., *El naturalismo español* (Madrid, 1965)
Davis, G., 'The Critical Reception of Naturalism in Spain before *La cuestión palpitante*', *HR*, XXII (1954), 97-108
——, 'The "Coletilla" to Pardo Bazán's *Cuestión Palpitante*', *HR*, XXIV (1956), 50-63
——, 'The Spanish Debate over Realism and Idealism', *PMLA*, LXXXIV (1969), 1649-56
Scatori, S., *La idea religiosa en la obra de Benito Pérez Galdós* Toulouse and Paris, 1927)
Pérez de Ayala, R., *Las máscaras* (Madrid, 1924)
Chonon Berkowitz, H., *Pérez Galdós: Spanish Liberal Crusader* (Madison, 1948)
Casalduero, J., *Vida y obra de Galdós, 1843-1920* (Madrid, 1951)
Río, A. del, *Estudios galdosianos* (Saragossa, 1953)
Eoff, S. H., *The Novels of Pérez Galdós* (St Louis, 1954)
Pattison, W. T., *Benito Pérez Galdós and the Creative Process* (Minneapolis, 1954)
Gullón, R., *Galdós, novelista moderno* (Madrid, 1960)
Correa, G., *El simbolismo religioso de las novelas de Galdós* (Madrid, 1962)
——, *Realidad, ficción y símbolo en las novelas de Benito Pérez Galdós* (Bogotá, 1967)
Ricard, R., *Aspects de Galdós* (Paris, 1963)
Hinterhäuser, H., *Los Episodios Nacionales de Benito Pérez Galdós* (Madrid, 1963)
Regalado García, A., *Benito Pérez Galdós y la novela histórica española, 1868-1912* (Madrid, 1967)

Nimetz, M., *Humour in Galdós* (New Haven, 1968)

Montesinos, J. F., *Galdós* (Madrid, 1968—; 3 volumes planned)

Anales galdosianos, Pittsburgh (now Austin), 1966—

Posada, A., *Leopoldo Alas, Clarín* (Oviedo, 1946)

Brent, A., *Leopoldo Alas and 'La Regenta'*, University of Missouri Studies XXIV (1951)

Ventura Agudiez, J., *Inspiración y estética en La Regenta de Clarín* (Madrid, 1970)

Gómez Santos, M., *Leopoldo Alas, Clarín. Ensayo bio-bibliográfico* (Oviedo, 1952)

Becarud, J., *'La Regenta' y la España de la restauración* (Madrid, 1964)

Brown, G. G., Introduction to Alas, *Cuentos escogidos* (Oxford, 1964)

Ríos, L. de los, *Los cuentos de Clarín* (Madrid, 1965)

Beser, S., *Leopoldo Alas, crítico literario* (Madrid, 1968)

Gramberg, E. J., *Fondo y forma del humorismo de Leopoldo Alas, Clarín* (Oviedo, 1958)

Blanquat, J., 'La sensibilité religieuse de Clarín', *RLC*, XXXV (1961)

Durand, F., 'Characterization in "La Regenta"', *BHS*, XLI (1964), 86-100

——, 'Structural Unity in Leopoldo Alas' "La Regenta"', *HR*, XXXI (1963), 324-35

Clochiatti, E., 'Clarín y sus ideas sobre la novela', *Revista de Letras de la Universidad de Oviedo*, LIII, LIV, LVII, LVIII, LIX, LX (1948-49)

Weber, F., 'The Dynamics of Motive in Leopoldo Alas' "La Regenta", *RR*, LVII (1966), 188-99

——, 'Ideology and Religious Parody in the Novels of Leopoldo Alas', *BHS*, XLIII (1966), 197-208

Archivum (Oviedo) II, i, 1952; (a Memorial Number)

González López, E., *Emilia Pardo Bazán, novelista de Galicia* (New York, 1944)

Brown, D. F., *The Catholic Naturalism of Emilia Pardo Bazán* (Chapel Hill, 1957)

Bravo Villasante, C., *Vida y obra de Emilia Pardo Bazán* (Madrid, 1962)

Chapter 10

Balseiro, J. A., *Novelistas españoles modernos* (New York, 1933)

Barja, C., *Libros y autores contemporáneos* (Madrid, 1935)

Aub, M., *Discurso de la novela española contemporánea* (Mexico, 1945)

Clavería, C., *Cinco estudios de literatura española moderna* (Madrid, 1945)

Baquero Goyanes, M., *Prosistas españoles contemporáneos* (Madrid, 1956)

Nora, E. G. de, *La novela española contemporánea*, I (Madrid, 1958)

Reding, K. P., *The Generation of 1898 as seen through its Fictional Hero*, Smith College Studies (1936)

Durán, M., 'La técnica de la novela y el '98', *RHM*, XXIII (1957), 14-27

Seeleman, R., 'The Treatment of Landscape in the Novelists of the Generation of 1898', *HR*, IV (1936), 226-38

King-Arjona, D., '*La voluntad* and *abulia* in Contemporary Spanish Ideology', *RH*, LXXIV (1928), 573-672

Espina, A., *Ganivet, el hombre y la obra* (Buenos Aires, 1942)

Fernández Almagro, M., *Vida y obra de Ángel Ganivet*, 2nd edn. (Madrid, 1952)

García Lorca, F., *Ángel Ganivet, su idea del hombre* (Buenos Aires, 1952)

Gallego Morell, A., *Ángel Ganivet. El excéntrico del 98* (Granada, 1965)

Franco, Jean, 'Ganivet and the technique of Satire in *La conquista del reino de Maya*', *BHS* (1965)

Herrero, J., *Ángel Ganivet, un iluminado* (Madrid, 1966)

Shaw, D. L., 'Ganivet's *España filosófica contemporánea* and the Interpretation of the Generation of 1898', *HR*, XXVIII (1960), 220-32

Revista de Occidente, 62 (1968); (Memorial Number)

H. Ramsden, *Ángel Ganivet's Idearium español* (Manchester, 1967)

Balseiro, J. A., *Blasco Ibañez, Unamuno, Valle-Inclán y Baroja* (New York, 1939)

Granjel, L. S., *Retrato de Pío Baroja* (Barcelona, 1954)

Baeza, F., *Baroja y su mundo* (Madrid, 1962)

Iglesias, C., *El pensamiento de Pío Baroja* (Mexico, 1963)

Arbó, S. J., *Pío Baroja y su tiempo* (Barcelona, 1963)

Flores Arroyuelo, F. J., *Las primeras novelas de Pío Baroja* (Murcia, 1967)

González Ruiz, N., 'Baroja y la España de Baroja', *BSS*, I (1923), 4-11

Owen, A. L., 'Concerning the Ideology of Pío Baroja', *Hisp*, XV (1932), 15-24

Bollinger, D. H., 'Heroes and Hamlets: The Protagonists of Baroja's Novels', *Hisp*, XXIV (1941), 91-4

Shaw, D. L., 'A Reply to *deshumanización*: Baroja on the Art of the Novel', *HR*, XXV (1957), 105-11
——, 'The Concept of *Ataraxia* in the later novels of Pío Baroja', *BHS*, XXXIV (1957), 29-36
——, Two Novels of Baroja, an Illustration of his Technique', *BHS*, XL (1963), 151-9
Livingstone, L., 'The Theme of the Paradoxe sur le comédien in the work of Ramón Pérez de Ayala', HR, XXII (1954), 208-23.
Shaw, D. L., 'Concerning the Ideology of Pérez de Ayala', *MLQ*, XXII (1961), 158-66

Chapter 11

Jobit, P., *Les éducateurs de l'Espagne contemporaine*, I: *Les Krausistes* (Bordeaux, 1936)
Schramm, E., *Donoso Cortés* (Madrid, 1936)
Monguió, L., *Don José-Joaquín de Mora en el Perú del 800* (Madrid, 1967)
Aranguren, J. L., *Moral y sociedad. La moral social española en el siglo XIX* (Madrid, 1966)
Entrambasaguas, J. de, 'Panorama histórico de la erudición española en siglo XIX', *Arbor*, XIV (1946), 165-91
López Morillas, J., *El krausismo español* (Mexico, 1956)
Cacho Viu, C., *La Institución Libre de Enseñanza* I (Madrid, 1962)
Menéndez Pelayo, M., *Obras completas* (Madrid, 1940), esp. XXXV-XLII, *Historia de los Heterodoxos Españoles*
Laín Entralgo, P., *Menéndez y Pelayo* (Madrid, 1944)
Alonso, D., *Menéndez Pelayo, crítico literario* (Madrid, 1956)
Ciges Aparicio, V., *Joaquín Costa, el gran fracasado* (Madrid, 1932)
Martín Retortillo, C., *Joaquín Costa* (Madrid, 1961)
Pérez de la Dehesa, R., *El pensamiento de Costa y su influencia en el '98* (Madrid, 1968)
Shaw, D. L., '*Armonismo*, the failure of an illusion', in *La revolución de 1868. Historia, pensamiento, literatura*, ed I. M. Zavala (New York, 1970)

INDEX

Printed in Great Britain by
The Garden City Press Limited, Letchworth, Hertfordshire, SG6 1JS